D1498376

"The uprising against the police in the summer of 2020 showed the United States, if not the world, what Black America has always known: the police are an enduring force of oppression and violence. Geo Maher's new book not only provides us the tools to understand the role of the police but the imagination to conceive of a world without them. This is the right book at the right time." —Keeanga-Yamahtta Taylor, *From #BlackLivesMatter to Black Liberation*

"An essential introduction to the case for abolishing the police." —*Publishers Weekly*

"From the ashes of the Third Precinct, Geo Maher looks for what grows when the deadly shadow of the police is removed. He writes an urgent history of the present. The ingredients of white supremacy, colonialism, and capitalism are baked into the cake called America, especially the institution of the police. You can't unbake that cake. Maher contends creating a world without police is not only possible, but necessary." —Nick Estes, *Our History is the Future*

"*A World Without Police* is provocative in the best possible ways: It dares the reader to imagine a future only without policing, but shorn of the capitalism and white supremacy that refashions a public in the image of the police. It situates the carceral and coercive institutions in the US within broader global currents of imperial violence. And it demands that we together build strong, antiracist, and egalitarian communities that can defend themselves here and across national boundaries." —Laleh Khalili, *Sinews of War and Trade*

"Thanks to the tireless organizing work of the 'stubborn agitators, zealots, and fanatics of the best sort' who inspire Geo Maher, police abolition is an increasingly widespread political demand. *A World Without Police* dismantles every argument cops and their supporters offer to defend our present world with police, incisively detailing their flaws and falsehoods. In our future world without police, Maher's persuasive book will serve as the institution's autopsy report." —Stuart Schrader, *Badges Without Borders*

"A clear-sighted and passionate case for abolition that is ultimately an argument for changing the world as we know it. Maher's work is steeped in historical understanding and revolutionary insight, but it is, above all, determinedly hopeful and humane in its vision of another way of living together that is absolutely possible." —Priyamvada Gopal, Insurgent Empire

"Maher's prose, trenchant and unapologetic, helps us write a poetry of abolition." —Tyler Wall, Police: A Field Guide

"We'll never be free as long as cops patrol our streets, and Geo Maher's book helps light our way in our struggle to build a world free from the plague of police." —David Correia, *Police: A Field Guide*

"In *A World Without Police*, Geo Maher considers modern day abolitionist movements against policing. Through the flames of the 2020 uprisings, he illuminates a long history of abolitionist struggles for freedom, for democracy, and for the radical transformation of the world. An urgent text for our times." —Christina Heatherton, *Policing the Planet*

"*A World Without Police* analyzes the unfinished business of 'abolition democracy' in the twenty-first century. Amid a cycle of rebellion, Geo Maher deftly illuminates how policing is a 'racket.' The power to transform society, he argues, lies in the visions of radical democratic movements to abolish the police." —Jordan Camp, *Incarcerating the Crisis*

A World Without Police
How Strong Communities Make Cops Obsolete

Geo Maher

VERSO
London • New York

First published by Verso 2021
© Geo Maher 2021

All rights reserved

The moral rights of the author have been asserted

1 3 5 7 9 10 8 6 4 2

Verso
UK: 6 Meard Street, London W1F 0EG
US: 20 Jay Street, Suite 1010, Brooklyn, NY 11201
versobooks.com

Verso is the imprint of New Left Books

ISBN-13: 978-1-83976-005-1
ISBN-13: 978-1-83976-008-2 (UK EBK)
ISBN-13: 978-1-83976-007-5 (US EBK)

British Library Cataloguing in Publication Data
A catalogue record for this book is available from the British Library

Library of Congress Cataloging-in-Publication Data
Library of Congress Control Number: 2021937561

Typeset in Sabon by Biblichor Ltd, Edinburgh
Printed and bound by CPI Group (UK) Ltd, Croydon CR0 4YY

Contents

Introduction

It was 9:53 p.m. on May 28, 2020, and Minneapolis's Third Police Precinct was surrounded. Hundreds of protesters, furious at the police killing of George Floyd three days earlier, had established a siege, flanking the building from the front, before then encircling it from the back as well. The panic on the police channels was palpable: "Our front door's fully breached . . . They're coming in, they're coming in the back . . . We need to move, we need to move!" Minutes later, police would abandon the precinct entirely, lobbing stun grenades and firing rubber bullets indiscriminately into the crowd before ramming a police SUV through the rear gate. Nine more vehicles followed amid a phalanx of officers on foot, fleeing under a hail of rocks and bottles punctuated by the occasional soft whoosh of roman candles. The precinct was soon fully ablaze.

To burn a building or a car is, like the riot itself, a form of communication. Too often, however, the enemy is out of reach, and so fires are lit for attention, to grab the headlines, or quite simply because nothing else has worked—a desperate bid to puncture the barrier between those who are and are not heard, those who matter and those who don't. Many buildings would burn that night and in the days that followed, but the Third Precinct was something different. Protesters had taken an enemy outpost, the direct object of their fury, and they had destroyed it. To burn down a police station was one thing; to do so *together*, as an act of collective mourning and celebration, was another thing entirely, and it was glorious indeed. So direct was the correspondence between the violence inflicted on George Floyd and the retaliation by protesters that, at the time, some 54 percent of Americans felt their actions were justified.

In front of the burning precinct, the scene was euphoric. Widely circulated images of the gathered crowds tell us much about those who would come to lead the George Floyd rebellions nationwide. Some faces, many masks. Multiracial, but mostly Black. Multigenerational, but mostly teenagers and Gen Z "zoomers" abandoned by the greed and fear of a dying white world. Those who might once have expected a level of comfort and security that is no longer possible, and those taught for centuries to expect very little, if anything—"the holders of empty promissory notes, and the holders of nothing at all," in the words of Joshua Clover.[1] But their exuberant faces betrayed more than fury at broken promises and rage at yet another brazen police murder: it gave us a glimpse of a different kind of world. And the parameters of that new world came immediately into focus. As protests leapt across the country like climate change–induced wildfires, grassroots pressure nationwide crystallized in an unprecedented way around a nearly unanimous demand: to defund and abolish the police.

Minneapolis is no stranger to police violence—the name Jamar Clark, shot dead in 2015, still rings loudly in our ears, as does that of Philando Castile, killed in 2016 in a nearby suburb. But it still came as a shock when city council president Lisa Bender tweeted dramatically on June 4: "We are going to dismantle the Minneapolis Police Department and replace it with a transformative new model of public safety." Flanked by councilors Jeremiah Ellison and Alondra Cano, Bender soon unveiled a veto-proof majority promising to make good on the plan. Cano describes her own realization, upon seeing the video of George Floyd's murder, that the Minneapolis Police Department "was never going to be repairable." She had seen police reform in practice, had heard the department lauded by Obama's police reform czars, and it still came to this: MPD officer Derek Chauvin's knee on George Floyd's neck. For nine eternal minutes.

No amount of cultural sensitivity or use of force training had prevented it. The current system of policing, Cano now realized, was the product of slavery and colonization, and no amount of reform had been able to change its fundamental nature. "This," she explained, "is why so many of us are unflinchingly committed to deconstructing that system altogether and creating a new system from the ground up with our communities." To do so, she insisted, doesn't mean "abolishing safety. We're not abolishing protection. We're abolishing a broken system."[2]

But as the city council was taking unprecedented steps toward dismantling the MPD and experimenting with alternative models for public safety, movements in the streets were not about to wait for elected leaders to make this new model of public safety—and this new world—a reality. As rolling protests continued across Minneapolis, an evacuated 136-room Sheraton hotel was quickly commandeered by organizers and transformed into a sort of self-managed commune, staffed by volunteers, to house local homeless residents. The Sheraton was but one part of a broader ecosystem of mutual aid that sprang up across Minneapolis during the George Floyd rebellions, providing a glimpse of the new forms of life that will be possible once the old are obsolete. "We are the petri dish," as one volunteer described it. "We are the experiment."[3]

Several months later, when Minneapolis police sought to rent a temporary space to house the Third Precinct, graffiti soon appeared promising James Baldwin's fire next time: "We could burn this one too." The building's owner canceled the lease, while rebels in Minneapolis and beyond channeled Malcolm X, praying for wind.

———

In the history of the United States, nothing has provoked mass rebellion more consistently than police brutality, but it has never been possible to predict *which* moments in the seamless fabric of anti-Black violence would toss forth the hottest spark. The

3

nationwide and even international response to George Floyd's killing was not an isolated event, but instead emerged within a global cycle of struggle that has been gaining velocity for more than a decade. At its broadest, this included the wave of global resistance to neoliberalism, often led by the poorest, that rattled Latin America and North Africa before crash-landing in the global North. In the United States, resistance to police murder broke out on the first day of the age of Obama, when Oscar Grant was shot dead by Bay Area transit police and Oakland erupted. Promised hope and change, people rebelled against what turned out to be more of the same—and they haven't stopped rebelling since.

Struggles against white supremacist violence and the mass impoverishment of poor communities spiraled unpredictably forth. Inequality had been growing for decades and was reaching an undeniable breaking point when the Occupy movement, warts and all, propelled anti-capitalist economic demands to the forefront of public consciousness. Meanwhile, persistent struggles precipitated by the racist killing of seventeen-year-old Trayvon Martin in 2012, and so many others, sparked a smoldering movement in defense of Black lives that soon found a powerful accelerant in the mass rebellions in Ferguson (after the shooting of Mike Brown by officer Darren Wilson) and then Baltimore (after Freddie Gray's deadly "rough ride") that indelibly transformed the political terrain of the country. At their best, Occupy and this emerging movement were able to find common ground; indeed, race and class are so powerfully intertwined in US history as to be inextricable.

More narrowly, Floyd was killed amid the surging wave of white resentment that had emerged in reaction to Obama and Black Lives Matter (BLM), thrusting Donald Trump into the White House. In his first days in office, Trump issued a statement denouncing a "dangerous anti-police atmosphere" and pledging to crack down on rioters and looters. This wasn't even a dog whistle, but a blaring alarm that declared racist violence by police and others to be acceptable, indeed laudable. In February 2020, Ahmaud Arbery was stalked and fatally shot by white vigilantes in Georgia, and the next month Louisville police stormed into Breonna Taylor's apartment in a no-knock raid, shooting her eight times. In May, newly released video of Arbery's murder went viral, sparking fury at both his death and the lack of arrests in the case. It was just a few weeks later that George Floyd lost his life under the knee of Derek Chauvin in Minneapolis, his last words an excruciating echo of those spoken eleven times by Eric Garner some six years earlier: "I can't breathe."

For the anti-colonial revolutionary Frantz Fanon, such asphyxiation was no accident, but the direct consequence of broader systems of global colonialism and white supremacy. After Garner's death, a powerful, if imprecise, quotation from Fanon's deathbed masterpiece, *The Wretched of the Earth*, began to circulate: "We revolt simply because, for many reasons, we can no longer breathe." The struggle to breathe, Fanon insisted, points toward liberation, in no small part because fire, too, needs oxygen.

—

Before long, a chain reaction of fierce struggles and astonishing victories was spreading across the country. Dozens of cities nationwide answered the call to defund the police, if only in symbolic ways.[4] In Minneapolis, a string of public agencies from the University of Minnesota to the public school district, parks and recreation board, and even museums all severed ties with the MPD. Other school districts from Saint Paul to Oakland voted to eliminate contracts for school police, or school resource officers (SROs), and San Francisco voted unanimously to declare schools a "sanctuary" from law enforcement. The sprawling Los Angeles Unified School District—with more than 400 officers— voted to cut its massive police budget by a third.

In popular culture, a broad cross section of celebrities openly declared their support for the street rebellions, and abolition was up for debate in the pages of the *New York Times* and among the stalwart radicals at *Teen Vogue*. The long-running reality television show *Cops*—which for decades epitomized the "copaganda" programming that was a hallmark of American entertainment— was abruptly canceled. Perhaps most surprisingly, NASCAR banned the Confederate flag, to the chagrin of many diehard stock car racing fans. The protests soon reignited a long-simmering controversy about monuments to racism and white supremacy, and Confederate leaders fell like dominoes throughout the month of June. A statue of Confederate president Jefferson Davis was defaced and later torn down by demonstrators in Richmond, Virginia, along with several of his compatriots. City and state leaders responded by voting to remove several more, including J.E.B. Stuart, "Stonewall" Jackson, and Robert E. Lee—but not before demonstrators had projected George Floyd's face dramatically onto the pedestal of the Lee monument under the words "No Justice, No Peace." In Raleigh, North Carolina, a Confederate monument was torn down and hung from a traffic light.

Colonizers met the same fate: Columbus statues were beheaded in Boston, torn down in Saint Paul, vandalized in Miami, thrown into a pond in Richmond, and ordered removed in St. Louis, Chicago, and San Francisco. In South Philadelphia, a Columbus statue was slated for removal after a violent standoff between anti-racist protesters and white reactionaries. Soon to follow were both the statue and mural commemorating police commissioner-turned-mayor Frank Rizzo, long a symbol of white supremacy in the city and a target of protesters. In Los Angeles, Sacramento, and San Francisco's Golden Gate Park, monuments to the Spanish priest Junípero Serra—who spearheaded California's cultural and actual genocide in the eighteenth century—were torn down by coalitions of Black and Indigenous activists. Protests also forced the removal of two monuments to Juan de Oñate, the bloody conquistador of what is today New Mexico.

The George Floyd revolt would soon go global, dovetailing seamlessly with ongoing struggles against colonial and imperial legacies. In Bristol, England, a statue of the slave trader Edward Colston was dragged from its pedestal and thrown into the river. Belgium removed several statues of Leopold II, who oversaw the death of some 10 million in the Congo, after protesters targeted them. Toppling statues was nothing new to the formerly colonized world, either. In Latin America, celebrations of the 1992 quincentennial of Columbus's arrival were marred when Indigenous movements toppled a monument to Diego de Mazariegos in Chiapas, Mexico—foreshadowing the Zapatista insurrection two years later. A Columbus statue in Caracas, Venezuela, met the same fate in 2004. In 2015, a movement emerged at the University of Cape Town in South Africa under the slogan "Rhodes must fall," demanding the removal of a statue of British imperialist Cecil Rhodes. The global revolt of 2020 reignited these demands: Indigenous protesters in Popayán, Colombia, hauled down a statue of the conquistador Sebastián de Belalcázar, and in Cape Town, Rhodes was decapitated.

To tear down monuments to white supremacy has nothing to do with erasing history, as the right likes to imagine. After all, most Confederate monuments are cheap knockoffs erected during waves of white reaction and often as a ploy to boost real estate values—not tributes to the past, but, in the words of University of Chicago historian Jane Dailey, harbingers of "a white supremacist future."[5] Struggles against such monuments, by contrast, point toward a different future, reinvigorating long-erased histories in the service of abolition and decolonization. In both of these unfinished battles, victories have been more formal than substantive: most slavery has been abolished in name, and formal colonies are few and far between. When movements target racist monuments, however, they insist on the need to build a world of real democracy and true human equality, and when they do so themselves, without asking politely, they demonstrate the boldness of their resolve.

White supremacy never goes quietly, however. The brutal repression and militarized force that police unleashed on protests nationwide only seemed to confirm what their critics had been saying all along, and the uptick in attacks by armed vigilantes only drove home the complicity between institutionalized policing and extra-institutional white supremacist terror. Far-right fascist and white supremacist attacks, on the uptick for years, now found a target for their resentment. Nationwide, white men drove cars into protests and opened fire on them. In Salt Lake City, a man tried to shoot at protesters with a bow and arrow, before being surrounded and disarmed by the crowd. At a protest against the Oñate monument in Albuquerque, a member of an armed militia known as the New Mexico Civil Guard shot one demonstrator; as the shooter was taken into custody, he loudly announced that his father was the former sheriff. And in Austin, Texas, an active duty soldier sought out protesters to attack and ended up killing Garrett Foster, a veteran who was carrying an AK-47 to defend BLM protesters.

In Buffalo, many were shocked by a video of riot police casually knocking 75-year-old Martin Gugino, a local Catholic peace activist, to the pavement. His skull fractured, Gugino lay stiffly, legs slightly crossed and fingers curling, as blood poured from his right ear onto the pavement. Dozens of black-clad officers continued forward, stepping over the bleeding senior citizen. Police initially claimed there had been a "skirmish"; later, they revised their story to say that Gugino had tripped and fallen of his own accord; and when two officers were suspended and later charged with felony assault, all fifty-seven members of the Buffalo Police Emergency Response Team resigned in solidarity. Scarcely a week later, on June 12, Rayshard Brooks, a 27-year-old Black restaurant worker, fell asleep at a Wendy's drive-through in Atlanta, only to be shot dead by police as he attempted to flee. In the post–George Floyd moment, however, reaction was swift: the police chief resigned almost immediately, and the officer involved was fired and criminally charged. In a defiant show of support for their colleague, nearly 200 officers engaged in a four-day "blue flu," calling in sick or refusing to respond to calls.

Then in late August, another young Black man, Jacob Blake, was shot seven times by police in Kenosha, Wisconsin, as his children looked on from their car. The shooting was caught on video, which shows Blake walking away from officers when they opened fire. That night, marchers faced off with armored personnel carriers, burning three garbage trucks positioned to block their advance. Two days later, on August 25, a seventeen-year-old white vigilante named Kyle Rittenhouse arrived in Kenosha, armed with an AR-15-style rifle. By nightfall, he had shot three protesters, killing two, becoming a hero to the white supremacist right in the process. Four days later, in Portland, Oregon—which saw more than one hundred days of uninter-rupted protests—a caravan of Trump supporters rolled through the city, firing paintballs and bear mace into crowds of demon-strators, and a member of the far-right Patriot Prayer organization was shot dead. Michael Forest Reinoehl—a self-identified anti-fascist—took responsibility for the shooting, claiming self-defense. Five days later, a joint federal-local taskforce retaliated, killing Reinoehl in a hail of gunfire.

The world was spinning palpably faster, entire decades compressed into the blur of weeks, to invoke Vladimir Lenin's apocryphal phrase. In Portland, middle-class moms were fight-ing the cops, while dads were using leaf blowers to turn tear gas back toward police lines. A strike that originated in the NBA and WNBA quickly spread to professional baseball and even hockey; a rising tide of athletes, so often painted as selfish indi-vidualists, thus moved in solidarity long before any union, and with a much more immediate and pronounced impact.

These are the parameters of the whirlwind into which we were collectively thrown in 2020. As a rotten system pulls out all the stops to stabilize the status quo, it's important not to forget those heady days of that long summer, when for a moment anything seemed possible and we were winning more than we had ever imagined.

—

We live in a world of police, a society built around policing and that presumes their necessity. The world of police is one where those in power see the police as a one-size-fits-all solution for every social problem: poverty, mental health, a lack of opportunity, or inadequate afterschool or sports programs—just send in the police, and if that doesn't work, send in some more. When you're holding a hammer, as the old adage goes, everything looks like a nail.

The catch-22 of this world of police is that those communities where the police do the worst are the same ones where safety is most needed, where entire sectors of the population are excluded from the formal workforce and left to hustle or starve, where poverty and mental health create a permanent feedback loop of crisis, and where there isn't always anyone else to call. But these are also the communities most in need of radical solutions. Without alternatives, it's difficult to tell people—especially those most marginalized and vulnerable—to simply stop calling the police on principle. People in physical danger, women and others in abusive relationships, families with loved ones suffering dangerous mental health crises—rich and poor, Black and white, people of all backgrounds call the police every single day because they have no one else to call.

And yet, as we will see, the police don't actually help. They don't prevent violence, and they don't make any measurable contribution to public safety. If anything, what the police are most adept at is eating up billions of dollars in resources that could be repurposed to build truly secure communities. The police have wormed their way into the very foundations of American society and work every day to make themselves—and their bloated budgets—seem indispensable. As a metaphor, think of cities built around highways and cars, where it's often difficult to walk or take public transit anywhere. So too are we accustomed to navigating a world where policing is built right into the structure of everyday life. The task of *undoing* these kinds of structural arrangements, putting an entire society in reverse, can seem overwhelming. It's no small job to tear the whole foundation from beneath a building, much less to reconstruct it anew. But to paraphrase novelist Ursula K. Le Guin, while the power of the police can seem inescapable, "so did the divine right of kings." Once upon a time there were no cops, and that day is coming again soon.

Abolition is not simply an *against*, however: it is also a *for*. As daunting as it is to imagine and begin to build a world without police, it is precisely in the simultaneity of these two tasks that the new world comes into focus. Despite its name, abolition approaches the task of dismantling oppressive institutions as an active process of rebuilding new and more human alternatives. "Abolition is about presence, not absence," in the words of the radical geographer Ruth Wilson Gilmore: "It's about building life-affirming institutions." Abolition is about laying a new foundation under, around, and in the cracks of the old world until the old foundation is no more. It is this double move, and the dynamic relation between the two parts—the negative and the positive—that scholar-activist Angela Davis gestures toward when she speaks of making prisons "obsolete."[6] Fighting against mass incarceration means building alternatives to prison, and insofar as these alternatives exist and the conditions underpinning the prison-industrial complex recede, the carceral state will wither away. As with prisons, so too with their handmaidens, the police: as organizer and educator Mariame Kaba has put it: "We are not abandoning our communities to violence. We don't want to just close police departments. We want to make them obsolete."[7]

This double task has been a part of abolitionist movements from the beginning, because the abolition of slavery has always meant more than the mere elimination of a single institution.

Intuitively, we know this to be true. We know the Thirteenth Amendment wasn't enough without the citizenship, equal protection, and suffrage conferred by the Fourteenth and Fifteenth Amendments. We know that abolition wasn't only about the vote, either, but about those educational and material transformations that would make Black votes matter. We know that abolitionists demanded not only emancipation but also the economic reparations denoted by the phrase "forty acres and a mule." We know, in short, that the brief period of post–Civil War reckoning that in some states saw self-rule by the Black majority was called *Reconstruction* for a reason.

For W.E.B. Du Bois, the dyad of abolition and Reconstruction marked out the most important moment in US history—"an eternal second in a cycle of a thousand years," whose failures and lessons ring deafeningly in our ears today.[8] His magnum opus, *Black Reconstruction in America*, showed how in its most radical moments, Reconstruction sought to build a society not just of political equality, but of *social* equality as well. Reconstruction governments pioneered public welfare for the poor and a public school system; created orphanages, schools for the deaf and blind, and mental hospitals; halted debt collection and abolished debtors' prisons; distributed land, expanded women's rights, and eliminated property restrictions on voting—extending the franchise to even many poor whites as well. These were accomplishments that preceded and rivaled those of the Paris Commune, and this experiment, what Du Bois called "abolition democracy," promised a better society for *everyone*. Abolition democracy "went beyond" simply abolishing slavery because mere political equality "was no logical stopping place; and it looked forward to civil and political rights, education and land, as the only complete guarantee of freedom, in the face of a dominant South which hoped from the first, to abolish slavery only in name."[9]

Even then, freedom was far from guaranteed. Black Southerners could not defend their vote with votes alone, and within a few years the material force of Black freedom was defeated by the equally material force of white terror and the Ku Klux Klan. Reconstruction was crushed, and if this was the supreme tragedy of American history, it was a tragedy for *everyone* the world over: "The slave went free; stood a brief moment in the sun; then moved back again toward slavery," and as a direct consequence, "the whole weight of America was thrown to color caste." Global war and imperialism divided and destroyed working-class movements, Du Bois concluded, because poor whites continued to choose their race over their class: "The plight of the white working class throughout the world today is directly traceable to Negro slavery in America."[10]

We find ourselves where we are today because the abolition of slavery after the Civil War was incomplete and one-sided— because it failed to create the kind of world necessary for slavery to really, truly cease to exist. This was not for lack of trying, however: abolishing institutions is far easier than reconstructing the world that upholds them, and many a struggle since has stumbled and stalled on the level of the formal. As a consequence, instead of forty acres and a mule there was sharecropping; instead of freedom there was convict leasing, "Black codes," Jim Crow, and mass incarceration. In short, instead of true abolition, we got *the police*.

For Angela Davis, the question of abolition democracy gets right to the heart of the dual and unfinished tasks of abolition and reconstruction today, which are

> not only, or not even primarily, about abolition as a negative process of tearing down, but it is also about building up, about creating new institutions ... Du Bois pointed out that in order to fully abolish the oppressive conditions produced by slavery, new democratic institutions would have to be created. Because this did not occur; black people encountered new forms of slavery—from debt peonage and the convict lease system to segregated and second-class education. The prison system continues to carry out this terrible legacy.[11]

Abolition democracy points not only to the failures of Reconstruction, however, but to its radically transformative potential as well. Abolition democracy means that *who* participates in political life changes *how* democracy functions and *what* alternatives become possible as a result. It's about the *kind* of democracy that comes into view when white supremacy is in retreat, and the fact that the participation of the most exploited, oppressed, and excluded leaves no structure of inequality intact.

"Democracy died save in the hearts of black folk," wrote Du Bois in 1935, and today, movements for Black liberation are once again setting the world into motion in ever more democratic directions.

—

If the flames that leapt up in Minneapolis cast police abolition suddenly into the mainstream imagination, these embers have been smoldering for centuries. From the very beginning, abolitionists have been stubborn agitators, zealots, and fanatics of the best sort who saw no room for compromise with the inhumanity of slavery and no way to reform away its evils.[12] They drew a hard line between good and evil, demanding Americans pick a side—are you with humanity or with the slave masters? At first, they were a tiny minority in a society that largely viewed slavery as natural, but within a few short years, abolitionist ideas went from fringe heresy to mainstream common sense. This shift didn't always—or even primarily—occur through reasoned argument and patient debate, but by unpredictable leaps and bounds and through the boldness and daring of Nat Turner, Harriet Tubman, Frederick Douglass, Sojourner Truth, John Brown, and so many other rebels and insurrectionists.

Thanks to their struggles and sacrifices, few would consider slavery a natural institution today, but the same can't be said of its carceral heirs: prisons and the police. When a group of scholars, activists, formerly incarcerated people and their families, and other community members got together to found Critical

Resistance more than a century later, in 1997, nothing seemed more natural than the ballooning prison-industrial complex (PIC), and nothing could have seemed more impossible than demanding its total abolition. The 1994 Clinton crime bill had seen the establishment of a broad bipartisan consensus in support of the unrestrained use of policing and imprisonment as the only possible solutions to social problems. But thanks to the tenacity of Critical Resistance and other grassroots organizations, the intervening two decades have seen a sea change in public consciousness.

Today, amid a torrent of mea culpas from a Democratic Party leadership complicit in jailing its own electoral base, there is little question that mass incarceration is a "crisis" in need of radical solutions.[13] While the prison population has declined in recent years, organizers from Critical Resistance are quick to insist that this work is far from over, and that we still live in a world of prisons to be dismantled and rebuilt on a different foundation: "Abolition isn't just about getting rid of buildings full of cages. It's also about undoing the society we live in because the PIC both feeds on and maintains oppression and inequalities through punishment, violence, and controls millions of people."[14] Since policing, like mass incarceration, has built our world in its own image, embedding and naturalizing the unnatural and inhuman, we can't talk about abolition today without talking about the police as well.

Even before the emergence of the BLM movement, police abolition was beginning to gain steam.[15] But it was the explosive resistance in the streets of Ferguson (2014) and Baltimore (2015), and the overwhelming military response, that propelled the question of the police squarely into the public eye. Movements once denounced for lacking a program soon found one, much to the chagrin of the powerful. The World without Police collective crystallized this emerging common sense by putting out a call for the three D's: disempowering, disarming, and ultimately disbanding the police entirely. "You can't reform a landmine," they argue, "but you can dismantle it, destroy the factories that made it, and dissolve the governments and businesses that profit off of its existence."[16]

Halfhearted responses, reports, and reform proposals from Barack Obama's Department of Justice seemed more concerned with containing Black rebellion than changing policing itself, and the questions left unanswered after Ferguson and Baltimore clamor for attention today with an unprecedented ferocity. While it shocked many to hear Chicago activist Jessica Disu insist on *Fox News* in 2016 that "we need to abolish the police, period," this idea—along with her further insistence that "we need to come up with community solutions for transformative justice"—has, just a few years later, become common currency for many organizers. Thanks to the tireless agitation of abolitionists and the bravery of the rebels in the streets of Minneapolis and elsewhere, we stand today amid a swirling sea change much like that of mass incarceration a decade ago.

Minneapolis shouted, and the nation and the world responded: What is to be done with the police?

—

This is both a book about the police and a book about abolition—about why we need to abolish the police, and what doing so might look like. While many books on the police tend to diagnose the problem of policing and only gesture toward abolition, and many books on abolition remain speculative about what the process might look like, this book grows out of a different context. Today, a new generation of struggles against white supremacy, policing, and capitalism throws forth new alternatives; new possibilities, strategies, and tactics; and new barriers and pitfalls. It is from within and amid this tumult that the experiments I discuss here are emerging and taking shape, however provisionally and tentatively. I can only hope that this book is faithful to the upsurge and, once the temperature has dropped and the forces of stabilization are in full force, that it provides a reminder of the fire of the streets.

Today, as a century ago, the positive, creative face of abolition, the building of the world we want to see—of security, equality, and freedom—is inseparable from the process of destroying those relics of the past that continue to stain our present. Abolition is a tight spiral, a double helix, of both processes. It is the rage of burning down a police station and the joy of doing it *together*, because to do so bespeaks a new world that both already exists and is permanently in the making. However, the precise relationship between the two, the center of gravity binding abolition to reconstruction, has not been fully ironed out, nor should we expect it to be. Abolition implies a plurality of approaches, many cooks in the kitchen, but this is not a book of recipes for the future. It's about what's cooking.

Writing in the *New York Times* in the midst of the global rebellion of summer 2020, Mariame Kaba warned against forgetting those glints of possibility that, like so many lightning bolts, illuminate moments of upsurge: "When the streets calm and people suggest once again that we hire more black police officers or create more civilian review boards, I hope that we remember all the times those efforts have failed."[17] Against this forgetting, which is actively encouraged by a system desperate to preserve itself in the face of total abolition, Kaba puts things as clearly as we could hope: "Yes, We Mean Literally Abolish the Police."

1

The Pig Majority

Ahmaud Arbery wasn't killed by an officer of the law. But he was killed by police. How else to describe Gregory McMichael, his son Travis, and William "Roddie" Bryan, when they decided to pursue Arbery—with a .357 Magnum and a shotgun in tow— while he was jogging through Brunswick, Georgia, on February 23, 2020? When the pursuers attempted to corral him with their pickup truck before ultimately shooting him in the chest with a shotgun, there is no doubt that, at that moment, they were the police. This intuition would soon be confirmed. The McMichaels were not arrested for a full seventy-four days after they killed Arbery, and it took the recusal of two prosecutors—the second of which only did so after penning a letter insisting that there were no grounds to arrest the three assailants. Why the recusals? Because the elder McMichael had been a longtime police officer himself.

Some have decried Arbery's killers as vigilantes or a lynch mob—both are certainly true. As one former federal prosecutor commented on the case: "the law does not allow a group of people to form an armed posse and chase down an unarmed person." But to draw a hard line between the state and its self-deputized enforcers betrays a woeful ignorance of US history, throughout which the police have rarely if ever been distinguishable from the white mob. After all, the power to convoke a posse, one still enshrined in Georgia criminal law (section 17-4-24), is a power that belongs to the police. While vigilante violence has taken distinct forms throughout US history, self-deputized defenders of property and whiteness have almost always served as a brutal adjunct to the police, and the line between the two has been far from clear. Vigilantism first emerged on the southern border to terrorize Mexican and Indigenous people, in support of and supported by the official forces of colonial order. The complicity of police with lynch mobs—in up to half of all lynchings—is well-documented.[1] And today, police membership in white supremacist organizations has been widely characterized as an "epidemic"; indeed, the name of one such organization, Posse Comitatus, says it all.[2]

In late August 2020, the smoldering embers of the George Floyd rebellion dramatically reignited after the videotaped shooting of Jacob Blake by police in Kenosha, Wisconsin. When protests broke out, armed white militias—bolstered by right-wing narratives about Antifa and Black Lives Matter (as well as a Republican National Convention that foregrounded racist vigilantes)—quickly arrived on the scene. Kyle Rittenhouse was among them. Rittenhouse's mother had driven her teenaged son, an aspiring police officer, across state lines with his AR-15-style rifle to defend the private property of others. Police greeted and thanked the militias, offering water to Rittenhouse and others. He was later seen speaking to an interviewer on camera: "Our job is to protect this business," although, as the *New York Times* quickly pointed out, "there is no indication that he was asked to guard the site."[3] This child-vigilante soon shot three protesters, two fatally.

In a video posted to Twitter, he can be heard speaking on the phone—"I just killed somebody"—before jogging, armed, toward the police, only occasionally raising his hands in the air. Despite protesters yelling to the police that Rittenhouse had shot someone, he was allowed to simply walk away from the scene of a double murder, crossing state lines before later being arrested. The Kenosha police chief blamed protesters themselves for the violence inflicted upon them: if they hadn't been out past curfew, they wouldn't have died. Kyle Rittenhouse, too, was out after curfew.

Seventeen-year-old Trayvon Martin wasn't technically killed by the police either, although George Zimmerman had certainly deputized himself to police the gated community in Sanford, Florida, where he would murder Martin in 2012. Nor was Jordan Davis, also seventeen, killed in Jacksonville nine months later, after white vigilante Michael Dunn became incensed by the loud "thug music" Davis and his friends were listening to at a gas station. Nor was nineteen-year-old Renisha McBride, who knocked on Theodore Wafer's door in Dearborn Heights, Michigan, for assistance a year later. Wafer fired a shotgun blast through his screen door and into McBride's head. And in 2020 alone, white vigilantes took it upon themselves to attack BLM protests nationwide with vehicles, firearms, bear spray, and even a bow and arrow.

When police attacked Black teenagers at a pool party in McKinney, Texas, in 2015, most of the subsequent uproar focused on Eric Casebolt, the raging police officer who grabbed a fifteen-year-old girl by the hair and pointed his gun at others. Less discussed, however, was the behavior of other civilians involved: the teenagers later attested to the fact that white women had attacked them and made racist comments, and video of the incident clearly shows a large, self-deputized white man physically intervening to help police detain the teenagers. When 22-year-old John Crawford III was shot dead by police in an Ohio Walmart in 2014 for holding a BB gun in an open carry state, police claimed he had ignored verbal commands. Surveillance video shows they fired immediately. In fact, police had been called to the scene by a white bystander, who was later found to have "intentionally" lied about Crawford behaving in a threatening manner. Whether this was a lie or white fear, the result was just as deadly. Vigilantes don't always need to pull the trigger; sometimes they just dial 911.

It was not the police but a grand jury of everyday citizens that declined to charge Crawford's killers. The same goes for the majority-white grand jury that declined to charge Darren Wilson, who gunned down Mike Brown in Ferguson, and the officers who shot twelve-year-old Tamir Rice in Cleveland. While grand juries are often seen as a rubber-stamp institution that, in the words of one judge, would "indict a ham sandwich" if prosecutors so requested, this clearly doesn't apply to cases involving Black people, where grand juries shield the system from scrutiny by letting police and white vigilantes walk free so prosecutors don't have to. Even in cases where grand juries or prosecutors *do* indict, as with Freddie Gray's death in police custody in Baltimore, judges often throw out the charges, or juries deadlock and acquit on flimsy claims of self-defense—rights not accorded to the victims of police violence.

This is what Ta-Nehisi Coates means when he writes, in *Between the World and Me*, that "to challenge the police is to challenge the American people, and the problem with the police is not that they are fascist pigs but that we are majoritarian pigs."[4] The pig majority includes the police, but it exceeds them as well. It comprises all those volunteer deputies eagerly doing their violent work alongside them. It is the judges, the courts, the juries, and the grand juries. It is the mayors and the district attorneys who demand "law and order" and denounce those who protest police brutality as "mindless rioters and looters." It is the racist media apparatus that bends over backward to turn victims into aggressors and—above all when the former are Black and the latter white—killers into saints. It is the same pig media that selects innocent-looking photos for white aggressors while their victims are painted as violent, that breathlessly reports drugs in the victim's bloodstream, previous encounters with the law, and scandalous social media posts. And it is the same media that, amid the wreckage of Hurricane Katrina in 2005, infamously coded white people as survivors and Black people as looters—legitimizing vigilante violence in defense of white property.

This expansive, amorphous pig majority comes into being long before violence occurs and continues to coalesce and expand after the body is cold. Its backbone is the self-deputized white majority that, with an effortlessness bordering on instinct, volunteers to police others, in part because it dreams police dreams and plays them out at home on wives and children, all while praying to a police god. This pig majority is fueled not only by overt racism and a white victimhood complex, but also by that perilous quantity that is white fear. It is part of the so-called implicit bias that leads police to shoot suspects of color—and Black suspects in particular—without hesitation. But white fear is deadly in other ways, too: when it calls 911 to report a suspicious person or a crime; when it describes a suspect; when it moves to a neighborhood and calls the cops on longtime residents and businesses for being too loud, too rowdy. It's apps like Citizen and local Facebook groups; it's cop-calling gentrifiers and the real estate developers behind neocolonial land grabs. And, as we will see, the pig majority that upholds white supremacy extends far beyond white Americans, conscripting many people of color—some voluntarily, some less so—to do its work as well.

The pig majority might include you, too. But it doesn't have to.

—

Policing and whiteness—white *power*—are inseparable. As W.E.B. Du Bois argued in *Black Reconstruction*, this has been true from the beginning, when "slavery demanded a special police force and such a force was made possible and unusually effective by the presence of the poor whites."[5] As slave patrols morphed into police forces, moreover, little changed, and the "police system was arranged to deal with blacks alone, and tacitly assumed that every white man was *ipso facto* a member of that police."[6]

After the abolition of slavery, when Black freedom threatened the plantation economy and terrified many whites, policing became *more* important, not less. "Black codes" across the South made Black labor mandatory under vagrancy laws, punishing those found in violation with forced labor. The objective was clear: to discipline a necessary workforce. Those who refused were imprisoned, and many were subjected to the regime of convict leasing—some of whom were returned in chains to the same plantations they had only just escaped. The broader result was a cheap labor force whose docility was ensured by the threat of re-enslavement, or worse. If policing disciplined former slaves, it provided concrete employment for many otherwise-destitute whites as overseers, slave breakers, and patrolmen. Whiteness, however, was not only about monetary wages, but also entailed what Du Bois called a "public and psychological wage" that "fed his vanity because it associated him with the masters."[7] Poor whites were bestowed with symbolic superiority and titles, but also material privileges: access to public functions and parks, public education, and leniency in the courts.

These petty privileges and "wages of whiteness" encouraged poor whites to identify as white rather than as poor, ensuring their loyalty to their class enemies and disarming any potential solidarity with poor Black people, slave or free. The police were thus the linchpin holding together a vast, cross-class alliance that, for Du Bois, marked the tragedy of post-emancipation America. Poor whites had betrayed their own class interests by entering into a devil's bargain with their "race," thereby setting American capitalism on a path of untrammeled greed and racial avarice from which it hasn't strayed since. This racial bargain had upheld the slave system, and the same bargain would doom Reconstruction, a radical experiment in social and racial equality that had improved the lives of *everyone*, poor whites included, by breaking the political power of the planter class, abolishing debtors' prisons, establishing public schools, and eliminating property qualifications for voting.

Having chosen their race over their class, these ipso facto police took on another name: the Ku Klux Klan. Through terroristic intimidation, the Klan-police disenfranchised Black Southerners and imposed "a double system of justice" that sought "to use the courts as a means of re-enslaving the blacks." "Gradually," Du Bois wrote, "the whole white South became an armed and commissioned camp to keep Negroes in slavery and to kill the black rebel."[8] The police stood against democracy from the very beginning, resisting with violent terror even its most limited representative form—one person, one vote. But this was in part because to grant basic suffrage to former slaves posed a threat to those limits and opened the door to more substantial demands. As Reconstruction governments showed, the vote was not an end in itself, but a means toward building that world of greater equality and more substantive participation that Du Bois called "abolition democracy." The Klan-police rolled back this ambitious vision, containing it within bounds acceptable for racists and capitalists alike.

While slave patrols provided the vicious blueprint, the policing of slaves in the South dovetailed with the policing of other "dangerous" classes like the poor and immigrant rabble of the North. It was in the context of Northern cities that professional policing had emerged in the United States, heavily influenced by the English model of Robert Peel's London Metropolitan Police. Even though their sources differed, there was no real contradiction between these two forms of policing—after all, in the development of American capitalism, slavery had been as important as industry, providing raw materials to the North and to London itself. In their genesis, police embodied the division of the poor, and in their practical function they uphold that division every day, patrolling the boundaries of property and that most peculiar form of property that is whiteness. American policing has always been about two things at once: controlling "dangerous" people and disciplining the workforce; assuaging the moral anxieties of white elites and the needs of capital accumulation; racist fear and economic profit.

Whether in the North or in the South, police have attacked workers and broken strikes, and they have policed the perceived vice and immorality that is primarily associated with people of color. After the abolition of slavery, policing helped keep the Black labor force on the plantations from which they had been momentarily freed, patrolling the boundaries of segregated neighborhoods for decades to come. And as deindustrialization set in in the 1970s and poor Black workers were pushed out of the labor market entirely, the police stepped in to enforce the violent feedback loop connecting ghettoes to prisons. This contemporary arrangement squeezes nearly free labor like blood from a stone, providing a never-ending stream of jobs for police and prison guards while protecting property—real estate values in particular—from the poorest. If Du Bois spoke more than a century ago of the role of the courts in re-enslaving Black people, the racist seeds of Jim Crow have borne fruit in the mass incarceration and the mass policing of today. How else to explain, more than a century after abolition, disparities in federal sentencing guidelines of one hundred to one between powder cocaine and crack?

It is no exaggeration to say that the South won the long Civil War, even if the fight rages on in the streets today. The racist policing pioneered under slavery and in the Jim Crow South have gone nationwide and metastasized—from Black codes to "broken windows," from convict leasing to the criminalization of Blackness. The watchword of American history is not change but continuity, not abolition but substitution. New structures of containment have replaced the old, in a seemingly interminable cycle driven by the irrepressible yearning of Black freedom dreams. Meanwhile, poor whites, dying of opioid addiction and preventable disease, choose the increasingly meager wages of whiteness over a better world for all, voting for more police as the coffers of the rich burst their hinges.

—

If whiteness were a job, it would be the police. But if policing emerged as historically indistinguishable from whiteness, and if white Americans continue to play a disproportionately heavy role in today's pig majority, what of the legions of Black and Brown police officers, commanders, and commissioners, district attorneys, mayors, and judges? What of the diversity among the ranks of border patrol, immigration and customs agents, and active duty foot soldiers of global imperialism abroad? And what of the complicity of the broader multiracial political class in what legal scholar James Forman Jr. has called "locking up our own?"

After a young client of his was handed a harsh sentence delivered via a speech about the virtues of Martin Luther King Jr. and the civil rights movement, it suddenly dawned on Forman that *everyone* in the Washington, DC, courtroom is Black:

> not just the judge, but the court reporter, the bailiff, and the juvenile prosecutor. So was the police officer who had arrested Brandon, not to mention the police chief and the mayor . . . I had been to the detention facility that would be Brandon's new home . . . and I knew that all the guards there were black, too. The city council that wrote the gun and drug laws Brandon had been convicted of violating was majority African American and had been so for more than twenty-five years. In cases that went to trial, the juries were often majority black . . . How did a majority-black jurisdiction end up incarcerating so many of its own?[9]

Although that particular situation could only have occurred in the past forty or so years, the dynamic is at least a century older: in his groundbreaking sociological study *The Philadelphia Negro*, Du Bois himself documented how Black police officers had been appointed in the city as early as 1884.[10] Almost exactly a century later in the same city, a Black mayor dropped a bomb on the MOVE Organization, burning down a city block and killing eleven—including several children—and a string of Black police commissioners have continued to this day to heap disproportionate brutality on poor people of color.

Policing is racist no matter who is doing the legwork. Even where intentions might be pure, racist fear is contagious, afflicting even officers of color, as repeated studies on implicit bias have demonstrated.[11] More importantly, however, individual intentions matter little in the face of the structural racism of policing, which dispatches officers onto the streets to patrol the boundaries of whiteness and wealth, reinforcing and deepening racial and class inequalities in the process. And just as more Black police doesn't mean less racism, it's no solution to brutality either.

The two different modes of policing that Du Bois had observed in the Jim Crow South and Philadelphia, respectively, remain in place today, revealed most clearly in the rebellions that shook Ferguson and Baltimore less than a year apart. In 2014 Ferguson rose up against a brazenly racist white power structure and Jim Crow police force that had systematically brutalized and looted a majority-Black city, functioning as a collection agency for what even the *Washington Post* called municipal "plundering."[12] By contrast, radical scholar Keeanga-Yamahtta Taylor underlines how in Baltimore,

> African Americans control virtually the entire political appara-
> tus. Mayor Stephanie Rawlings-Blake and police commissioner
> Anthony Batts were the most prominent faces of political power
> in Baltimore during the rebellion, but Black power runs deep in
> the city . . . If the murder of Mike Brown and the rebellion in
> Ferguson were reminiscent of the old Jim Crow, then the murder
> of Freddie Gray and the Baltimore uprising symbolize the new
> Black political elite . . . Even with the involvement of a Black cop,
> a Black prosecutor, and a Black judge, justice remained elusive
> for Freddie Gray.

Even Marilyn Mosby, the state's attorney touted by many as heroic for charging the officers involved, was largely grandstanding for political clout: just weeks prior to his murder, she "had personally directed the police department to target the intersection where they first encountered Gray."[13]

Black leaders occasionally even went beyond even their white counterparts, as when Representative Charles Rangel urged Richard Nixon to wage a disastrous war on drugs.[14] The Congressional Black Caucus supported Ronald Reagan's 1986 drug laws—which included the racist sentencing disparities between crack and powder cocaine. Moreover, Taylor notes, they were similarly conscripted into the pig majority under Bill Clinton, when

> Black elected officials lined up to sign off on legislation that was literally intended to kill Black people. In 1993, President Bill Clinton unveiled a new "crime-fighting" bill, the Violent Crime Control and Law Enforcement Act of 1994, that included expanded use of the death penalty, life sentences for nonviolent criminal offenses, 100,000 more police on the streets, and a gratuitously punitive elimination of federal funding for inmate education.[15]

When the Congressional Black Caucus hesitated, a coalition of Black mayors shoved them across the goal line. According to Taylor, Black leadership came to support unchecked policing and mass incarceration not from a position of weakness, as is sometimes argued, but out of growing strength and comfort in the halls of power. And due to their ability, "as members of the community, to scold ordinary Black people in ways that white politicians could never get away with," Black officials provided crucial leverage for the Clintonite reform package.[16] In the aftermath of the 1994 bill—championed by Hillary Clinton and Joe Biden alike—Black incarceration rates tripled as the devastation of police violence reached an unprecedented zenith.

This is the truly galling reality of the right-wing obsession with so-called Black-on-Black violence. The causes of the racist brutality meted out by police and vigilantes on poor communities of color—the far more prevalent white-on-Black crime that the right doesn't discuss, because it's baked right into the structure of American society—are exactly the same as the causes of violence within poor communities of color: systematic neglect and active looting, a lack of social welfare programs, and unequal access to education and opportunities. Far from "ignoring" the problem of intra-community violence, moreover, the Black political class has been, in Forman's words, "consumed by it," swallowing hook, line, and sinker the racist pathologization of poor communities of color in support of a bipartisan project of police power.[17] What *has* been ignored across the political spectrum is the fact that even when poorer Black and Brown communities demand more police in their communities, they have never asked for *just* the police, and have never seen the police as the sole solution to all social ills.

More often, "these communities also ask for better schools, parks, libraries, and jobs, but these services are rarely provided" because they "lack the political power to obtain real services and support to make their communities safer and healthier."[18] Even many Black leaders, Forman argues, "adopted an all-of-the-above approach to fighting crime" in the 1970s that included social welfare and jobs programs alongside police and prisons. But instead, "black America had gotten only one of the above: punitive crime measures."[19] In fact, as historian Elizabeth Hinton crucially adds, those most radical grassroots voices that "collectively defied the legitimacy of new policing and carceral strategies" have been largely erased from a historical record dominated by more conservative "segments of the black middle class, political leaders, and clergy."[20] This hasn't stopped many from trying, however, in a series of struggles, to establish community control over not only the police but also public institutions like schools and other community resources.

If Chicago is a code word for racist fear today, there is no better proof of policing's colossal failure than that massively over-policed city, which has nearly twice as many officers per resident as Los Angeles. The Chicago Police Department has spared no degree of brutality—even creating a secret torture regime—in the name of law and order, and yet, despite everything, the city has seen dozens shot in a single weekend.[21] While many see such crime statistics—and their own fear of becoming victims—as incontrovertible proof that the police are a necessity, the reality is that violence persists in Chicago and elsewhere *despite* policing. This speaks to a broader point. If someone robs your house or assaults you, the truth is that the vast policing apparatus of the United States—unmatched anywhere on earth—has done *nothing* to prevent that from happening.[22] But by a bizarre sleight of hand, American police continue to cite their own abysmal failures as proof of their indispensability.

The inverse is true as well: mass incarceration did not correspond to an increase in crime rates and much less did it prevent future crimes. More specifically, the "War on Drugs" that contributed disproportionately to ballooning prison populations beginning in the 1980s was not a response to any noticeable uptick in drug crime, but simply an excuse to invent new and harsher criminal categories that were used to lock people up. Exactly the same is true of the police. The dramatic expansion of policing in every aspect of our lives—their proliferation and militarization, their callousness and arrogant refusal of oversight—is the result not of some desperate social crisis in need of a solution, but of the everyday functioning of a social system based on inequality and white supremacy.

Today's pig majority extends far beyond white people, but it is nonetheless fundamentally about white *power*. The presence of "Black faces in high places"—from the ranks of the police to political power—has done little to transform the deep structures of white supremacy in American society. What's more, they have actually provided the system with a powerful alibi, a Black mask for the perpetuation of white supremacy and capitalist exploitation—the spokespeople of the system and the storm troopers enforcing it. We live in a world of both Fergusons and Baltimores. But just as both names conjure the specter of police murder, they also bespeak a spirit of revolt among those who haven't been fooled by the post-racial hype.

—

While the pig majority has always been bigger than the police, policing as a concrete institution has expanded massively in recent decades, suffusing American society, sinking its invasive roots ever deeper and choking out all else. The number of police in the United States has grown exponentially, fueled in no small part by Clinton's 1994 crime bill. According to the FBI's Uniform Crime Reporting database, the sheer number of uniformed police has grown from 195,000 in 1960 to more than 1.1 million in 2007. In other words, there are *five times* as many cops walking the streets today as there were sixty years ago, and even in per capita terms, twice as many. Moreover, this growth accelerated markedly after the crime bill, which promised federal funding for 100,000 new cops. But the problem went deeper: that funding accounted for only one-third of new police during that period. According to the Urban Institute, state and local spending on the police increased astronomically between 1977 and 2017, from $42 billion to $115 billion.[23] In cities like Chicago, growth was more extreme still: per capita spending on the police nearly *tripled* from 1964 to 2020.[24] Both of these trends—numbers and budgets—continued to grow even as crime rates began to fall sharply in the 1990s.

Police at all levels have become increasingly militarized, too. The 1033 program, established in 1997 but ramped up dramatically after the 9/11 attacks, has seen more than $7.4 billion in military hand-me-downs distributed to more than 8,000 police departments nationwide. While the police and the military have never been truly distinct, and while militarization is more a symptom of the excesses of police power than its fundamental cause, police access to massive arsenals of military hardware has had a major impact on the way police view their role in the world and the violence they commit. As Ryan Welch, a political scientist at the University of Tampa, puts it: "Our research suggests that officers with military hardware and mindsets will resort to violence more quickly and often."[25] Bigger, militarized hammers mean even more nails, as civilians are viewed increasingly as counterinsurgents, and police militarization fuels an escalating dialectic of police–military entanglement.

School police, often benignly euphemized as "school resource officers," date to the 1950s, but their usage was initially sparse. From the 1970s to the 2000s, however, the proportion of schools with SROs rose from 1 to 40 percent.[26] The dramatic increase in SROs also tracked that of police more widely, seeing a sharp upturn in the 1990s, even as crime rates were dropping. This rise was fueled by both push and pull factors: on the one hand, criminalization seeped into schools in the guise of zero-tolerance policies, and on the other, the federal government began to subsidize SROs. A decade later, 70 percent of high school–aged children had an officer or security guard in their school, and the Department of Education reported nearly 100,000 arrests during the 2011–12 school year. Between 2006 and 2011, according to the Southern Poverty Law Center, police in Birmingham public schools subjected more than 1,000 students to pepper spray.[27]

Although campus police existed at universities like Yale as far back as the 1800s, their expansion in the present came in response to the student movements of the 1960s—in particular, the deaths of students caused by outside police and the military. According to a 2011–12 Department of Justice survey, some 4,000 police departments span 92 percent of public and 38 percent of private institutions university and college campuses, and these numbers have continued to grow. While some argue that campus police are more focused on student well-being than outside forces, high-profile incidents like the brutal pepper-spraying of student protesters at University of California, Davis, in 2011 would suggest otherwise. Further, sometimes protecting students is itself the problem: since campus police, especially in urban areas, understand their task as protecting campus *from* nonstudents outside of it, shootings of poor and homeless local residents are routine. Again, campus police have continued to expand despite falling campus crime rates, and they have "increasingly gained the ability to arrest and patrol outside jurisdictions" without mechanisms of municipal oversight.[28]

Transit police, like the Bay Area Rapid Transit officer that killed Oscar Grant on the Fruitvale BART platform in 2009, have also seen their numbers increase. And as with campus police, Grant's killing revealed that accountability for nonmunicipal police agencies is even more evasive than for municipal police forces (BART's board of directors appoints a general manager who then hires the police chief without any input from the public).

All told, the United States today spends more per capita and dedicates a larger part of its total budget to policing than any other major country—some $389 billion, according to the Organisation for Economic Co-operation and Development—all while dedicating far less to social welfare.[29] This hypertrophic growth of the American police state has no relationship whatsoever to crime rates, nor has it made us safer. Quite the opposite: policing has continued to expand despite two decades of falling crime rates, and poor communities of color continue to bear the twin brunts of social abandonment and police violence.

Even this is far from the whole story, however, since as we have seen, policing is about far more than the police. Today it involves a ballooning private security apparatus as well—across society as a whole, but especially in heavily policed essential industries like health care. Like militarization, privatization is faithful to policing's origins in the protection of private property and the security of some over others, and in all likelihood, this continuity will lead to consequences that are no less dire. Already in the 1980s there were more private security officers than police, and that number has surpassed 1.1 million today according to the most recent data from the Bureau of Labor Statistics.

The quantitative expansion of policing has gone hand in hand with—and arguably fueled—an even more sinister *qualitative* shift, in which society as a whole has been refashioned in the image of the police. This is what critical theorist Mark Neocleous has called the fabrication of social order by the police. For Neocleous, too many criminologists and self-styled "police scientists" pare the question of policing down to a discrete institution, surgically excising the police from their historical genesis and broader collusion with other institutions. "Policing," he writes, "is undertaken partly by the uniformed public police, but their actions are coordinated with agencies of policing situated throughout the state"—notably, institutions of social welfare.[30] On the other hand, those sympathetic to French philosopher Michel Foucault's equation of prisons, schools, and mental institutions, as comparable structures of surveillance and discipline, can bend the stick too far in the opposite direction. In a sort of bloodless Foucauldianism, policing can become a pure metaphor in which everything is *like* the police, but the actual police are rarely mentioned.

Neocleous resists both extremes, locating the police as a specific institution in relation to a broader structure he calls the social police: one that doesn't simply reflect society or repress the population, but actively *fabricates* a new vision of social order and rebuilds the world in its image. This crucial insight is not a new one. The German philosopher Walter Benjamin pointed out a century ago that the police use violence not only to uphold and preserve the law, but to make and remake the law as well. This remaking has reached new heights in the century since, extending even into the realm of language, in what David Correia and Tyler Wall call "copspeak."[31] A police murder becomes an "officer-involved shooting" that strangely lacks an acting subject; the growing arsenal of weapons in the hands of police are celebrated as "less lethal" while still killing hundreds; and sexual assault by police, including rape, is routinized as a "body cavity search" or swept under the rug as "sexual

misconduct." The sanitized language of policing forms a protective cocoon around the institution that makes the need for police
unquestioned and unquestionable, and copspeak delineates a
horizon—the world of police—that clouds our vision and blocks
out all other possibilities.

The history of the United States would attest to this need to
expand our understanding of the police even further still, beyond
the realm of the state, to understand policing, in the words of
historian Peter Linebaugh, as "inseparable from conquest, slavery,
debt, industrial discipline, and social hierarchies. Armed settlers,
'pioneers,' militia, army units, slave patrollers, Texas rangers,
posse comitatus, slave catchers, factory guards, troopers, private
security forces, vigilante groups, MPs, lynch mobs, Ford's 'service
department,' death squads, night riders, and the KKK have all
served police functions."[32] If, as Robin D.G. Kelley adds, "it is
important to make a distinction between the police as a formal,
modern institution and 'policing' as a broader set of practices
and procedures that operate beyond (but sanctioned by) formal
state structures," this is in part because we need to retain the
specificity of the latter and understand the crucial importance
of the police as an anchor for the broader policing apparatus of
racial capitalism.[33] While policing operates through thousands,
if not millions, of self-deputized surrogates, uniformed police are
the glue binding the pig majority. And, as we will see, police
power—expressed largely through so-called police unions—is
the tip of the spear.

Many abolitionist scholars and activists have drawn our attention to both the broader social policing apparatus and its efforts
to remake the world on the blueprint of police and prisons. For
Beth Richie and Kayla Martensen, this "carceral expansion" has
created a full-fledged "Prison Nation," where "punitive and social
services can become indistinguishable" in terms of "control,
surveillance, and punishment."[34] Institutions like child protective services and family court have arguably played racialized
disciplinary roles from the very beginning, not only tearing

families apart but also concretely feeding police violence and mass incarceration; indeed, Walter Scott was killed by police in North Charleston, South Carolina, in part over a warrant for unpaid child support.[35] This carceral expansion has been sharpest in recent decades, however, as even many well-intentioned social workers and feminists have turned to police and prisons as the only solution for domestic and community violence—raising challenges, as we will see, for abolitionist movements today.

Schools too, which Foucault and others have long compared to prisons, have increasingly become more *like* prisons. In this sense, the "school-to-prison pipeline" is less a clear line in the sand than a continuous spectrum. Schools were performing a policing function before the advent of school police, and this function is furthermore built right into the history of school segregation and contemporary processes of resegregation. Not only do segregated schools reflect and further contribute to deepening racial and economic inequalities, but school police themselves have come to play sharply opposed roles depending on where they work. In public schools in poor communities of color, SROs police the students—threatening to send them to a real prison if they misbehave or run truant. In white suburban citadels, police are increasingly deployed to protect the student body from mass shooters—even if, as we will see, they often fail spectacularly to do so. Here, too, the question doesn't stop at the schoolyard fence or the disciplining of students themselves, but bears upon the policy agenda of the nation's highest office: infamously, Vice President Kamala Harris once laughed when recounting her efforts as San Francisco district attorney to criminalize truancy and jail parents.

Policing is a cancer, and it is powerfully malignant, metastasizing and spreading uncontrollably throughout the social body. Or better still, policing is a virus, because rather than simply spreading its own cells—proliferating school police, campus police, prison police, private police—it hacks into the

DNA of existing institutions, communities, and even the everyday consciousness of individuals, corrupting their code and infecting them with a single idea: that every problem can be solved by the police. Family conflicts, neighborhood disputes, schoolyard bullying and brawls, gendered violence, poverty, mental illness, homelessness, and, in a cynically perverse turn, even racism itself—all become objects of policing, and the only solution the police offer is violence. This is the world of police, and we are in its terminal stage.

The pig majority and the world of police it underwrites doesn't stop at the US border, either. Domestic policing has always been shaped by and inseparable from colonial expansion and the deployment of imperial power abroad, which in turn became a mode of policing unto itself. Robert Peel, the architect of British policing, honed his ideas during the colonial occupation of Ireland. Similarly, the Pennsylvania State Police, notorious for the brutal repression of a largely immigrant workforce of miners, were modeled on US occupying forces in the Philippines, and, as sociologist Alex Vitale notes, "Marine General Smedley Butler, who created the Haitian police and played a major role in the US occupation of Nicaragua, served as police chief of Philadelphia in 1924."[36] August Vollmer, the father of "police science," often cited his experience in the Philippines, and we can trace the dialectic of imperial policing back further still, to domestic colonization: "Many American troops involved in the 'Philippine Insurrection' (1898-1902) had experience in fighting the Indian Wars," and would come to play a pioneering role in developing later counterinsurgency technologies.[37]

Nowhere was the complicity of policing with colonial expansion so evident as along the rapidly shifting Southwest border. There, the Texas Rangers functioned, in the words of Alfredo Mirandé, as a species of hybrid "police vigilantes," enforcing colonialism, imperialism, and domestic white supremacy all at the same time, "taming the frontier and displacing Indians and

Mexicans from the land."[38] Through their brutal work, Texas was effectively stolen twice: first formally from Mexico and then later, more substantively, through a series of genocidal massacres and lynchings that ethnically cleansed the state and made stolen land available to white settlers. In her history of the US Border Patrol, Kelly Lytle Hernández describes the Rangers' multifaceted role in upholding racial and capitalist domination in the state:

> They battled indigenous groups for dominance in the region, chased down runaway slaves who struck for freedom deep within Mexico, and settled scores with anyone who challenged the Anglo-American project in Texas. The Rangers proved particularly useful in helping Anglo-American landholders win favorable settlements of land and labor disputes with Texas Mexicans. Whatever the task, however, raw physical violence was the Rangers' principal strategy.[39]

In later decades, the Rangers came to function as the racist Texan equivalent of the Pinkerton Agency—doing the bidding of private ranchers and political leaders while resisting racial integration. In one incident stemming from an alleged cattle raid against the King Ranch—to this day, the largest in all Texas—Rangers "began a systematic manhunt and killed ... 102 Mexicans," using even the thinnest pretext to "kill Mexicans almost at will."[40] For this brutal history of violent ethnic cleansing, the Rangers are glorified to this day, and celebrated as models for policing by presidents Lyndon B. Johnson and Richard Nixon alike.

Thus, where Du Bois spoke of two systems of American justice, there were in reality at least three: justice and equality before the law (within certain bounds) for many white Americans, alongside two parallel systems of injustice for Black and Brown people. Mirandé refers to the last of these as "gringo justice," a system of aggressive dispossession and land theft masked as white self-defense that later stabilized as a regime of "Juan Crow" segregation running parallel to Jim Crow in the South. While "the agencies that have undoubtedly elicited the most fear, resentment, and distrust are the Texas Rangers and the Border Patrol," many Mexican Americans were historically abused by *la placa* (the badge) as well, from the 1943 Zoot Suit Riots—an anti-Mexican pogrom by vigilantes, soldiers, and off-duty police—to the 1971 police riot in East Los Angeles. Little surprise that many Latinx people today view the police "not as a symbol of law and justice, but rather of lawlessness, injustice, and abuse."[41]

The line between official border policing and vigilante violence against Mexican and Central American migrants has never been clear, and remains blurry to this day. As one *Intercept* headline puts it, "The bloody history of border militias runs deep—and law enforcement is part of it." This entanglement underwrites what Monica Muñoz Martinez, a professor of American studies at Brown University, deems a "culture of impunity" that "allowed state police officers and local law enforcement in many instances to collaborate with vigilantes. But, she adds, "they wouldn't have called them vigilantes. They would have said they were pulling together a posse."[42] From the Texas Rangers hunting escaped slaves to Louis Beam, who organized patrols of the state's southern border under the aegis of the Ku Klux Klan, however, anti-Mexican border vigilantism and anti-Black racism were never separate or separable. And like the police themselves, official institutions like the US Border Patrol grew out of informal, white supremacist mobs.

As with all policing, moreover, border policing doesn't respond to the threat of violent crime, much less solve or prevent it. Instead, it too grows from the cross-fertilization of economic interest with racial fear, inventing entirely new categories of crime and creating criminals, just as the Black codes did in the South. Meanwhile, with every measure taken to reinforce the border, the potential profits to be gained from ferrying people or products across it only increase—and with them, violence. From colonial expansion to white supremacist fears of "white genocide" and the threat of a "great replacement" today, the violent policing of the boundaries of whiteness is motivated by a powerful and dangerous victim complex. When white settlers flooded into Texas, they painted those who resisted their land grab as the aggressors, and little had changed by 2019, when Patrick Crusius, a 21-year-old white man, walked into an El Paso Walmart, killing twenty-three in a targeted attack on those he perceived to be Mexican. In a manifesto posted to the message board 8chan, Crusius decried a "Hispanic invasion" of what had only recently been Mexican territory and, before that, Indigenous land. "They are the instigators, not me," he wrote.

The white supremacist magic by which perpetrators become victims and the dispossessed become targets of legitimate violence operates more broadly still. When neighborhoods are gentrified, poor longtime residents suddenly become a problem population. When Black people are murdered by police or vigilantes, they are transformed in the courtroom and the media into aggressors guilty of their own killing—as the City of Cleveland put it, twelve-year-old Tamir Rice's death in a hail of police bullets was "directly and proximately caused" by his own failure "to exercise due care to avoid injury."[43] When movements take to the streets to insist that Black lives matter, moreover, police cynically appropriate the status of victims, contending that "blue lives matter," that police are the most oppressed minority, and that there is a "war on police."

What is the "thin blue line" if not a border?

——

This vast and expanding policing archipelago, and the pig majority underpinning it, stretches far beyond the police as an institution, beyond the bounds of whiteness, and even beyond national borders. This, too, Du Bois knew. When the

Confederate States seceded, he reminds us, they did so with an internationalist vision: the dream of building a "great slave empire in the Caribbean." If the South lost this battle, once again it won the longer, global war. While formal slavery was defeated, the fall of Reconstruction cleared the way for white supremacist rule both at home and abroad. "The United States was turned into a reactionary force," Du Bois wrote. "It became the cornerstone of that new imperialism which is subjecting the labor of yellow, brown and black peoples to the dictation of capitalism organized on a world basis."[44]

Long before the Global War on Terror and even the Vietnam War—described by its perpetrators as a "police action"—American policing went global in a series of Marine landings in Cuba, Puerto Rico, Chile, Nicaragua, Honduras, Panama, the Philippines, the Dominican Republic, and elsewhere. In *Badges without Borders*, Stuart Schrader shows how policing in the United States has always been a global affair bound up with imperial power. Long before New York police commissioner Bill Bratton pioneered "broken windows" or proactive policing—targeting small quality-of-life issues to deter more serious offenses—counterinsurgency, or "small wars," was framed as "a police-led, less-lethal, preemptive, and anticipatory approach."[45] Bratton himself would later play a major role in exporting broken windows across the globe—quite literally "policing the planet," in Christina Heatherton and Jordan Camp's apropos phrase.[46] "Across the globe," Schrader writes, "counterinsurgency was policing. At home, policing was counterinsurgency."[47]

Over time, these global counterinsurgency methods came home to roost, most recently in the deployment of overwhelming military force against protesters on the streets of Ferguson in 2014, and against the Dakota Access Pipeline protesters two years later. While these events rightly shocked many, however, they were really nothing new. People of color have long been defined as an insurgent class and treated like a dangerous fifth column. For instance, under Commissioner Bull Connor, police in Birmingham, Alabama, bought two armored personnel carriers to confront the early 1960s civil rights movement. Partly in response to such treatment, Black and Brown radicals have long described their communities as internal colonies that are, in James Baldwin's haunting phrase, "policed like occupied territory." As hellfire rains down on Black and Brown people abroad, the same occurs at home under the perverse veil of "law and order." Today, in Baltimore as in the neo-colonies, those doing the policing often look just like the "insurgents" they are tasked with containing, and from Plan Colombia to the Mérida Initiative in Mexico, the language of fighting crime has provided cover for bloody counterinsurgent war and the projection of US power.

If policing is bigger than the police, imperialism is bigger than the military. The proliferation of privatized police domestically coincides with the emergence of a vast and expanding mercenary apparatus masquerading under the sanitized name of "private contractors." Of these, Blackwater is of course the most notorious (which is precisely why it has changed its name repeatedly, first to Xe Services, and today, Academi). During the Iraq War, Blackwater was implicated in multiple massacres, and even the US Congress had difficulty investigating. Despite being plagued by the same kinds of accountability problems as private police everywhere, the contracting of mercenaries has exploded since Afghanistan and Iraq. The ratio of private contractors to troops tripled under Obama—between 2007 and 2012 alone, the Pentagon spent $160 billion on private security contractors, and by 2017 there were nearly three contractors for every US troop stationed in war zones.[48] Moreover, as governments and private corporations covertly turn to mercenaries worldwide, there is no way to estimate the true scope or cost of this expanding mercenary apparatus.

What happens abroad doesn't stay abroad, however. Just as countries like Colombia and Mexico, where decades of civil war and drug violence have created a surplus of unemployed violence workers, so too are US mercenaries returning home and infiltrating an already-violent society. Many join the police or work in private security, while others offer their skills to organized crime, or even join right-wing militias in their spare time. The result has been predictable: attacks on protesters, mass shootings, and domestic violence have proliferated. America is not only a police nation, but a counterinsurgent nation as well. Inversely, moreover, the domestic vigilante can easily become the international mercenary, sanctioned or not, as the botched coup attempt against Venezuelan president Nicolás Maduro in May 2020 makes clear.

Under the self-important name of Operation Gideon, mercenary startup Silvercorp recruited Venezuelans for a doomed mission to kidnap Maduro. Founded by Canadian-born US Special Forces veteran Jordan Goudreau, Silvercorp, which had provided security for Trump rallies, sought support from the US government and right-wing Venezuelan leaders before launching the harebrained assault. Unsurprisingly, the operation was fully infiltrated by the Venezuelan government from the start, and as failure became inevitable, Goudreau desperately tweeted at Donald Trump directly in a vain attempt to gain official backing. The mercenary equivalent of a wannabe Instagram influencer, Goudreau's previous hustle had sought to embed armed agents in schools disguised as teachers, purportedly to prevent school shootings.

———

Ta-Nehisi Coates's provocation that "to challenge the police is to challenge the American people" is at once undeniable and insufficient. To speak of the police is to describe both a discrete institution and something far broader, at the expansive overlap of whiteness, capitalist greed, and global imperialism. None of this is to suggest that the police as an institution are any less important, however—far from it. If policing is a broad practice that functions as the linchpin of US capitalism, buying off poor whites with the wages of whiteness and destabilizing class solidarity, then uniformed police represent the glue binding policing together today.

Through the everyday street discretion police exercise from their brick-and-mortar precincts, they make and remake the color line in all its classed dimensions. They provide self-deputized white vigilantes with a legal backdrop and a model to emulate. They claim to provide security from the ravages of capitalist inequality, while in reality they only reinforce and deepen these inequalities. They incorporate a multiracial cohort of recruits into the broader white supremacist project—providing it with a powerful alibi. And if the policing of imperial power has developed in conjunction with with the domestic policing of colonized and formerly enslaved populations, the police today stand as a concrete interface point with settler colonial projects like Israel and counterinsurgency efforts worldwide, policing the boundaries of wealth and whiteness on a global scale.

This pig majority can appear so overwhelming and the global policing apparatus so sprawling that even the idea of resistance may seem daunting. To abolish the police means abolishing capitalism and white supremacy as well, to which Schrader adds, "To dismantle the carceral state, the national security state will also have to be dismantled."[49] Taken as a whole, this is a tall order indeed. But understanding the police in their international context also turns the balance of forces upside down. America's pig majority is, in fact, a global minority, and the constituency for abolition far broader than we might first assume. It encompasses what Du Bois described as a vast, "dark proletariat . . . that basic majority of workers who are yellow, brown and black," but it exceeds it as well.[50] Resistance to the global police state has always existed, and there have always been more of *us* than *them*.

Black movements have long diagnosed the historic complicity between police and white supremacists, rallying behind the slogan "Cops and Klan, hand in hand." But so too have Latinx migrant organizers emphasized a similarly tautological equation:

"La migra, la policía, la misma porquería" (Border patrol, the police, the same bullshit). Between and at the intersection of Black and Brown movements today, the constituency for abolition is a global majority, and the history and contemporary practice of global struggles against capitalism, colonialism, and white supremacy offer a vision of a different kind of world entirely.

2

Who Do You Serve? Who Do You Protect?

Let's start with some basic arithmetic. Most Americans have been raised to believe that it is the mission of the police to "protect and serve" the public, and that any failure to do so would be to violate that mission. But *who* do the police serve, and *who* do they protect?[1]

Certainly not communities of color. According to most calculations, Black Americans are about three times more likely to be killed by the police than their white counterparts. And when we look more closely at the data, the gaps only widen further: by age, Black males aged fifteen to nineteen are up to twenty-one times more likely to be killed by police than their white peers, according to ProPublica; by geography, the disparity in police killings of Black people is 6.5 to 1 in Chicago, according to a recent statistical analysis by two Harvard scholars.[2] Nor do police truly protect Latinx, Indigenous, or Pacific Islander communities—even if we set aside histories of genocidal dispossession, these groups are often twice as likely to suffer death at the hands of law enforcement as white people. And while many Asian communities do not figure prominently in police brutality data and remain internally divided over the question of policing, long histories of forced labor, exclusion, and internment mean that any meager privileges afforded to so-called model minorities are tenuous at best—as the racialization of the coronavirus pandemic and recent uptick in anti-Asian violence has made clear.[3]

White people, roughly 60 percent of the population, certainly tend to enjoy more police protection than others, but even this protection is far from universal. When asked in mid 2020 why so many Black people are killed by the police, Donald Trump responded: "So are white people. More white people, by the way." On the one hand, it's unsurprising that Trump would echo right-wing fallacies about policing in the age of Black Lives Matter. Yes, police kill numerically more white people than Black people (just under half of those killed in an average year are white), but to take this fact as meaningful betrays an astonishing obliviousness to proportion. While white people are underrepresented in police killings, Black people are—dramatically and indisputably—overrepresented. But on the other hand, this was also strange coming from someone who claims to support the police as vociferously as Trump. Surely there's no better argument for abolition than the fact that the police murder even those they were established to protect!

Some conservative commentators have gone further, however, seeking to discredit claims of racial disparities in police violence entirely. Writing in the *Wall Street Journal* after the police murder of George Floyd, Heather Mac Donald, author of *The War on Cops*, sought to debunk what she calls "the myth of systemic police racism." Citing a study published in the *Proceedings of the National Academy of Sciences* (*PNAS*), Mac Donald argued that police killings of Black people are "less than what the black crime rate would predict, since police shootings are a function of how often officers encounter armed and violent suspects."[4] You can't be killed by the police if you are a good, law-abiding citizen who never interacts with the police—so goes the argument. The problem is that the argument is utterly false, and deeply racist in its own right.

Statistical analyses of data from New York City's stop-and-frisk program make clear that there are huge disparities in who the police target, in what communities, and why—disparities that far outstrip crime rates.[5] As Princeton researchers have recently demonstrated, simply combining one racially determined variable (police encounters) with another (police killings) proves exactly the opposite of what Mac Donald and others would have us believe.[6] If anything, by increasing the number of nonviolent encounters, the constant harassment of racial profiling has the effect of watering down the data and making police encounters by Black people with the police seem *less* deadly than they actually are, by "perversely using one kind of discrimination, over-policing, to mask another: the greater use of deadly force against Black suspects."[7] Moreover, according to the Mapping Police Violence project, most police killings begin from interactions involving the suspicion of a nonviolent crime or no crime at all, and "Black people were more likely to be killed by police, more likely to be unarmed and less likely to be threatening someone when killed."[8] Writing at *Slate*, data analyst Rob Arthur has shown that even among police killings, Black people are less likely to have resisted than white people.[9]

When several teams of researchers made this exact point, the authors of the study Mac Donald cites withdrew their article, prompting her to throw a very public fit.[10] But the goal of her op-ed and others like it was never rational argument; indeed, we give Trump and right-wing talking heads too much credit if we take their arguments as factual claims to be debated. Instead, adjusting police killings to crime rates is yet another dog whistle that reinforces and relies on the racism of the target audience: of course they are criminals, so they deserve what they get. Nevertheless, the damage was already done: Mac Donald's piece had been syndicated nationwide, to very concrete effect. Less than a week later, Travis Yates, a high-ranking member of the Tulsa Police Department—which already boasts an astronomical per capita rate of police killings—provoked widespread outcry by suggesting that police are "shooting African Americans about 24 percent less than we probably ought to." Yates cited Mac Donald and the *PNAS* study directly.[11]

Sadly, it isn't only the right that minimizes police killings of people of color. Some on the left have wasted a great deal of breath and ink doing much the same. The Marxist intellectual Adolph Reed, for example, in his obsessive zeal to discredit a

Black Lives Matter movement that he sees only as a "branding exercise," bends over backward to minimize and explain away racial disparities in police violence.[12] As usual, Reed's facts don't match his penchant for hyperbole, and rather than simply admit that whites are killed at a lower rate, Reed explains—in tortured prose—that "whites are killed by police at a rate between just under three-fourths (through the first half of 2016) and just under four-fifths (2015) of their share of the general population." Racial disparity, he argues, is a distraction from the fact that police killings occur in poorer areas (the overlap of race and poverty goes unmentioned), and that many whiter states have higher rates of police homicide. Never mind that he counts New Mexico among these "whiter" states despite its Latinx majority and ongoing police brutality against Indigenous people.[13] And never mind that numerous studies show Black people "to be at greatest risk in predominantly White neighborhoods."[14] "Racism and white supremacy," Reed concludes, "don't really *explain* how anything happens."

Nothing except, say, the clear disparities in who is stopped and searched, who is perceived as a threat, and those all-important split-second decisions about who to shoot or not—all of which, when not explicit policy, are governed by a racial bias demonstrated in countless studies.[15] Or how a rich Harvard professor like Henry Louis Gates Jr. can be arrested for allegedly burglarizing his own home. Or that Ferguson police officer Darren Wilson perceived Mike Brown as a "demon" in the moments before shooting him dead, or that Derek Chauvin, in Minneapolis, felt that George Floyd could survive nearly nine minutes of sustained pressure to his neck.[16] Or that police and others often see Black teenagers (and even preteens) as older and less innocent than white children, and Black girls as larger and more masculine—and thus more threatening.[17] Reed's attempts to minimize racial disparities are hard to distinguish from Trump's own whataboutism, and he struggles and fails to explain away the fundamental question: Why is it that certain people walk out of their homes every day into a world in which they are more likely to die at the hands of police?

Ultimately, however, numbers tell only part of the story. After all, nearly *all* those killed by police are men, but it would be absurd to argue that this is due to some underlying anti-male discrimination. Let's not entertain the same absurdities when it comes to white people: while white people are killed by police in unacceptably high numbers, they are not killed because they are white, but *despite being white*. They are killed in increasingly outrageous numbers because, faced with an expanding policing apparatus that thrives on total impunity—on the ability to brutalize and kill anyone, anywhere—not even their whiteness can protect them.

In *From #BlackLivesMatter to Black Liberation*, a book that Reed has derided, Keeanga-Yamahtta Taylor shows that it is possible to take police racism seriously while also recognizing the broader devastation that the police wreak across many different communities. While Black Americans, she observes, "suffer most from the blunt force trauma of the American criminal justice system," the increasingly heavy-handed nature of law-and-order politics means that even white people are jailed at rates far higher than in other countries, and "*thousands* of white people have also been murdered by the police."[18] We don't need to erase these differences in order to build solidarity against the police, nor does this solidarity begin from denying police racism. It comes, rather, from confronting it head on.

Solidarity means recognizing that policing has always been about both economic profit and racial control, that police have always been strikebreakers and a uniformed lynch mob at the same time, and that law-and-order politics emerged as a strategy that was not only overtly racist, but also sought to destroy those social movements capable of uniting the poor. It means recognizing—as Taylor does—that racist policing has conscripted *both* poor whites (from the beginning) and Black officers and elected officials (more recently) into functional roles, and that, far from proving that racism is irrelevant (as Reed insists), Black leaders have functioned both as mouthpieces for condescending sermons and as foot soldiers of oppression against the poor. And solidarity means understanding that the racism of the police is more than skin-deep, that Black and Brown officers are just as likely to be violent and racist (sometimes more so), and that the racist function of the police spans the entire (multiracial) pig majority.

—

Our calculations are just getting started. We know that the police protect wealth and private property, not the poor—this, too, helps explain the massive and growing number of white people killed by police. Since the late 1960s, moreover, when wages stagnated and American capitalism began to rely on ballooning real estate, consumer, and student debt, funneling wealth to the top while generating mass impoverishment at the bottom, fewer and fewer Americans have had any wealth left to protect at all—especially not the millennials and zoomers leading the struggle against the police in the streets today. You don't call the police to protect your student loan debt or the cramped apartment you don't even own. An estimated 9 percent of white families have zero or negative net wealth—literally *nothing* for the police to protect. Leaving aside the fact that this number skews far higher for younger generations, even this very low bar brings the "serve and protect" ratio—those who enjoy some small property the police might deign to protect—down from about 60 percent to around half of the population .

But we aren't done yet. The nationwide dismantling of access to mental health care and treatment, especially among the poor and people of color, has meant that those suffering a mental health crisis and their families "have little choice but to call 911—and it's typically the police who respond."[19] Police are not trained mental health workers, however, but trained *violence* workers. The results have been predictably devastating. In

October 2020, the videotaped killing of Walter Wallace Jr. just blocks west of my home in Philadelphia reignited the wave of mass protests that had exploded months earlier, provoking several more days of looting and the return of the National Guard. Wallace was suffering a mental health crisis, and despite the fact that he was apparently holding a knife, none of his friends, family, or neighbors considered him a serious-enough threat to warrant deadly force. After Wallace's brother called an ambulance, the police arrived instead. "They weren't trying to help us, they didn't give a damn about us," his mother Cathy recounted.[20] Despite her efforts to calm the tension, two officers fired a total of fourteen shots, killing Wallace.

A *Washington Post* database counts 1,244 people with confirmed mental illness killed by police just since 2015, while another report indicates that one in four deadly police encounters involve mental illness. This would make those with untreated mental illness an astonishing sixteen times more likely to be killed by police, and even this is almost certainly a low figure. Extrapolation from other studies suggests a much higher rate of one in two—a full half of all fatal encounters.[21] Nearly half of all Americans will suffer a mental health crisis at some point in their lives, and some 4 million are untreated today. While mental illness and access to treatment overlap heavily with race, class, age, and sexuality, these figures nevertheless take another significant slice out of that "serve and protect" pie, and there are plenty of examples of just how quickly racial and class privilege can evaporate once the police arrive on the scene of a crisis. Moreover, because police violence is itself a key trigger for further mental health problems, policing and mental illness constitute a vicious cycle.[22]

The police don't protect the homeless, either, and just as mental illness has been increasingly criminalized, so too has the epidemic of homelessness sweeping the United States since the 1980s. Rather than attend to the root causes of homelessness, cities nationwide—under pressure from real estate developers and newly arrived gentrifiers—have simply banned homeless people from existing in public spaces, creating another vicious cycle in which the very same forces making homes too expensive for the poor pressure local leaders to make criminals of those forced onto the streets. This criminalization has powerfully dehumanizing effects as well, turning the poor into lawbreakers and vagrants. Under law-and-order capitalism, this means they are responsible for their own misfortune.

The results are predictable: vigilante killings of homeless people run rampant, and the 2011 death of Kelly Thomas was a painful reminder that the intersection of homelessness and mental illness can be fatal once the police get involved. Thomas, a white man with diagnosed schizophrenia, was unarmed when he was repeatedly tased and viciously beaten by six members of the Fullerton, California, police department. In gut-wrenching videos of the assault, Manuel Ramos, who would eventually face second-degree murder charges, can be seen taunting Thomas: "Now you see my fists? They're getting ready to fuck you up." Thomas can be heard crying, apologizing, and screaming for his father. A paramedic would later testify that officers demanded treatment for their minor (and self-inflicted) injuries while their victim lay nearby, beaten to a bloody and unrecognizable pulp. He died five days later. Ramos and another officer were acquitted of all charges.

———

By far the largest constituency left unprotected by the police is women. This might seem ironic, since the most frequent response to calls to abolish police and prisons today asks: What about the rapists? But while the specter of sexual assault is deployed to justify the need for police to prevent rape and arrest rapists, and prisons to lock them away, this has never been the reality. The police don't prevent sexual assault or other forms of violence against women; perpetrators are rarely investigated, indicted, or convicted; and mass incarceration does nothing to "keep society safe" from the "worst of the worst." In reality, the police inflict far more violence on women than they prevent.

For the anti-lynching campaigner Ida B. Wells, lynching—often the result of spurious rape accusations—was designed to send a message not only to Black men but to white women as well. If lynching claimed to protect the "honor" of white women from the sexual appetites of free Black men, it also contained a tacit threat: that such protection could be withdrawn. Lynching was therefore key to patriarchal power, because it served to conscript white women into a devil's bargain not unlike that which bound poor whites to their class enemies. White women were forced to sacrifice certain freedoms and rights in exchange for protection from imaginary threats. For more than a century, police have enforced the same bargain. From vagrancy laws to criminalize nineteenth-century sex workers in New York to "vice squads" targeting interracial nightclubs in South Central Los Angeles a century later, policing has long sought to enforce an ideal of moral purity by disrupting interracial intimacy and solidarity.[23] Moreover, the devil's bargain Wells identified more than a century ago has been reborn in the carceral feminism of today, which appeals to police and prisons to protect the vulnerable.[24] The tendency to see police as the only possible protection against rape today, and rape as the last-ditch argument for policing, reflects this longstanding double bind.

But today as in the past, the numbers are absolutely clear: not only do police not prevent sexual assault, they rarely even investigate it, much less does the criminal justice system deliver the convictions that are its raison d'être. Most sexual assaults—some two-thirds—are not reported, and even when they are, investigations are often halfhearted.[25] According to a 2019 investigation published in *The Atlantic*, 200,000 rape kits were found sitting untested across the country. That's 200,000 women who, after 200,000 assaults, jumped through the emotional and procedural hoops to report an assault only for *nothing* to happen. In one case, a serial rapist in Detroit committed eleven assaults in eleven years while his DNA sat untested in police custody.[26] After mass public outcry about the untested kits, significant progress has been made in working through the backlog, but this is only the first step. Despite the fact that most survivors of sexual assault know their attacker, official police "clearance rates" (meaning arrest, not even conviction) remain abysmal (an estimated 32 percent nationwide in 2017), and even these are exaggerated.[27] Once so-called "exceptional clearances" are excluded, the true clearance rate is likely only half the official rate, and as low as 8 percent in some cities, including Chicago.[28] Once you do the math, less than 6 percent of rapes lead to arrest, and less than 1 percent to conviction.[29]

Even this is only half of the equation at best. Not only do police fail to *prevent* violence against women and sexual assault in particular, they *contribute* actively and disproportionately to gendered and sexual violence both on and off the job. Sexual assault by on-duty officers is what former career cop Norm Stamper calls policing's "nasty little secret," something that "happens far more often than people in the business are willing to admit," as shown by his vivid descriptions of his own stomach-turning experience. His "cautious guess" is that around 5 percent of officers will commit sexual assault at some point— which amounts to some 50,000 predators walking around with a badge and a gun every day.[30] According to the conservative Cato Institute, the second most common complaint against police, after excessive force, is "sexual misconduct"—which, once we strip away the sanitized copspeak, means "rape by cop or attempted rape by cop," or more accurately still, "police sexual terror."[31]

Rape by cop, moreover, is not simply a sexual assault that happens to be carried out by a police officer. It is a specific and pervasive technique that takes advantage of the greatest power disparities in American society. Police intentionally and systematically target the young and the powerless, those with a history of drug addiction, mental illness, or run-ins with the law—in short, those most vulnerable. One study suggests that a full *half* of survivors are minors, and according to the United Nations Committee on the Elimination of Racial Discrimination, "rape and sexual abuse by police [in the United States] are primarily reported by women of color."[32] Rape by cop is itself a form of policing, and here the case of Daniel Holtzclaw—"the most famous of all police rapists"—is especially instructive. As David Correia and Tyler Wall explain,

> All of his victims were Black women. To hunt his prey, Holtzclaw used the basic tools and methods of all patrol officers: running background checks on police databases as a way to locate people who have criminal histories. Holtzclaw would then exploit this knowledge by coercing women into performing sexual acts on him. This highlights a key feature of rape by cop: the least powerful in society are often targeted the most since they have fewer options for legal recourse, and this is only exacerbated when victims have to turn to the very institution that employs the person causing them injury.[33]

Ultimately Holtzclaw proved too embarrassing for the police and the criminal justice system to sweep under the rug. Unlike most police rapists, he was tried and convicted of eighteen counts and sentenced to 263 years in prison.

By combing through news reports and court documents, the *Buffalo News* found a case of sexual assault by police occurring every five days nationwide, concluding that "the numbers are almost certainly higher."[34] A 2015 Associated Press report identified 1,000 cops who had been fired for sexual misconduct over the course of six years, but here too, "the number is unquestionably an undercount."[35] Indeed, it is only the tip of a massive iceberg: already-low reporting rates for sexual assault in general are much lower—abysmally so—for those assaulted by police. In the words of attorney and activist Andrea Ritchie, "Survivors of sexual assault by police are the only survivors of sexual assault who have to report the assault to the people that committed it. That's a huge reason they're not reported."[36]

Those courageous enough to report are subjected to a gauntlet of threats and intimidation. When a teenager known online as Anna Chambers accused two NYPD officers of raping her while handcuffed and in custody, her mother recalled that no fewer than thirteen officers approached them in the hospital to dissuade them from filing charges. Consent in custody, as journalist Natasha Lennard has argued, is "impossible." Someone in an inherently coercive power relationship like police custody "cannot give consent, in any meaningful sense of the word, to the officer holding them."[37] While previously illegal for prison guards, it was not until after Chambers's case that New York law was changed to make sex in police custody nonconsensual by definition. However, Chambers's rapists were not prosecuted according to the new law; they pleaded guilty to minor charges and were given probation.[38]

At home, things are scarcely better than they are on the job. Existing data based on two studies from the 1990s shows that some 40 percent of police officers have abused their partners or children, but because both studies rely on self-reporting and are limited only to recent cases of abuse, this is almost certainly an undercount as well.[39] Since the prevalence of domestic violence across society as a whole is estimated to be around 10 percent of families, this means that cops are at least four times as likely to abuse their partners or children—the highest rate of *any* occupation. And again, why would a woman report domestic violence when "her chances are at least two out of five that the officer who responds has recently beaten his own partner," and when the consequences of reporting can be terrifying, if not deadly.

After reporting her husband, one survivor recalls, "I started receiving phone calls with the sounds of a gun-racking, the metallic sounds of a clip of bullets being loaded into the chamber of a .45, his service weapon."[40] The National Center for Women and Policing paints a picture of near-total impunity: only 19 percent of departments terminate officers after a second instance of abuse, and their service weapons are rarely confiscated.[41] Some departments do not prosecute officers for domestic violence at all, while others prosecute at half the rate of the general public—many actively promote abusers. Not only are cops who abuse their partners rarely jailed or disciplined, but they are armed, trained to pursue, and given access to police databases and the location of domestic abuse shelters.

Why don't police departments fire officers who abuse their partners? Quite simply because they would run out of cops. To expect anything else is to confuse policing with a peaceful affair. As violence workers, police inject that violence into every situation they enter, with little to no likelihood of consequences. The same goes for other violence workers, namely the military, where data collected by the National Coalition against Domestic Violence shows that between 1995 and 2001, 30 percent of active duty women reported domestic abuse, while there were at least 217 domestic violence homicides.[42] Likewise for Border Patrol, which has seen several cases eerily similar to Holtzclaw's in which agents have taken sexual advantage of the extreme vulnerability of migrants—again, most are never reported, and in some cases, witnesses to abuse have even been deported.[43]

—

The police don't protect sexual minorities, either. Some 5 percent of the population, LBGTQ people are far less likely to be able to rely on police for safety, and far more likely to be abused themselves. Given the breadth of the category, these numbers vary widely: from mainstream middle- and upper-class gay people in the upscale Castro district of San Francisco to young trans people of color living in homeless shelters or on the streets of the Tenderloin, the differences within the community can be as dramatic as those outside of it. According to the National Transgender Discrimination Survey, more than a quarter of respondents have been physically assaulted for their gender identity, and an astonishing three-quarters of all deadly anti-LGBTQ hate crimes are directed at trans women. The report explains:

> Unfortunately, law enforcement is often part of the problem . . . Half of transgender people report they are uncomfortable seeking police assistance. More than one-fifth (22%) of transgender people who had interacted with police reported police harassment, and 6% of transgender individuals reported that they experienced bias-motivated assault by officers. Black transgender people reported much higher rates of biased harassment and assault (38% and 15%).[44]

According to data from the National Coalition of Anti-Violence Programs, trans people are almost four times as likely to experience police brutality, and for trans people of color the ratio is as high as six times that of white cisgender people.[45]

Sex workers, too, are not only left unprotected but actively targeted by police for sexual extortion, even (or especially) among minors. In *Playing the Whore*, journalist Melissa Gira Grant speaks of

> a matrix of widespread police misconduct toward sex workers and people profiled as sex workers. In New York City, for example, 70 percent of sex workers working outdoors surveyed by the Sex Workers Project reported near daily run-ins with police, and 30 percent reported being threatened with violence . . . when street-based sex workers sought help from the police, they were often ignored . . . 14 percent of those who primarily work indoors reported that police had been violent toward them; 16 percent reported that police officers had initiated a sexual interaction.

"Police violence against sex workers," Grant writes, "is a persistent global reality."[46]

In but one disturbing illustration this persistent reality, an Oakland, California, woman known as Celeste Guap revealed in 2016 that when she was underage, she had been involved in a police prostitution ring involving dozens of officers across several departments. Ultimately, the revelation led to the resignation of several officers, while others were disciplined, and the city settled for nearly $1 million—although most criminal charges were dropped or thrown out. Speaking of the Oakland case, Nola Brantley, who was herself abused by a school police officer at age fourteen before later founding an organization to support survivors, insists that police routinely coerce sex workers with threats of arrest: "You're talking about a highly vulnerable population of individuals. It's very, very common . . . We'd have girls that would come in all the time and talk about being raped by police officers . . . police would not put pressure on their traffickers as long as they were allowed to have sexual contact with the girls."[47]

Sex workers, like people of color, homeless people, and the mentally ill, are considered "acceptable" targets for violence by society and the police alike. This explains not only why serial killers routinely target sex workers, for example, but also why police often dismiss the victims of serial killers as sex workers, even when this isn't the case.[48] In every single one of these categories, moreover, the question isn't simply about a failure to "serve and protect," and much less is it an accident. Rather, like American society as a whole, police view vulnerable communities as disposable, meaning that they aren't worth protecting and that there will be no consequences for sexual misconduct and violence; their lives are not valuable, nor are their deaths meaningful. But if the police don't protect women—not even white women and not even their own partners—why is so much weight given to the argument that women, more than any other group, *need* the police?

For Isabel Cristo of *The New Republic*, the question "What about the rapists?" is a "conceptual trap" into which even abolitionists can fall if we are not cautious. To concede that vulnerable people need "someone to call" for protection on the road to abolition—and that, consequently, we need the police in the short term—betrays a fundamental misunderstanding of what the police do. Simply put, "policing doesn't protect women," or many others for that matter—not now, not ever. Moreover, to argue that we need police pending abolition is to obscure the very real violence police *cause*, since, as Cristo observes, "far from being protected, it's under the guise of 'fighting crime' that Black women, trans women, indigenous, undocumented, and poor women have been subjected to a system of violent policing that continually exposes them to gender-based harm."[49]

—

I have a confession to make: this chapter's argument has been based on a false premise from the jump. The motto "To protect and serve" was never a sincere declaration of principle at all, but one coined by the Los Angeles Police Department in 1963 under the tenure of police chief William Parker, an "avowed white supremacist" who turned the LAPD into "a redneck army of occupation" by actively recruiting white officers from the Jim Crow South.[50] In other words, the idea that police protect and serve the majority of the American public has been little more than window dressing for racist policing from the very beginning, an empty slogan and nothing more. The real question has always been: *Who* precisely do the police serve? As we have seen, the constituency is narrow indeed, even when measured purely in terms of police killings—death by the numbers. This doesn't even account for the everyday dehumanization of constant harassment, which runs much broader and deeper, leading to immeasurable consequences. Police murder is a symptom of a much-deeper sickness.

The police only serve the interests of the select few: the whitest and the wealthiest, those in positions of power and with significant property to protect, the owners of businesses and real estate, and those who—as a result of their own opulence—live in fear of the poor, dark masses. Even then, what percentage of those most protected—rich, white men—have friends, family members, children, or loved ones who are poor or homeless, who are queer or trans, who are people of color or suffer mental illness, and who are therefore at a much-higher risk of violence or death at the hands of cops? Ultimately, as police become more arrogant, impervious to accountability, and militarized, increasingly seeing *everyone* as a potential target for brute force, even some police officers—like William "Dub" Lawrence—are learning the hard way that the violence of policing is powerfully contagious. The subject of the award-winning documentary *Peace Officer*, Lawrence is a former Utah sheriff who helped found and train one of the state's first SWAT teams in the 1970s, only to watch in horror three decades later as the same unit killed his son-in-law during a mental health episode.

As proposals to defund and even dismantle the police took center stage in the aftermath of the George Floyd rebellions, police and their allies doubled down on the idea that we *need* them for protection—and that their absence would unleash a frenzied paroxysm of violence on the scale of *The Purge*. But according to David Bayley, a Princeton-trained political scientist and former dean of the SUNY Albany School of Criminal Justice, "one of the best kept secrets of modern life" is that "police do not prevent crime."

Experts know it, the police know it, but the public does not know it. Yet the police pretend that they are society's best defense against crime and continually argue that if they are given more resources, especially personnel, they will be able to protect communities against crime. This is myth.

What evidence is there for this heretical and disturbing assertion? First, repeated analysis has consistently failed to find any connection between the number of police officers and crime rates. Second, the primary strategies adopted by modern police have been shown to have little or no effect on crime.[51]

Bayley is no abolitionist, and no opponent of the police: he is simply stating incontrovertible fact. He goes on to cite dozens of studies: latitudinal research comparing different large cities that show no relation between the number of police and crime rates; longitudinal analyses of historical trends over time showing that the massive growth of the policing apparatus has not impacted crime statistics—indeed, quite the opposite. Most interestingly, Bayley cites cases in which police went on strike or were laid off en masse and—you guessed it—crime did not increase.

If we need confirmation of this, we can find it in the New York City Police Department's ham-fisted strike against Mayor Bill de Blasio in late 2014. When de Blasio expressed dismay at the non-indictment of officer Daniel Pantaleo for strangling Eric Garner, the police went postal (no shade to the US Postal Service), fuming that the demand for accountability was putting officers at risk. Deemed a "blue coup" by its detractors, striking officers hoped that by throwing a tantrum and working-to-rule (i.e., doing the bare minimum required by law), they would prove their indispensability and communities would clamor for their return. But the opposite was the case: not only did arrests decline by half, but crime too fell—and dramatically so. Through a combination of Freedom of Information Act (FOIA) requests and complex statistical analysis, researchers have shown that complaints of serious crimes dropped some 3 to 6 percent during the slowdown. And since the particular program the police were rolling back was so-called broken windows policing, they provided ample evidence that the strategy doesn't work, and that it can even "inadvertently contribute to serious criminal activity" by establishing a "vicious feedback between proactive policing and major crime" that can "exacerbate political and economic inequality across communities."[52] If the cops want to keep striking, more power to them—it's just another reminder that we don't need them at all.

Bayley goes on to show that the three central strategies deployed by police—patrols, rapid response to the scene of a crime, and investigation after the fact—have each been separately shown to have no impact on public safety whatsoever. Even if one were to believe, as most supporters of police do, that arrests and convictions prevent future crime, what to make of the 2020 study by a University of Utah law professor concluding that among serious crimes, only 2 percent result in arrest and conviction?[53] The oft-held truism is actually true: as singer-songwriter Tracy Chapman once put it, "The police always come late, if they come at all."

This is no accident: the police were never designed to prevent crime or to protect all citizens. They were created to safeguard the *specific* interests of wealthy, white, property-holding men— and to expand those interests by providing the muscle for colonial land grabs, breaking workers' strikes, ensuring the availability of the poor, people of color, and migrants as a disciplined and compliant workforce, and locking up in the warehouses we call prisons all those whose labor is no longer useful. Ever since, they have helped to produce a society that is not only increasingly policed, but that is shot through with all those same elements of racial, capitalist, colonial, patriarchal power. When it comes to this function, policing, as Michelle Alexander has said of prisons, has not been a failure but "a fantastic success ... creat[ing] far more crimes than it prevents, by ripping apart fragile social networks, destroying families, and creating a permanent class of unemployables."[54] This is what police, like prisons, have *always* done—why would we expect them to do anything different today?

It will surprise many to learn that the police don't prevent crime, but what might be even more surprising is that they *aren't even required to try*—or, for that matter, to protect the public at all. When Nikolas Cruz opened fire at Marjory Stoneman Douglas High School in Parkland, Florida, in 2018, killing seventeen, what did the armed sheriff's deputy stationed at the school, Scot Peterson, do? He *hid*. For forty-five minutes. Despite outrage from mourning parents, a federal court ruled in

Peterson's favor, finding that "the Sheriff's Office had no legal duty to protect students during the shooting at Marjory Stoneman Douglas High School."[55] This was just the most recent in a spate of federal and Supreme Court rulings upholding the "no duty to protect" rule. In a pair of decisions dealing with child abuse (*DeShaney v. Winnebago County* in 1989) and domestic violence (*Castle Rock v. Gonzales* in 2005), the Supreme Court ruled that despite documented proof of threats, police and other public agencies could not be held liable for not protecting the public from a private, third-party actor. Unless we are explicitly in their custody or some other form of "special relationship," the police are not obligated to protect and serve *at all*. As absurd as it sounds, the Parkland ruling argued that no such special relationship existed between the students and the sheriff's deputy explicitly hired to protect them.

The point here is not to debate the intricacies of legal precedent but to note the vast gulf that exists between what the police are *required* to do and what the public *believes* they are supposed to do, a gap concealed by the myth of "serve and protect." This example is especially relevant given that the question "What about the rapists?" is almost always followed with "What about mass shooters?" The answer is Parkland, and "no duty to protect." Indeed, there's zero evidence that school police have *ever* stopped a mass shooting. What happened in Parkland was, in fact, a replay of the massacres in 1999 at Columbine High School in Colorado, and in 2016 at the Pulse nightclub in Orlando, among others. Writing exasperatedly about the "cowardly cops" who failed to stop Pulse shooter Omar Mateen, Michael Parenti observed at the time that "while they are shy about confronting killers in nightclubs or schools . . . the police continue to perform fearlessly against unarmed individuals."

And just as police are not legally required to protect and serve, they are not trained to do so, either. On the contrary, they are trained to protect themselves first and foremost, even if it means harming others, and they are taught that their safety exists in a zero-sum relationship to a presumed aggressor. According to Seth Stoughton, a law professor who spent years working as a police officer in Tallahassee, the problem isn't a *lack* of training but what the police are actually trained to do. Starting at the police academy, "the concept of officer safety is so heavily emphasized that it takes on almost religious significance." Rookies are taught that their prime directive is survival, and that "every encounter, every individual is a potential threat"—a strangely Hobbesian vision for those claiming to be "public servants."

Stoughton goes on to describe "hands-on exercises" in which

> one common scenario teaches officers that a suspect leaning into a car can pull out a gun and shoot at officers before they can react. Another teaches that even when an officer is pointing a gun at a suspect whose back is turned, the suspect can spin around and fire first. Yet another teaches that a knife-carrying suspect standing 20 feet away can run up to an officer and start stabbing before the officer can get their gun out of the holster. There are countless variations, but the lessons are the same: Hesitation can be fatal. So officers are trained to shoot before a threat is fully realized, to not wait until the last minute because the last minute may be too late.

While occasionally encouraged to avoid mistakes fatal to the public, "officers are taught that the risks of mistake are less—far less—than the risks of hesitation. A common phrase among cops pretty much sums it up: 'Better to be judged by twelve than carried by six.'"[56]

But the reality is that it isn't really dangerous to be a cop, hyperbolic ranting about a "war on police" notwithstanding. According to the Bureau of Labor Statistics, being a police officer is less dangerous than being a logger, fisherman, roofer, pilot, garbage collector, truck driver, farmer, steelworker, construction worker, landscaper—the list goes on. My own father was nearly killed in a logging accident, not because he was a hero, but because he was a poor, disposable worker. But loggers don't declare war on the trees. Fishermen don't believe the seas are out to get them. And I have yet to see a "Garbage Collectors' Lives Matter" T-shirt.

Poor people go to work and risk their lives every day without exaggerating their heroism, even when that heroism is exceptional: nurses, doctors, and other frontline health care workers; the USPS workers and garbage collectors who are only beginning to get their fair due; and the migrants picking fruit in the fields of California as wildfires bear down on them. It is only the police who are forever describing themselves as the bravest of public servants but are trained to see everyone they encounter as a mortal threat. It is no surprise that this topsy-turvy view, in which armed aggressors paint themselves as victims, bears the same logical structure as the victim complex of settler colonialism in the past and white nationalism today. Cops today are increasingly, and by design, *cowards* who never stop talking about how brave they are.

Why do we have public employees trained in the use of violence if they aren't even required to use that violence to protect and to serve, and if even when they do, it has no positive impact whatsoever on community safety? Why would the public pay billions of dollars in salaries just to then pay hundreds of millions more—$100 million in Chicago in 2018, and $880 million in Los Angeles between 2005 and 2018—to settle cases of police brutality?[57] There is no Hippocratic Oath for police, and if they were actually held to the standards of *primum non nocere* (first, do no harm), policing would be nothing like what exists today. Instead, the only oath binding police today is to avoid any possible danger to themselves; to shoot first and ask questions later, killing those armed with cars, knives, sticks, wallets, cell phones, or nothing at all. What happens when the public realizes that the police don't protect us, and that they aren't even required to do so?

Trying to understand the police can sometimes feel like staring into a fun house mirror. The right-side-up reality of a policing apparatus that systematically fails to protect the vast majority instead appears flipped upside down, in an expansive pig majority that underwrites, supports, and votes for ever more police as the sole solution to all of society's ills. What explains this optical illusion whereby an American public that jealously guards its tax dollars nevertheless throws billions at a violent and useless system of policing? To be sure, false promises can be tempting, especially when there seems to be no alternative to the world of police. But the mirror is cracking, and the idealized image of the police is splintering. Even the tiniest fractures offer glimpses of a new world.

The only people police protect and serve are *themselves*.[58] And just like any other corrupt and self-serving bureaucracy living parasitically off the public dime, they should be abolished.

3

The Mirage of Reform

Scarcely a week before Baltimore police killed Freddie Gray in April 2015, officer Michael Slager gunned down Walter Scott in North Charleston, South Carolina, shooting the fleeing man in the back five times from a distance of more than twenty feet. After footage of the killing sparked widespread outrage, and Slager was quickly arrested and indicted for murder, a deafening chorus emerged, insisting that "the system worked." And they were right. The system *did* work, just not in the way that most mean.

The system lurched into motion immediately, as Slager cuffed the dying man and then ran (*ran!*) back to grab his alibi, the Taser that he would then plant near Scott's failing body. As rapper and activist Boots Riley noticed at the time, Slager did so in an eminently *practiced* way: "This was done so readily and so smoothly that it can't be the first time he's done it, and the nonchalance shows that it's commonplace."[1] The machinery continued to whir smoothly as the second officer on the scene— Clarence Habersham, who is Black—ignored the planted evidence, raised no questions, and did not administer CPR to Scott. Habersham later insisted that he had immediately applied pressure to Scott's wounds, but audio recordings from the scene suggested that he was instead counting bullet holes in the still-dying man. After all, multiracial policing is still just policing. The North Charleston Police Department parroted Slager's account in a preemptive attempt to exonerate the officer, calling the killing a "traffic stop gone wrong" that had been "unfortunate and difficult for everyone."[2]

The media—an essential component of the system if ever there was one—immediately ate up a story so thoroughly predigested as to not raise any eyebrows. The police are to be believed, so we are told. Among those who also believed that the system worked, because they are an essential *part* of that system, were groups like Al Sharpton's National Action Network, whose local representative was clear about his priorities: "I don't want to see another Ferguson." The system purred along smoothly when a superior officer briefly interviewed Slager, only to make it clear that he had nothing at all to worry about: "They're not gonna ask you any kind of questions right now."[3] The system worked because it performed the function it was designed to perform: to kill Black people and either justify it, cover it up, or both. This is the system, this has always been the system, and yes: *the system worked*.

Michael Slager wasn't arrested because the system worked—if this were the case, killer cops would be arrested all the time. He was arrested due to a glitch in the system, and that glitch's name is Feidin Santana. Not only did Santana courageously capture the murder of Walter Scott on video, but crucially, he released the video not to the police, but to Scott's family instead. Santana knew better than to trust the police with evidence, and he feared for his own personal safety. On both counts, he was justified. When Johannes Mehserle shot Oscar Grant dead in Oakland, other officers immediately attempted to confiscate the phones of bystanders like nineteen-year-old Karina Vargas. She released her footage, which went viral. Ramsey Orta, who filmed Eric Garner's killing, was harassed by police, imprisoned at Rikers Island, and—he believes—poisoned as retribution.[4] Slager was arrested not due to the normal functioning of the system, but because Santana operated outside it.[5]

Policing isn't a few bad apples: it's a violent system that generates corruption, brutality, and inhumanity, recruiting self-selected bullies and teaching them how to bully more effectively. It is famously shielded by the so-called blue wall of silence, behind which, with a tiny handful of exceptions, even the "good cops" cower, protecting their own in the knowledge that they might be next. And it's a system in which the very worst of those apples float to the top, promoted internally or elected to leadership positions in the Fraternal Order of Police. Policing is not a fundamentally sound system that has simply become too heavily armed or militarized. On the contrary, policing—especially of poor communities of color at home and abroad—has always been a militarized affair. Likewise, policing isn't suffering an unfortunate crisis of community relations; the "community" is the explicit target of its control and repression. No number of town hall meetings and soothing words, barbecues and softball leagues, can obscure this fundamental reality.

Policing isn't broken, and police reform hasn't failed. Just as policing is doing what it was designed to do, so too has police reform been largely successful in its own task: to legitimize the police. And just as every "failure" of policing is turned into the need for more funding and more police, the same goes for police reform—every failed reform means we just need to try again. Police reform is always a "failure," but the answer is always more reform. This is why the various quick-fix, silver-bullet solutions to police violence and misconduct have done nothing more than strengthen policing as a system. Ironically, it is by claiming to be broken—repeatedly, loudly, and publicly—that policing has historically distracted attention from its own rotten foundations. Reform doesn't seek to change and correct the problem of policing from the outside: it is itself an essential part of that problem.[6]

To borrow a phrase from Critical Resistance co-founder Rachel Herzing, we can understand police reform as a sort of magic, an incantation that—no matter how absurd—is believed to cure all ills through mere repetition. This magic takes the form of a historical disappearing trick, concealing the failure of all previous reforms behind the magician's cape of the present. Were this trick not already obvious enough, consider the fact that one central target of police reform in the present—"broken windows," or proactive policing—was itself once offered as a magical fix by a previous generation of violent magicians.[7] What could be more magical than solving crime proactively, before it even happens? Or, consider that police once held up the kind of "neck restraint" that killed George Floyd as an alternative to beating suspects with their nightsticks. The magic of reform is its power to hypnotize, to dazzle, especially those who want to believe (or at least want an excuse to ignore). We should be wary of similar incantations in the present: body cameras, racial sensitivity training, diversification, procedural justice, community policing, "less lethal" weapons.

By the same token, police reform is also a mirage: it tantalizes from a distance, promising relief that never arrives. The closer you get, the further it recedes into the distance, but not without enticing you to continue walking in vain. We *know* that police reform doesn't work, because we've seen it all before; because in the densely packed years from Ferguson to today, all we have had is reform proposals and blue-ribbon commissions. None of this was enough to save George Floyd's life.

—

Police reform is as old as policing itself. The earliest sheriffs, the shire-reeves of Norman England, were empowered both to collect local taxes and to enforce the law—a perfect recipe for corruption and brutality (Robin Hood's antagonist, the Sheriff of Nottingham, was hardly a caricature in this respect). Later constables and night watchmen, established around the thirteenth century, were scarcely better—"unarmed, untrained, under-supervised, often unwilling, and frequently drunk," not to mention "wandering about with lewd Women."[8] In fact, the very founding of the modern police was an attempt to rein in the corrupt bands roving the countryside and brutalizing the poor in the name of the Crown. Ever since, the response has been the same on either side of the Atlantic: to professionalize the police along military lines and on the model of colonial domination.

Within a few short decades of the NYPD's founding, the 1894 Lexow Committee discovered a level of corruption so widespread that officers were guilty of "almost every conceivable crime."⁹ Police affiliated with the Tammany Hall political machine would buy promotions before recouping their money through extortion and by running prostitution rings—all while cracking down on independent sex workers—and they were fully embedded in the widespread political corruption and electoral tampering that defined the era. These early reforms had little effect, and the Prohibition era saw the explosive growth of both corruption and police abuse, including the use of torture to extract confessions. A 1931 report by the Wickersham Commission was penned in large part by diehard police reformer August Vollmer himself, who often boasted about his own colonial experience, advocated the use of "military tactics" to fight crime, and described policing as "a war against the enemies of society."

Vollmer argued that police should be professionalized even further along military lines by incorporating a vertical structure and adapting colonial methods. As LAPD chief, he had previously modeled an elite crime-fighting unit on counterinsurgent forces in the Philippines.¹⁰ This was a strange response indeed if torture was a concern: US counterinsurgency training has seen the most brutal forms of torture exported globally, with those chickens later coming home to roost in cases like Jon Burge in Chicago. If Vollmer's counterinsurgent policing initially involved a campaign for hearts and minds through community engagement, however, he and other police reformers soon abandoned this vision in favor of inward-oriented process of professionalization. Early police forces in the United States had been "catchall health, welfare, and law-enforcement agencies" that "cleaned streets and inspected boilers in New York, distributed supplies to the poor in Baltimore, accommodated the homeless in Philadelphia, investigated vegetable markets in St. Louis, [and] operated emergency ambulances in Boston."[11] Before long, the professionalization drive of the 1930s stripped police of what little role they had played in social welfare to focus more narrowly on crime, setting the stage for the crisis of today.

Fast-forward to the late 1960s, when three separate federal commissions—Katzenbach, Kerner, and the National Violence Commission—all struggled with the questions raised by mass rebellions against police violence. All three commissions pointed squarely toward underlying social issues: police brutality may have provided the spark, but structural racism, poverty, unemployment, and housing were the kindling. The Kerner report, in particular, famously diagnosed the existence of "two societies, one black, one white—separate and unequal," concluding that "white society is deeply implicated in the ghetto. White institutions created it, white institutions maintain it, and white society condones it." The vast social divide that produced the riots was not the product of policing as such, and would not be resolved without job programs, investment in public housing, and the broader desegregation of American society.

Lyndon Johnson would largely ignore these recommendations in favor of an emphasis on security that saw the dramatic expansion of policing. While for many this is an indication of the unfulfilled promise of the Kerner Commission, it also paradoxically shows how Kerner, by pairing far-reaching statements about social welfare that political leaders would inevitably ignore with a by-now standard menu of minor reforms, became a model for almost every subsequent police reform proposal. And while recognizing that "recruitment of more Negro officers alone will not solve the problems of lack of communication and hostility towards police," Kerner nevertheless concluded that such diversification efforts should be "intensified" anyway.

The New York Knapp Commission, empaneled in 1970 following corruption revelations by detective Frank Serpico, showed just how little the NYPD had changed over the course of a century. While not focused on use of force against civilians, Knapp was a window into how corruption stitches police together like a gang or a mafia. Low-level corruption, so-called "grass eating," was the disciplinary glue binding together the blue wall of silence and protecting more aggressively corrupt "meat eaters." After all, you can't snitch if you're a little guilty too. Serpico himself learned the hard way what happened to those who betrayed the brotherhood: he was shot in the face under suspicious circumstances while his fellow officers refused to provide backup, later denouncing "an atmosphere in which the honest officer fears the dishonest officer." A 1994 report from the Mollen Commission later found that attempts to reform the NYPD had actually made things worse: the department had cracked down on the low-hanging fruit of everyday graft while commanders, in part worried about public embarrassment, had discouraged investigations of more serious corruption. Whereas cops had previously accommodated criminals, the report argued, now they *were* the criminals—more meat eaters than grass eaters.

The 1980s saw multiple riots and multiple commissions in Miami, a prelude to the televised beating of Rodney King in Los Angeles in 1991, and the massive explosion that ensued when his assailants were acquitted a year later. This time it was the Christopher Commission, which unearthed a culture of impunity in the LAPD in which even repeat abusers were often promoted, and the parallel Kolts Commission, which found the same in the LA County Sheriff's Department. Both made what were effectively the same proposals prescribed by independent reviews throughout nearly three decades of explosive unrest triggered by police terror: more training, more diverse recruitment, more oversight, more discipline, better processing of complaints—and of course, community policing, which seeks to make policing more effective through close cooperation with community members. Another instance of brutality, another rebellion, another series of commissions, another set of useless proposals that don't grapple with the reality of police power. From the LAPD Rampart scandal in the 1990s to the Oakland Riders a decade later, and the 2020 case of a Compton sheriff's deputy who killed eighteen-year-old Andrés Guardado while "chasing ink"—seeking initiation into a police gang known as the Executioners—policing is a violence machine that produces brutality, impunity, and corruption with every turn of its gears.[12]

With the killing of Mike Brown and the rebellions in Ferguson, the interminable cycle of police reform began its grinding motion once again, this time generating not one but two commissions and reform proposals. On March 4, 2015, the Civil Rights Division of the Department of Justice released a scathing indictment of the Ferguson Police Department (the *Ferguson Report*), finding wide-ranging and racially motivated violations of the First and Fourth Amendments, the unrestrained use of excessive force, discriminatory intent violating the Fourteenth Amendment, and court and city practices that were effectively funding the city budget on the back of poor Black residents. When it came to recommendations, however, the report simply offered more of the same: more training, better reporting and tracking, more civilian input (not even oversight), public information sharing, and above all, the implementation of "a robust system of true community policing."[13] Were it not already perfectly clear that these proposals were mere window dressing, the DOJ issued a report on the very same day finding no reason to pursue charges against Darren Wilson for killing Brown.

Just two months later, Obama's President's Task Force on Twenty-First Century Policing came to many of the same conclusions as the Ferguson Commission for policing nationwide. As if announcing that the goal was to simply manage public opinion, everywhere one might expect mention of police misconduct, the report instead speaks of public perception. The task is to "promote effective crime reduction while building public trust," and the first pillar for doing so is not rooting out police misconduct (the cause of distrust), but "building trust and legitimacy." As

Stuart Schrader put it at the time, the point was to encourage obedience, not justice.[14] And the litany of reforms was familiar: "less-than-lethal" technology, better training, community relations and feedback, better use of social media, officer wellness, diversification of the police force. Both reports, moreover, emphasize that magician's sleight of hand—non-enforcement activities—distracting attention from actual police practices while conceding that reform is impossible.

Tracey Meares, a professor of law at Yale, served on Obama's police reform commission, and was nothing if not a true believer in police reform. But she saw firsthand how even the most uncontroversial measures, including the mere acknowledgment of past abuses, have proven "incredibly difficult for many if not most agencies. Further steps, such as holding officers criminally accountable for killing unarmed civilians, seem almost impossible." Like so many others in recent years, Meares became a sort of unwilling abolitionist, even writing in 2017 that, "policing as we know it must be abolished before it can be transformed."[15] Meares's abolitionism was apparently short-lived, however: in recent months, she has openly advocated the same Obama-era reforms that she had once considered futile.

That Obama's police reform efforts were in bad faith was obvious to many Philadelphians as soon as he named Charles Ramsey to lead the commission. As police chief in Washington, DC, Ramsey had overseen mass arrests during 2002 protests against the World Trade Organization and International Monetary Fund, for which he was later found personally culpable for violations of the Fourth Amendment, costing the city millions in damages before moving on to Philadelphia.

Just three days before Obama tapped Ramsey, Philadelphia police shot Brandon Tate-Brown in the back of the head during a traffic stop. The unnamed officers claimed Tate-Brown, a 26-year-old Black man, was reaching for a gun in his car—his family said there was no gun. In early 2015, as Ramsey traveled the country, local organizers—myself included—refused to leave

A WORLD WITHOUT POLICE

the streets, marching through driving snow in Northeast Philadelphia to demand the names of the officers and surveillance
footage of the killing. When then–district attorney Seth
Williams—currently sitting in federal prison for extortion,
bribery, and fraud—announced that no charges would be sought
against the officers, protesters took over a police–community
town hall featuring Ramsey and Williams, both of whom are
Black, in heavily white Northeast Philadelphia, sparking a melee
that led to ten arrests. Larry Krasner defended our comrades
who, much to Ramsey's embarrassment, were acquitted.

It was only as a result of this pressure that, a month after the
Twenty-First Century Policing Commission published its report,
the city finally released the officers' names and the video of the
shooting. Ramsey himself was forced to admit what the video
clearly showed: that Tate-Brown was not reaching for a gun at
all. In other words, the whole time that Ramsey was crisscrossing
the country on Obama's dime preaching police reform and
civilian oversight, he was stonewalling at home and lying to
Tate-Brown's family about their son's murder by cop. The
struggles around the case revealed to many organizers and community members alike that so-called police reform is little more
than a façade, an ideology, and an alibi, marking a turning point
for grassroots struggles in the city. Two years later, riding a
wave of community organizing, Krasner was elected district
attorney over ferocious opposition from the police, and all told,
Philadelphia paid some $40 million in settlements for police
"misconduct" under Ramsey the reformer.[16]

———

When it comes to police reform, there's nothing new under the
sun—just old, discredited solutions dressed up in new language:
body cameras, demilitarization, diversification, training, and
chokehold bans, accompanied by vague phraseology like community policing, and today's preferred (if uninspiring) magical
incantation: procedural justice.

80

Body cameras. In the wake of the Ferguson rebellions, the Obama administration touted no solution with more confidence than body cameras, for which it requested $75 million in federal matching funds for the purchase of 50,000 units by local and state police. But while video of police killings has played a key role in stoking outrage and resistance, there is little evidence that body cameras make cops less violent or lead to heightened accountability. Body cameras would not have saved Eric Garner—after strangling Garner on film, NYPD officer Daniel Pantaleo even waved at the camera. As Walter Scott's killing in North Charleston shows, however, the existence of video *does* matter, but only when the police don't control the cameras or the footage. Police routinely disable their cameras or raise the hoods of patrol cars to obstruct dashcams. Others tamper with or delete footage later, and more often it simply isn't released at all. Feidin Santana's bystander footage of the shooting of Walter Scott mattered precisely because he didn't hand it over to the cops.

In a study conducted on the Rialto, California police department, officers were fitted with body cameras on randomly determined shifts, while on others they were not. The initial findings of the study pointed to an 88 percent reduction in civilian complaints against the Rialto police and a 60 percent reduction in the use of force, and these numbers were immediately trumpeted nationwide by activists and policymakers alike, creating the body camera myth that we have today.[17] But as it turns out, William "Tony" Farrar, the study's main author, was the department's police chief at the time, and officers at the scandal-ridden department knew they would be fired if they didn't shape up. For scholars like Ben Brucato who have looked more critically at the idea that body cameras offer a magical solution to police violence, this is enough to question the integrity of the research entirely. The Rialto study, simply put, is junk science.

According to Brucato, the argument that body cameras can provide a solution to police brutality depends on the idea that the images they capture reflect a neutral viewpoint, but the reality is that footage is most often used against defendants and always subject to the interpretation of experts.[18] In fact, the recorded image is never neutral in a racist society, as the brutal beating of Rodney King made perfectly clear. During the trial of the officers involved, footage of the attack was used to make King himself, bloody and prone, look like the aggressor, while the officers bludgeoning him did so in self-defense. As Patricia Williams described it:

> It's a kind of game we Americans play ... Candid Camera and a Rorschach test all mixed up into one. You just take a big chunk of material reality, freeze it frame by frame, mix all the frames up, and then play them backward, forward, upside down at randomly varying speeds, for a nice kaleidoscopic effect. When you start to feel a little dizzy, you bring in a team of players, called experts, who interpret the designs as creatively as they can, and then the jury has to pick the meaning that they like the best.

Through this kaleidoscope of white supremacy, defense attorneys "turned Rodney King's body into a gun ... King's body helplessly flopping and twitching in response to a rain of blows, became in the freeze-framed version a 'cocked' leg, an arm in 'trigger position,' a bullet of a body always aimed, poised, and about to fire itself into deadly action."[19]

This lack of neutrality has become increasingly clear. In fact, one Temple University statistical analysis showed *higher* rates of civilian deaths at the hands of police where body cameras were deployed, especially among victims of color. "Expecting that a wearable video camera would provide evidence to justify the use of force," the study concludes, "the officer becomes less reluctant to deploy deadly weapons."[20] In other words, police use violence more because they believe body cameras will absolve them, and absolve them they have: police control the on/off switch and determine what footage sees the light of day, while district attorneys and grand juries often refuse to charge or indict.

While body cameras are widely touted as protecting the public—including by Obama himself—that is not how they were conceived or pitched to police departments. Axon, formerly Taser International, originally advertised its body cameras to police by telling them, "Your perspective matters," even citing the relevant Supreme Court decision (*Graham v. Connor*) according to which reasonable use of force "must be judged from the perspective of a reasonable officer on the scene." A commercial for Taser's online evidence hosting service is even clearer: "When controversy hits, the public usually hears one side of the story—make sure it's yours."[21]

Body cameras were designed to protect the police, not the people. As abolitionist organizer Mariame Kaba has put it, "The camera is pointed at you!"

Demilitarization. Outraged at the overt military occupation of Ferguson in 2014, many well-meaning critics have proposed rolling back the dramatic militarization police have undergone in recent decades. As columnist Jamelle Bouie put it at the time, "They're treating demonstrators—and Ferguson residents writ large—as a population to occupy, not citizens to protect."[22] The question has never been *whether* police would use military-grade force, but *who* they were prepared to use it against. In 1960s Birmingham, Public Safety Commissioner Bull Connor deployed military vehicles against Black protesters, and in 1985, Philadelphia police dropped a bomb on Black radicals that burned an entire city block. Indeed, communities of color have long been coded as insurgents and given the same treatment as occupied territories abroad. And Ferguson police, like many others nationwide, were trained in settler colonial Israel.[23]

While we should of course demand an immediate halt to the 1033 program that provides civilian police departments with surplus military equipment, and strip them of the hardware they already have, we shouldn't fall for what criminologist Brendan McQuade calls the "demilitarization ruse."[24] In the end, killing with a nine-millimeter handgun or a chokehold isn't much different from killing with a fully equipped SWAT team, and very few of the cases that have sparked the most public outrage have even involved military force. Derek Chauvin only needed arrogance and a knee.

Diversification. Reform commissions from Kerner to the present have argued that recruitment of officers of color would improve community relations. The problem is that it doesn't work, and the intervening decades have shown that *who* is doing the policing doesn't make much of a difference at all. And, as Alex Vitale reminds us, some studies have even indicated that "black officers are *more* likely to use force or make arrests, especially of black civilians."[25] The problem isn't the individual but the structural function they are tasked with carrying out. Targeted harassment policies like stop-and-frisk, for example, come from above, as does the targeting of certain neighborhoods and the demand for results or else. Nonwhite officers are subject to many of the same internalized biases as white officers when determining who constitutes a threat. They are likely to be under even more pressure than their white counterparts to prove themselves by force.[26] And if the *Ferguson Report* recommended diversification in response to the killing of Mike Brown, the same could not be said for Baltimore after Freddie Gray.[27]

Training. In the aftermath of the George Floyd uprising, many have insisted that training is the key to correcting police abuse, but this too misses the mark. Derek Chauvin was a field trainer, and he was training recruits when he killed Floyd.[28] Garrett Rolfe, who shot Rayshard Brooks at an Atlanta Wendy's a few months later, had undergone 2,000 hours of training (equivalent to almost a year's worth of full-time work) in de-escalation, cultural awareness, and use of force. That didn't stop him from shooting Brooks as he fled. Rolfe had previously shot into a vehicle in 2015, even voicing concerns on body camera footage that he might be charged, but the very next year he was reprimanded for again pointing a gun at a car.[29]

The reality is that training doesn't improve police behavior and is more often part of the problem, since it teaches cops to prioritize their own safety over the lives of others. General studies of bias training across different spheres of life, including but not limited to policing, have shown that while training can reduce *implicit* bias, this reduction doesn't last very long and, more importantly, it doesn't translate into a reduction in *explicit* bias or behavior.[30] If bias is difficult to train away under normal circumstances, sensitivity training can't compete with police academies that teach cops to view the public as a threat, or with on-the-job pressures that view violence as an inevitable part of police work. When warrior cops hit the streets, whatever de-escalation training they have been required to participate in quickly evaporates in the mist of fighting the bad guys.

Dave Bicking, a Minneapolis-based organizer with Communities United against Police Brutality, agrees, labeling anti-bias training an "unscientific fraud" that lets "police officers off the hook": "It's something that looks nice, something that makes it look like a police department is doing what it needs to do—and at the same time, it's not actually going to threaten any entrenched interests or cause any significant change in policing."[31]

Chokeholds. Minneapolis has also seen calls to ban chokeholds and other "neck restraints" like the one that killed George Floyd. To be clear: chokeholds should absolutely be banned—Minneapolis was rare in allowing these, and department data has shown that they were used 237 times since 2015, with 44 percent resulting in unconsciousness. They were also used disproportionately on Black people.[32] But as this racial disparity only underlines, the problem isn't the chokeholds—it's racism, which dehumanizes and determines who can be killed with impunity. Chokeholds had been banned in New York for more than two decades when police strangled Eric Garner to death, but it was pressure from the top and broken windows policing that led police to target Garner. The officers involved were following orders and upholding departmental policy, even as they violated aspects of the written rules. The NYPD responded with more training for an already highly trained force, without addressing the utter lack of concern shown for Garner's well-being. Like broken windows, chokeholds—"vascular restraint" or "pain compliance" in copspeak—were themselves framed as reform measures: more chokeholds meant less beatings, according to the peculiarities of pig logic.[33]

Calls to ban chokeholds today are, therefore, yet another example of seizing on the narrowest legal reform to avoid broader accountability and placate an angry public. Similarly, when George Zimmerman killed Trayvon Martin, many rightly scrutinized so-called stand-your-ground laws, state-by-state provisions according to which the victim of an attack is not required to retreat before using deadly force in self-defense. However, Zimmerman's defense didn't even rely on stand-your-ground, opting for a more basic legal claim to self-defense. The more fundamental question wasn't stand-your-ground, but why Trayvon Martin didn't also have the right to defend himself from Zimmerman, who stalked, pursued, and attacked him. If the answer wasn't already clear enough, it was perfectly illustrated when Zimmerman's lawyers arrived at closing arguments with a life-size cutout of Martin to dramatize just how scary the unarmed Black teenager was. Changing the rules isn't enough to stop racist cops or vigilantes, and the problem isn't chokeholds: it's the racist cops who use them.

Community policing. A staple of twentieth-century reform proposals, so-called community policing offers a panacea for all policing's ills. Community policing is never a true reflection of the community, however. At best, it represents a comforting myth, and at worst a dystopian model of counterinsurgency. For Alex Vitale, the structural function of the police puts them on an unavoidable collision course with the community: "When their job is to criminalize all disorderly behavior and fund local government through massive ticket-writing campaigns," we can't expect community relations to be positive. This is why the "community" in question is always of a very specific kind: local business owners and gentrifiers promising "development," rather than the poorest and most vulnerable to police harassment and violence. For Vitale, "research shows that community policing does not empower communities in meaningful ways" but only "expands police power."[34]

Community policing accomplishes this through a direct attack on the community as a source of power and a barrier to police authority. Justin Hansford, a professor of law who was a legal observer during the Ferguson uprising, has seen this play out in practice. First, he argues, "authentic communal feeling" is "strategically dismembered" by policing itself. "After eviscerating communal bonds, the police insert themselves into the vacuum of uncertainty around the idea of community to generate a community in their own image (and their own likeness), granting legitimacy only to community groups who conform to state conceptions of law, order, and propriety." Rather than listen to those most impacted by policing—young people of color, the homeless, sex workers, drug users—police tend to "solicit opinions from business owners and church leaders and disproportionately seek out whites," letting this "narrow slice of the population" stand in for the community as a whole while deepening rifts within that community. Hansford even recalls attending a local meeting of Obama's Twenty-First Century Policing task force, during which the police chief in Sanford, Florida—where Trayvon Martin was killed—credited community policing efforts like a "Sweet Tea Day" for calming angry protests that followed the killing.[35]

The ultimate goal of community policing is to *destroy* any sense of true community, leaving only a community of snitches and bootlickers in its wake.

Procedural justice. Vague-sounding proposals for greater police accountability, similarly, offer little hope. Civilian review boards are almost universally toothless, making good-faith recommendations at best, while the binding decisions are left to the police brass. Federal oversight will certainly be stronger under Biden than it was under Trump, but we shouldn't forget that Obama's DOJ was unwilling to charge Darren Wilson or the officers who killed Freddie Gray. Even independent investigators run into constant stumbling blocks because the system simply wasn't built to hold cops accountable. Grand juries are cynically used to defuse an angry public by providing a cooling-off period after police abuse. District attorneys are reluctant to charge cops who they often see as colleagues and who they depend on every day to do their own jobs. When killer cops are charged, it is often halfheartedly; majority-white juries are hesitant to convict; and they are usually given lesser charges like involuntary manslaughter as a compromise. Accountability remains a pipe dream so long as it fails to account for these barriers and for police power more broadly.

This goes double for today's magical talisman of choice: so-called procedural justice. The basic idea is that if the police are *perceived* to be acting fairly, support for policing will increase and people will be more likely to obey the law. But this is simply old wine—a reiteration of the Kerner and Katzenbach Commissions—repackaged in new bottles to be sold to a gullible public. Not only is there no demonstrated statistical connection between fairness and support for policing, but to even speak of fairness grossly misunderstands what police are designed to do and what they do in practice every day. The police are sent out into poor communities and communities of color to uphold and exacerbate social inequalities. Their job is to oversee and manage systematic unfairness, and this fact is not lost on those they are tasked with controlling. No amount of rhetorical magic can disappear this function into a hat.

Accountability, community policing, procedural justice—all impossible chimeras at best and expansions of police power at worst. And whether it's the officer, the district attorney, the jury, or the media, white supremacy is the common denominator that determines who can be killed or abused with impunity. For Mariame Kaba,

> the philosophy undergirding these reforms is that more rules will mean less violence. But police officers break rules all the time. Look what has happened over the past few weeks—police officers slashing tires, shoving old men on camera, and arresting and injuring journalists and protesters. These officers are not worried about repercussions any more than Daniel Pantaleo, the former New York City police officer whose chokehold led to Eric Garner's death; he waved to a camera filming the incident. He knew that the police union would back him up and he was right. He stayed on the job for five more years.[36]

Police reform, in the words of David Correia and Tyler Wall, "has only intensified the policing and caging of the poor and people of color"; it "never ends police violence, because police reform has always and only sought to improve the image of police and to shore up police legitimacy more generally."[37] As Obama's blue-ribbon commission transparently admits, the target of reform isn't the police but the *public*, and the point is to repair the public perception of the police rather than actual police policies, functions, and behaviors.

All of which leads us to another sleight of hand of policing that is indeed quite magical. Just as every outbreak of violence or criminality indicates not a failure of policing but the need for *more* of it, so too with reform: no matter how lawless, corrupt, or violent the police, no matter how ineffective the commissions and the reforms, the reformers insist that *this time, it will work.* Every reform inaugurates "a new era for police"—a temporal erasure that is more than transparent in the case of Obama's "Twenty-First Century Policing." Reform attempts to wash away the sins of the past by rewarding the most ineffective and violent departments with grants, advanced weaponry, and new technological fixes.

But as we have seen from chokeholds to broken windows, today's reforms have a tendency to become tomorrow's deadly problems. For Correia and Wall, it is only our "collective amnesia" that prevents us from recognizing the reality: that "without reform there is no police."[38]

———

What we learned from a century of failed police reforms was made crystal clear in the more than nine minutes that Derek Chauvin pressed his knee into George Floyd's neck. In the exasperated words of a local journalist covering the city's busy police brutality beat:

> Minneapolis did everything Barack Obama asked it to.
>
> Its mayor and city council appointed a reform-minded police chief who emphasized a guardian mentality instead of a warrior one. They held listening sessions with the community and updated policies to create more transparency and accountability. They promoted officer wellness by offering yoga and meditation classes.
>
> Yet none of this stopped officer Derek Chauvin from pinning his knee on the neck of George Floyd until he lost consciousness and died.[39]

After Ferguson, Minneapolis was one of six cities trained by the DOJ-funded Center for Policing Equity to build trust and correct bias. Derek Chauvin had eighteen prior complaints against his record and had been involved in several shootings—one fatal. In one incident, he shot an unarmed man in his own bathroom, but rather than being removed or even reprimanded, Chauvin was rewarded with a medal of valor for the shooting.[40]

As a result of Floyd's death and many others, the mirage of police reform is collapsing, the spell finally wearing off. However, this hasn't stopped politicians from cynically invoking Floyd's name to justify yet more police reform. The 2020 George Floyd

Justice in Policing Act, a Democratic-sponsored House bill that was resurrected and passed in March 2021, proposes mostly minor changes and reiterates a blind faith in discredited proposals like body cameras. Even welcome changes to no-knock warrants would only apply to federal officers, while merely pressuring other agencies to comply. The most important change would be without a doubt the rollback of the so-called qualified immunity that protects most police from civil suits as a result of misconduct. Strangely however, the bill excludes federal officers like immigration, customs, and border patrol agents, and it fails to close the Section 1983 loophole, which provides feds double protection from liability.[41] In response, Representative Ayanna Presley introduced a bill that would close the loophole, but it remains to be seen whether Senate Democrats will leverage their newfound majority to abolish qualified immunity once and for all. More galling still, while movements in the streets continue to demand the defunding of the police, the George Floyd act earmarks an additional $750 million for the cops. As the human rights lawyer Derecka Purnell puts it: "The George Floyd act wouldn't have saved George Floyd's life."[42]

It is only as a result of 2020's mass rebellion in the streets and the increased circulation of abolitionist demands that police reform is once again on the agenda—the perennial containment strategy of an imperiled system. While pressing for total abolition, how do we navigate such reform proposals, knowing full well that they are designed to undermine more radical demands? Many prison and police abolitionists have sought to do so by drawing a working distinction between two categories: on one hand, those reforms that merely reinforce the carceral status quo, and on the other those potentially transformative changes that make communities freer and safer while creating space for movements to demand more radical change. Abolitionist geographer Ruth Wilson Gilmore, for example, speaks in terms of André Gorz's distinction between ineffectual "reformist reforms" that function fully within the logic of the system—"tweaking

Armageddon," as Gilmore's has described it—and the kinds of "non-reformist reforms" that actually help *weaken* the systems we oppose.[43]

Building on this distinction, Mariame Kaba provides some simple guidelines for assessing police reform proposals. For Kaba, we should uniformly reject those proposals that allocate more money to the police, advocate more police as a solution, or offer a technological fix—which is both distracting and "more likely to be turned against the public"—and those that seek to individualize what is in reality a collective, structural problem.[44] Non-reformist reforms are the opposite: they do not strengthen policing, but operate outside and beyond the logic of the world of police, in which every problem can be solved with more police. At best, they can even help to strike symbolically and materially at the heart of police power.

Abolitionists, Kaba argues, should support reforms that provide reparations to survivors of police violence, that require officers to carry individual liability insurance to cover the costs of their misconduct, and that increase transparency, along with the creation of civilian oversight boards with real authority to discipline police. Most importantly, we should back those reforms that siphon funds away from the police and toward the community, that disarm them, and that facilitate the ultimate dismantling of the police. To these, the abolitionist organization Critical Resistance adds some other specific proposals: to end the paid administrative leave for police undergoing misconduct investigations; to withhold pensions from police fired for use of force; and to block overtime pay for military and warrior-style training sessions.[45] And the broad framework known as #8toAbolition has sought to introduce the idea of abolitionist reforms into the mainstream.

While the central thrust of reform proposals put forth since Ferguson seek to salvage the legitimacy of the police, there are some other specific proposals on the table—particularly those that emerged from the more advanced position of the 2020

George Floyd rebellions—that we can, and should, support without losing sight of the abolitionist horizon. We should support, for example, disarming the police and pushing back on their capacity to use force with impunity—priorities that can be advanced through both changes to departmental policy and heightened accountability and civilian oversight. While demilitarizing the police won't fundamentally change the nature of policing, abolitionists should advocate for an immediate suspension of the 1033 program that has seen $7.4 billion in military equipment handed over to police departments, as well as efforts to roll back the use of paramilitary SWAT raids.

We should absolutely support outright bans on chokeholds and other measures like those that killed Eric Garner and George Floyd, while recognizing that changing the law doesn't necessarily change street-level practices. We should support an immediate ban on no-knock raids like the ones that killed Breonna Taylor in 2020, seven-year-old Aiyana Stanley-Jones in 2010, and dozens of others in between. But we should also recognize that fifty long years have passed since the radical spoken-word poet and musician Gil Scott-Heron denounced the practice. For Scott-Heron, advocates of no-knock raids cynically claimed that the policy was designed to protect its victims—"legislated for the people you've always hated," in Scott-Heron's terms—whereas the real question was and remains: "Who's gonna protect me from you?"

By far the most widely debated reform thrown forth by the George Floyd rebellions is actually not a reform at all: defunding the police. An empty signifier that can mean different things to different people, the vagueness surrounding defunding has been both key to its spread and an indication of its potential shortcomings. Do we mean *fully* defunding the police or merely shifting a small part of the police budget toward social programs? Is defunding simply a cosmetic change that gives cities an alibi for more of the same, or does it open a door to radically rethink the overbearing role of the police in our society? As usual, the answer is *both*. Before the fires in Minneapolis had even cooled, cities under pressure from grassroots movements were scrambling to cut their policing budgets. While some cuts were substantial—in Austin, New York, Los Angeles, the Bay Area, and elsewhere—others have been purely symbolic. In Philadelphia, for example, what was advertised as a cut to police funding instead simply rescinded a proposed increase while shifting crossing guards to a different budget line.[46]

While we should be on guard against such deceptive budget shuffles, and while cutting police funding is not the same as abolishing the police, the hidden power of defunding as a strategy lies in how it can symbolically disrupt the world of police and provide a practical bridge toward a world with no police at all. By gradually taking money away from the police, we can show that more police doesn't mean more safety. When we dedicate those resources to social programs and non-carceral alternatives, people will begin to realize that their lives haven't gotten worse but better, not more dangerous but safer, and that there are far better ways to spend the massive resources squandered by already overburdened and underfunded cities. Not only is defunding a net social good in this sense, but as Kaba emphasizes, "fewer police officers equals fewer opportunities for them to brutalize and kill people."

The fraught potential of defunding as both an alibi for the system and a possible strategy for its undoing is emblematic of the inescapable challenges that face any reforms pending abolition. Even minor reforms are only on the table today because of pressure from organized grassroots struggles, and that pressure must remain relentless if we want to deepen those gains. All reforms are two things at once: a containment strategy whereby those in power seek desperately to maintain the status quo, and a concession to—and index of—the power of our movements in the streets. We must remain cognizant of both levels as we navigate the treacherous straits of reform. We should work to change laws while remembering that the police break the law every day.

And we should leverage our small victories to roll back police power while sowing the seeds of abolition.

There is no alternative to this slow accumulation, leveraging moments of open rebellion to force small but important concessions, before then using these as stepping-stones to strengthen movements and to make ever more ambitious demands. But abolition is about far more than this, and if we must keep one eye on the punitive structure of the state, our central focus must be elsewhere. Abolition is about organizing community alternatives to policing and mass incarceration, about using the breathing room afforded by these small victories not to propose a slightly better version of the same, but to shoot for something radically different. It's about pushing back the world of police *and* building something new in its place.

—

Police abolition is a fantasy. We are told as much every day. But like all mantras, this refrain belies a doubt. Indeed, abolition must be dismissed as fantastic to protect a greater fantasy: the notion that police reform, which has never worked, and that for structural reasons *cannot* work, simply needs one more shot. Sisyphus was cursed by the gods to forever roll his boulder—liberal police reformers today have no such excuse.

Confronted with patients stuck in a constant loop of repeating their own traumatic failures, Sigmund Freud spoke of what he called "repetition compulsion." While the perennial failure of police reform might seem to reflect such an inexplicable compulsion, however, psychic phenomena never map cleanly onto class society, and those doing the repeating today are not the same people who will suffer the consequences—and the trauma—of yet another cycle of futile reforms. For those in power, a far more cynical and material dynamic is at play, in which political leaders and police executives build entire careers as "reformers" while rank-and-file cops jealously defend their own impunity. Seen in this light, the best metaphor might instead be that of an abusive relationship—the repeated promise that this time, things will be different. Given what we know about domestic violence at the hands of police and the chronic abuses of the system writ large, perhaps it's no metaphor at all.

The police cannot be reformed—more than a century of experience proves this beyond a reasonable doubt. Even if we tried, and we do continue to try, police resist tooth and nail even the smallest reforms and the most minimal accountability. They do so, in part, because ultimately they want zero accountability. They also do so simply because they can. As we have seen, the history of American police is the history of their expanding power, and it is a voracious power that accepts no limits: a fascist power. While some non-reformist reforms can help to chip away at policing and undercut the ideological foundations of the world of police we inhabit, the question of power remains. Any path to abolition passes through a confrontation with the foundations of police power and must systematically *break* that power.

4

Breaking Police Power

It's September 30, 2012, and Philadelphia's annual Puerto Rican Day parade is just winding down. A crowd of revelers can be seen on video heckling a group of police officers when one, a white-shirted lieutenant, wheels around and takes several steps forward before throwing a hard right hook into Aida Guzman's jaw. At six foot three and 215 pounds, the officer, Jonathan Josey, who is Black, is easily twice Guzman's size, and when police drag her past the camera, she is visibly bleeding from her mouth.

This was the scene captured in viral footage that immediately garnered a million YouTube views. Within days, Commissioner Charles Ramsey was playing the oxymoronic role of good cop, suspending Josey with the intention to fire, and he was quickly charged with misdemeanor assault. Officers accused Guzman of throwing water on them, but even this bogus charge was eventually dropped, with the city paying her a $75,000 settlement for the attack. What did the Fraternal Order of Police do? They threw Josey a party, or more specifically, a thirty-dollar-a-head fundraiser advertised with fliers reading: "Come on out and support ONE OF OUR OWN." The event drew protests from the left and the Puerto Rican community, and I was among those who showed up to express disgust at the FOP's brazen display of solidarity with the cop who delivered the cowardly sucker punch. This was only the beginning, however.

Early the next year, Josey was acquitted in a bench trial by a judge who pointedly dismissed viral footage of the assault as a "social media contest." Only later did it come out that the judge in question is married to a police officer, and that she had been present in the courtroom during the trial in support of Josey. Acquittal wasn't enough for the FOP, however. They wanted to do more than simply show their support and fundraise for an abusive cop: they wanted him back on the force, and they filed an arbitration grievance to that effect. In the words of John McGrody, vice president of the local FOP, "sometimes police work isn't pretty, but it's actually correct." In August 2013, Josey was reinstated with back pay to the tune of $100,000. If this were not proof positive of the brutal arrogance of the police, their unions, and the judicial apparatus that supports them, the story had yet one more twist. When Josey was later passed over for promotion by a committee clearly worried that the Guzman incident would undermine police–community relations, the FOP filed a lawsuit in federal court demanding Josey be fully promoted with, you guessed it, back pay. After all this, Lieutenant Jonathan Josey had the audacity to complain on Facebook about how, as a Black cop, he feels "ostracized" by both his community and colleagues, declaring in a faux plea for sympathy, "I'm a jurisdiction away from being George Floyd."

It says a lot that anyone familiar with the FOP won't find this story surprising in the least, and there are dozens more I could mention.[1] Like the fact that when San Francisco 49ers quarterback Colin Kaepernick kneeled during the national anthem at a 2016 preseason game to draw attention to police brutality, the San Francisco Police Officers Association threatened to withhold security from 49ers games if Kaep wasn't punished. "A work stoppage to punish a player for expressing his opinion may seem extreme," James Surowiecki wrote at the time in *The New Yorker*, "but in the world of police unions it's business as usual."[2] Or the fact that after the killing of Mike Brown, the local FOP surreptitiously sponsored a crowdfunding campaign for his murderer, Darren Wilson.[3] John McNesby, the bloviating, red-faced president of the Philadelphia FOP, once called Black Lives Matter protesters "a pack of rabid animals," while his Baltimore counterpart—impervious to irony—called them a "lynch mob." Not to be outdone, Minneapolis police union head Bob Kroll, who denounced George Floyd as a "violent criminal," has also called BLM a "terrorist movement." More recently, the head of the Portland Police Association even proposed a ballot initiative to limit freedom of assembly in the city.[4]

Police unions routinely harass and threaten elected officials who cross them. The head of the St. Louis police union referred to special prosecutor Kim Gardner, who is Black and has pressed for police reform, as a "menace to society" who needed to be removed "by force or by choice." Most notoriously, the New York City Police Department "declared war" on Mayor Bill de Blasio for expressing even the meekest concern about the police killing of Eric Garner. After two cops were shot dead in Brooklyn in 2014, Patrick Lynch, the head of the Police Benevolent Association (PBA) blamed BLM and the mayor directly, and officers turned their backs on the mayor at the hospital and the funeral— a performance they would repeat in 2017. And amid the George Floyd protests of 2020, the Sergeants Benevolent Association (SBA), doxed the mayor's daughter by releasing private information on her arrest, in an effort to twist the mayor's arm to approve mounted police units.

—

Police power doesn't just exist on the street or in the local precinct, it doesn't rest in the chief or commissioner, and it doesn't originate in the mayor or other civilian authorities who are its formal overseers. The power of the police is much bigger, much more ambitious, and far more dangerous than many realize—although this is getting harder to deny by the day. The central weapon for guarding and expanding the power of the police is not the department itself, but a parallel structure: the benevolent association, the fraternal order, all those organizations that masquerade misleadingly under the heading of "police unions." Behind closed doors, it is these organizations that negotiate police contracts—placing impunity from accountability front and center—and lobby for special legal protections. In public, police associations smear the victims of police abuse, engage in racist attacks on social justice movements, and seek to leverage public fear toward openly authoritarian ends. They are a bully pulpit that has increasingly made leaders like New York's Lynch and Minneapolis's Kroll fixtures on the right-wing media circuit and at conservative political rallies for former president Trump.

To abolish the police, we must first break police power, and breaking police power begins with confronting and destroying these so-called police "unions." To be clear, police associations aren't like other unions; in reality, they aren't unions at all. Police themselves are little more than glorified slave catchers and strikebreakers with a long history of providing their muscle as hired guns for big business and white supremacy—which are often the same thing. American police emerged to contain slave resistance prior to the mass exodus from plantations during the Civil War that W.E.B. Du Bois called a "general strike"—and after the war had ended, hand in hand with the Klan, the poor-whites-turned-police helped crush the emancipatory project of Reconstruction.

As labor battles heated up in the early twentieth century, nascent police forces like the Pennsylvania State Police—modeled on the colonial troops that occupied the Philippines—earned the nickname "Pennsylvania Cossacks" for brutally crushing coal strikes in the western part of the state.[5] In the 1921 Battle of Blair Mountain, the largest labor rebellion since the Civil War, thousands of armed miners faced off against Pinkerton-style private detectives, local deputies, and county and state police. An estimated 1 million rounds were fired, and when the smoke cleared, more than a hundred lay dead. As they had a generation prior, and as they continue to do today, police collaborated openly with right-wing vigilantes like the American Legion, which viciously attacked the IWW throughout the 1920s, and later with the Black Legion, an anti-leftist heir to the Klan.[6]

Given this history, it's strange that police would have—or even *want*—unions at all, but the twentieth century has seen police shift opportunistically, in the words of anarchist author and preeminent historian of the police Kristian Williams, "from strikebreakers to strikers (and back again)," their power increasing at every turn. In fact, at the same time that police were crushing workers' movements, their own early labor aspirations were being defeated. Grasping cynically at the coattails of a labor movement they were actively undermining, what were at the time poorly paid police formed their first unions in the early part of the century under the aegis of the American Federation of Labor (AFL). But a disastrous police strike in Boston in 1919 saw these early unions discredited and crushed after rioting and looting left eight dead. Police lost this early battle, but they won the longer war, trading away union status for special privileges, thereby setting the template for what was to come. Police unions were outlawed nationwide, but the demands of the striking cops were met regardless—in some cities, police salaries were doubled.[7] It's a strange strike indeed that wins in the process of losing.

Since Boston, most police organizations have not been unions strictly speaking. Legally, they could only be associations like the PBA (an independent association of beat cops) or fraternal orders like the FOP (a national organization open to any officer—including the top brass). As we saw in the previous chapter, the 1920s and '30s saw a push toward police professionalization, and police associations came to reflect a rank-and-file resentment toward management—police chiefs and commissioners, often tasked with balancing the demands of officers with those of city leadership. This tension has never been a true contradiction, however. As a result of their nonunion status, not to mention their function as a means of social control, police orders and associations developed in isolation from the broader labor movement, and instead collaborated with commanders and city leaders eager to grant them special privileges. Though once drawn from the working class and poorly paid, police were soon treated differently and paid far better than other workers.

Moreover, police organizations gained their privileged position as separate from and above workers precisely by leveraging two related threats: from the labor movement itself, and from the surging Black freedom struggle. When the American Federation of State, County, and Municipal Employees (AFSCME) and Jimmy Hoffa's Teamsters started to recruit cops to their organizations in the 1950s, PBA and FOP leadership were as eager to protect their own positions as police departments were desperate to prevent broader labor solidarity. Both management and rank-and-file cops won when police associations traded the right to strike for binding arbitration—stability for city leaders, negotiating power for police associations. The labor insurgency of the beat cops had been a flash in the pan: now they were a part of the system. From this point on, all labor-like activity by police would in reality be a ploy to leverage special privileges, and an incredibly successful ploy at that.

The real turning point in police power, however, would come a decade later, in reaction to the burgeoning radical and anti-racist movements of the 1960s. Police brutality had provided the spark for rebellions in Harlem, Watts, Newark, and elsewhere, provoking public outrage and scrutiny. Police, in turn, felt that their hands were unduly tied by Warren-era Supreme Court decisions like *Mapp* and *Miranda*, upholding Fourth and Fifth Amendment protections against illegal searches and coerced confessions. When John Lindsay, the incoming mayor of New York, restructured the city's police review board in 1966 to ensure a civilian majority, the PBA debuted what would become central tactics in the arsenal of police unions. In a two-pronged campaign, the PBA stoked fear with an openly racist law-and-order media blitz, and even cynically denounced dissenting Black officers for "put[ting] their color before their duties as policemen."[8] This public campaign provided the PBA with the necessary ammunition to force a ballot initiative to overturn the mayor's civilian review board. The victory sent shock waves nationwide, discouraging civilian oversight of the police elsewhere.

Police continued to leverage the twin fulcrums of their expanding power: capitalist fear of organized labor and white fear of Black people. The two coincided the following year when Detroit police engaged in what would become a standard police tactic: the sick-out or "blue flu." While the head of the Detroit Police Officers Association denied that the action constituted a strike—these were prohibited—his denial was also couched in the threat that police were "beginning to think and act like a trade union." The message was clear: police *weren't* unionized workers, but they wouldn't rule out using union tactics or seeking support from allies in the AFL-CIO if their demands were not met. The deadlock was broken in the most traditional of ways, however: to suppress the 1967 Detroit rebellion. As Williams notes, "With the Black community in open revolt, the cops, the city government, and local elites very quickly rediscovered their previous affinity." And once again, "the cops got their raises."[9]

The tragic origin story of policing—white solidarity against Black insurgency—was thus repeated. Just as countless poor whites had sided with their class enemies during and after the Civil War, so too did police unions show that their class solidarity was exactly skin deep. Rather than joining labor, they opted for a fraternity stretching "from the highest commander to the rookie on the beat," which helped commanders maintain loyalty from the rank and file, and ensured brutal and corrupt cops the silence of their brothers-in-arms. Those in power showed they were willing to buy police off with the wages of whiteness—which by now included very real and rapidly increasing salaries—even if nonwhite officers also benefited. From this point on, policing would be defined by a corporatist partnership between commanders and the rank and file, with police unions playing the prized role of mediators. This cross-class solidarity of the police brotherhood set the stage for an ambitious power grab that would mark a return to their role in the machine politics of a century prior.

Already in the late 1960s, political elites from New York to Los Angeles began to speculate that the police had become more powerful than civilian authorities, and during the 1970s police became local kingmakers in many cities—with unions as their muscle. In Philadelphia, Frank Rizzo made the most of this violent symbiosis. The openly white supremacist police commissioner, best known for stripping members of the local Black Panther Party naked in a humiliating press display, rode police power to the mayor's office in 1972. And from City Hall, Rizzo only expanded the power of the police even further: in the words of a former city manager, "the police were bulletproof, especially under Rizzo." Soon they were fielding their own candidates and sponsoring local, state, and federal legislation. The direction of this activism was uniformly conservative, as exemplified by the Los Angeles Fire and Police Protective League (the Fi-Po), which "lobbied for counter-subversive laws, promoted right-wing rallies, sponsored conservative speakers," and in a display of anti-labor solidarity even "sold businesses a blacklist naming union organizers and radicals."[10]

The conservative, corporatist, white supremacist agenda of police unions has changed little in the past half century. History even repeated itself in New York in 1992, when police fought back against yet another effort at civilian oversight, this time under David Dinkins, the city's first Black mayor. Thousands of off-duty cops rioted while on-duty cops passively looked on: "Several officers, including one captain and two sergeants, failed to hold police lines, and a uniformed officer—Michael P. Abitabile—waved protesters through the police barricades while shouting racial slurs." In retrospect, the 1992 police riot looked a lot like a "municipal-level coup": catapulting Rudy Giuliani to the mayorship on a tough-on-crime platform, and with him

Commissioner Bill Bratton and broken windows policing, continuing the cycle of expanding police power.[11]

American police were created to safeguard class domination and white supremacy, and they have built their own power by playing up popular fear of unions and people of color—and repressing the movements of both. But these twin objectives produced a tension—if not a contradiction—between racial solidarity and police solidarity, one that cuts across an increasingly multiracial police force, and even into the associations representing them. As Williams documents:

> Historically, most police associations barred Black members, and police in Detroit and St. Louis threatened strikes to keep Black people off the force. The police departments accommodated the White officers in various ways, sometimes by refusing to hire Black people, in other cases by keeping Black officers out of uniform, restricting them to Black neighborhoods, or barring them from arresting White people. As recently as 1995, a group of Black LAPD officers sued the Police Protective League for its role in preserving discrimination on the force, describing the union as a "bastion of white supremacy."[12]

To this day, dozens of cities, like St. Louis, maintain a separate-but-equal division between Black and white police associations.[13]

The racist and classist history of police unions has produced what Williams calls the "collusive bargaining" of today, in which the police, their commanders, and city officials perform antagonism toward one another, even though they ultimately, with some minor exceptions, want the same things. In this sense, the relationship between beat cops and the top brass is not a class relationship, but a symbiotic one: racial capitalism needs the police, and the privileges and power that the police enjoy depend on racial capitalism. Rather than seeking to change the underlying inequalities that govern society, the police are the vicious glue holding those inequalities together. Such corporatist collaboration is always anti-worker at best and a hallmark of fascism at worst, and the police are no exception. Thus, while many commanders feign antagonism toward police unions, we shouldn't take such displays seriously. So long as police associations embrace with open arms those most reactionary elements that even the commanders don't want, this is little more than a game of good cop versus bad cop.

If you know the game, you know the trick: they're both the bad cop.

—

Police are not workers, their unions are not unions, and despite the name, their associations are far from "benevolent." Indeed, "fraternal orders" seems far more fitting, given all that they share with the racism, the violence, the unearned privilege, and the toxic masculinity of college fraternities (which are also worth abolishing).[14] Developing in isolation from the labor movement and following a different trajectory, police associations came late, and no sooner did they become antagonistic to the institutional order than they were fully incorporated into its functioning.

While drawn from the lower classes a century ago, their wages quickly leapfrogged those of other workers—today, "police officers are among the best-paid civil servants," and "they've been extraordinarily effective in establishing control over working conditions."[15] While most unions have gotten weaker, police unions have only grown stronger, and the power and privileges police enjoy today are unheard of in any sector of the labor movement—perks afforded not through working-class struggle but as hefty bribes paid to the essential workers of racial capitalism for their betrayal of broader solidarities. If the police emerged as poor, white slave catchers—ensuring a docile labor force and assuaging white fear— these two elements tell us much about the power police associations wield today and the nature of their demands.

Today, nearly 80 percent of uniformed police—some 600,000— are represented by an association. The majority, around 340,000, belong to the more than 2,000 lodges of the arch-reactionary FOP, which is not affiliated with a broader labor federation, while others belong to a range of local and regional associations. Of the remaining 20 percent that are technically union members, the largest organization is the International Union of Police Associations (IUPA), chartered by the AFL-CIO in 1979, which formally represents 20,000 members but claims closer to 100,000. The International Brotherhood of Police Officers (IBPO) is nearly as large with 15,000 members, and organizes with its sibling organization, the International Brotherhood of Correctional Officers under the umbrella of SEIU's National Association of Government Employees (NAGE). Often confused with a union, the National Association of Police Organizations (NAPO) is a lobbying body. While police associations have become increasingly notorious for media scare tactics, intimidation campaigns, and thinly veiled racism, the backbone of police power comes from the work these associations do behind the scenes.

While police power is occasionally written into local law and guaranteed in city charters, more often it manifests through collective bargaining between police associations and elected municipal leadership. This bargaining certainly includes wages—and indeed, has led to near-constant pay hikes while other public sector workers have suffered austerity budgets. Unlike real unions, however, the true centerpiece of these negotiations is *impunity*. Faithful to their origins, police associations, as David Correia and Tyler Wall note, "have transformed police violence into a contractually protected condition of their employment."[16] While police first flexed their collective power in opposition to civilian oversight, negotiated impunity has accelerated since the 1980s, when cash-strapped cities found themselves unable to pay raises and offered special rights instead.

In most cities, this negotiated impunity works just as it did for Jonathan Josey in Philadelphia. Cops accused of misconduct cannot be compelled to speak until after a mandated "cooling off" period, and when they do speak it is often to their own colleagues, before then appealing to a binding arbitration board composed of their peers. The time frame for accountability is contractually narrow: misconduct complaints must be filed immediately (in some cities, within thirty days), and disciplinary records are quickly scrubbed—sometimes after only six months. Officers under investigation continue to collect their pay under suspension, and if they are fired and reinstated—which occurs in 46 percent of cases, according to one study—it's with back pay.[17] The result is a clear pattern of misconduct, in which repeat offenders are rewarded with a clean record every six months and can continue to abuse the public.

In 2013, San Antonio police officer Jackie Neal was fired and briefly jailed for raping a woman in his police cruiser. According to a *Reuters* investigation, however, Neal had a history of sexual misconduct that included sex with a teenage participant in a police youth program and a history of domestic violence, but had never been meaningfully punished, aside from a brief suspension that he swapped out for vacation days—a perk negotiated into the union contract. When city manager Sheryl Sculley, outraged by Neal's case, sought to eliminate the contract clause that scrubbed previous disciplinary records, the San Antonio Police Officers Association "targeted Sculley with a $1 million advertising campaign." Her reform failed. An investigation by *Reuters* uncovered similar patterns of contractually-enabled abuse elsewhere, including in Columbus, Ohio.[18]

While police power on the local level is mostly about contracts, on the state level it manifests primarily as legislation through which police associations institutionalize their negotiated privileges in the form of Law Enforcement Officers' Bills of Rights (LEOBoRs). After Freddie Gray was killed in a "rough ride" orchestrated by a multiracial squad of officers, Baltimore mayor Stephanie Rawlings-Blake openly complained that the Maryland LEOBoR prevented her from compelling the officers involved to give statements. While Rawlings-Blake was far from innocent, she wasn't lying, either: Maryland law enshrines one of the most aggressive packages of special rights for police in the country. When pressed, police advocates insist that they don't enjoy special rights and that LEOBoRs simply uphold the due process of officers who might otherwise be scapegoated by elected officials trying to pass the buck. Indeed, according to Vince Canales, president of the Maryland FOP, "The police have rights like anyone else." But this begs the question of why the FOP has dedicated seemingly endless resources to the proliferation of such laws if they add nothing not already promised to everyday citizens.[19]

The reality is that LEOBoRs do more than reinforce basic constitutional rights: they promise a special set of rights specific to the police as a special category of citizens. Not only that, but these special rights exist in a zero-sum relationship to everyone else, contributing to the systematic violation of the rights meant to be enjoyed by the public. LEOBoRs emerged simultaneously with police unions, amid calls for civilian oversight and the reining in of police impunity. While police resented Supreme Court decisions like *Mapp* and *Miranda*, they selectively embraced others, notably *Garrity v. New Jersey* in 1967 and *Gardner v. Broderick* in 1968, both of which found that police had been unjustly deprived of their ability to plead the Fifth. Speaking to Eli Hager of the Marshall Project, Samuel Walker, an emeritus professor at the University of Nebraska and expert on police accountability, argues that LEOBoRs grant police a sort of due process on steroids—one that "impedes accountability, and truly is a key element of our lack of responsiveness to these cases." Walker adds, "It's a scandal, really."[20]

Like local contracts, LEOBoRs often include a so-called cooling-off period—in Maryland, an absurd ten days—during which officers accused of misconduct can find a lawyer and access all evidence against them before even having to settle on a story. When they eventually are questioned, police are guaranteed perks like bathroom and snack breaks and are not to be threatened or plied in any way—thereby, in Hager's words, "assuring police officers treatment that they themselves do not consistently offer to suspects they are questioning."[21] Some legislation specifies that police can only be questioned by other police, and the accused can appeal to a binding arbitration board consisting of three of their own colleagues. In Rhode Island, which boasts the strongest LEOBoR in the country, accused officers are even allowed to name one of the arbitrators. Like local contracts, these usually include a statute of limitations, often one hundred days but sometimes as short as a month, after which officers can no longer be disciplined, and a period after which disciplinary proceedings are purged. And of course, they continue to draw paychecks while suspended from work.

All in all, the process is so difficult that many departments are hesitant to even undertake the task of disciplining officers, leading to cases where "an officer can rack up a number of complaints but be given a pass until he does something more serious."[22] Today, fourteen states have LEOBoRs, and eleven more are considering them, while a federal version is regularly proposed to Congress—all thanks to the efforts of FOP lobbyists and a vociferous pig majority. The predictable result of such a thick protective layer is what Walker describes as a "culture of impunity."[23] But if many Americans have generally been willing to grant special rights to police, for all the racial and class reasons we might assume, these laws have come under heightened scrutiny today, with some turning the police justification for special rights around on them. If, as police unions argue, they make life-and-death decisions on a daily basis, then shouldn't this imply a special level of scrutiny, not a special layer of protection?

"If a doctor commits malpractice," writes James Surowiecki in *The New Yorker*, "it's a matter of public record, but, in much of the country, a police officer's use of excessive force is not."[24] As Jeffrey Fagan, a professor at Columbia Law School, asks with more than a bit of incredulity, "They want better treatment than other criminal defendants? They already have 95 percent of civil-rights law on their side, starting with qualified immunity"—that special layer of protection that shields police from civil miscon-duct claims, and has been applied with increasing stringency by the Supreme Court. Unless police brazenly violate the law *and* this violation has been upheld by precedent under almost iden-tical conditions, most claims can be peremptorily dismissed before trial. As the nonprofit law firm Institute for Justice has described it, qualified immunity means that the police and other government officials "can get away with violating your rights as long as they violate them in a way nobody thought of before."[25]

However, no amount of special protection is too much for the police. As the bizarre ressentiment that goes by the name "Blue Lives Matter" makes clear, police suffer a perennial victim complex that they share with their white supremacist brothers-in-arms—armed guardians of the state competing in a perverse Oppression Olympics with those they brutalize on a daily basis. The FOP has recently sought to turn this slogan into federally legislated fact, pushing Congress to amend the federal Hate Crimes Prevention Act to include police as a protected category. Little surprise, then, that the FOP endorsed Trump in 2016, even re-upping its endorsement during his 2020 reelection campaign with a declaration of "full and enthusiastic support" for the then-president. The FOP was joined by many local police frater-nities and the IUPA, whose president, Sam Cabral, complained in his endorsement that many Democrats "still refer to the tragedy in Ferguson as a murder."[26] Yes, Sam—it was a murder.

Where all of the special rights that police have strong-armed from the public through decades of extortion fail, they don't hesitate to turn to more extreme measures. Writing in *The New Republic*, Sam Adler-Bell describes how "police unions deploy ominous social media campaigns to vilify and intimidate reform-minded legislators. They exploit racialized law-and-order rhetoric to polarize the public. And they threaten liberal mayors with widespread civic chaos and destruction if their demands aren't met."27 There is a direct line that connects police unions and the special rights they demand to the continuing epidemic of police violence that killed George Floyd in Minneapolis. Collective bargaining and special legislation are the main reason that officers like Derek Chauvin were still walking the streets with a badge after multiple use-of-force incidents. The connection is more direct still: after Minneapolis Mayor Jacob Frey sought to rein in aggressive police trainings in 2019, police union president Bob Kroll openly flouted the mayor by offering free warrior-style trainings to his members. Shortly after Floyd's death a year later, the IUPA shared an article from *Police* magazine that upholds kneeling on a suspect's neck as a "non-deadly force option."28

When you multiply this single case by the thousands of cities and police associations nationwide, a dark picture emerges. Indeed, a paper authored by three professors at the University of Chicago Law School has shown that the right to collective bargaining correlates to a 40 percent increase in violent police misconduct.29 By demanding the right to kill, maim, and abuse with impunity, these violent fraternities are directly responsible for police brutality and murder.

—

The case against police associations seems cut-and-dried, especially for the left: they are not unions, and they "organize police *as police*, not as workers."30 In the churning wake of the George Floyd rebellions, calls for major union federations to expel police from their ranks grow louder by the day. Within the AFL-CIO in particular, a veritable revolt quickly spread, with the president of the Minnesota branch demanding Kroll's resignation almost immediately following Floyd's killing. This was soon followed by a powerful statement by the Association of Flight Attendants, which under the leadership of socialist Sara Nelson unanimously approved a resolution "demanding law enforcement unions immediately enact policy to actively address racism in law enforcement and especially to hold officers accountable for violence against citizens, or be removed from the Labor movement."[31]

Many more are not waiting around to see if the police reform themselves before demanding the immediate disaffiliation of the IUPA from the AFL-CIO. While graduate student employees in California were ahead of the curve when they made this demand in 2015, five years later the consensus had become more widespread. The Writers Guild of America, East (WGAE) approved a resolution demanding the expulsion of the IUPA, citing the AFL-CIO's stated commitment "to vanquish oppression, privation and cruelty in all their forms," and was soon followed by Workers United of Upstate New York.[32] The young president of the South Dakota AFL-CIO, Kooper Caraway, has called for the same, and similar calls have spread to other affiliated unions, like the call for a "Cop-Free AFSCME" (home to Alaska's Public Safety Employees Association, among others).[33]

Campaigns have spread outside the AFL-CIO as well. Citing the vicious attacks on the Service Employees International Union's 1990 Justice for Janitors strike in Los Angeles, as well as the fact that Rayshard Brooks's killer, Garrett Rolfe, is formally represented by the SEIU-affiliated NAGE, members have launched a campaign under the tagline "SEIU drop the cops" (the broader Change to Win federation of which SEIU is a part also represents the IBPO, and the Teamsters actively organize police and prison guards).[34] In a major victory, a county labor council in Seattle successfully voted to expel the Seattle Police Officers Guild, the largest police association in the Northwest.

So far, labor federations have largely resisted these calls, however, closing ranks around their affiliated "brothers."[35] Unwilling to alienate more conservative members or to lose the most heavily unionized sector of the US workforce, not to mention the resources and leverage that comes with organizing police, prison guards, and border patrol, the AFL-CIO has argued that the best way to change the behavior of police is not to expel them, but to pressure police unions from within by establishing the kind of "code of excellence" demanded of other trades. For his part, AFSCME president Lee Saunders, who is Black and has denounced Floyd's killing, has nevertheless refused to consider disaffiliation. Saunders has even echoed a Blue Lives Matter logic of equivalence by insisting that "just as it was wrong when racists went out of their way to exclude black people from unions, it is wrong to deny this freedom to police officers today."[36] The real reason that labor leaders are resisting calls to disaffiliate police unions, however, is a broader anxiety shared by many on the left that *any* attack on unionized workers will only accelerate the demise of already-beleaguered public sector unions.

Some, like law professor Benjamin Levin, are critical of police unions but seek to distinguish the *police* from their *union*. For Levin, demands for transparency and public accountability are "risky" because they echo arguments made against other public sector unions like teachers, and because "attacking police by arguing for stripping organizing rights legitimates anti-union arguments."[37] This suspicion is not entirely unjustified: right-wing libertarian think tanks like the Cato Institute have jumped on the police reform train, with Cato affiliate Ilya Somin arguing that it is possible to weaken police unions if "liberal civil liberties advocates can work together with conservatives who dislike public sector unions more generally."[38] Longtime union organizer Bill Fletcher Jr. agrees with Levin, insisting that "the central issue is police repression, not police unions," even going so far as to argue that "law enforcement unions are not the problem; the history, culture and practices of the U.S. law enforcement system are the problem." Absent a broader "reckoning" with the role of police in colonialism and capitalism, Fletcher argues, "police would just find ways other ways to wield political power, and elected officials would find other excuses to hide behind."[39]

Even the organized left has struggled to find a unified perspective on police unions. Take the recent dustup within the

Democratic Socialists of America (DSA) over the 2017 election of Austin organizer Danny Fetonte to a national leadership post. Fetonte had spent years organizing cops and prison guards under the aegis of the Combined Law Enforcement Associations of Texas (CLEAT), which has resisted police oversight and accountability, including in the shooting of mentally ill seventeen-year-old David Joseph, who was naked and unarmed. At the time Fetonte was elected, DSA had only recently endorsed prison and police abolition, and many had a hard time reconciling this abolitionist vision with organizing inside police unions. In the end, the organization's national committee failed to remove Fetonte, issuing a halfhearted statement that stressed "the complicated nature of police union affiliations with large unions." Under pressure from chapters nationwide, Fetonte—who argued that police deserve collective bargaining rights—resigned a few weeks later. While disagreements over police unions persist, DSA as a whole has consistently reiterated its commitment to abolition.

—

It is impossible to distinguish between the police and their so-called unions, however, or to blame white supremacy in the abstract without confronting the most virulently white supremacist institutions in policing—and broader society—today. Moreover, the concern that any attack on police associations will boomerang back onto the broader labor movement is exaggerated, and the benefits far outweigh any possible risk. The reality is that it is only by expelling and ultimately abolishing police unions that we can begin to glimpse a broader and more radical horizon for inclusive working-class struggles without and against the police.

The best response to those who argue that the disaffiliation and dismantling of police unions will undermine other public sector unions was offered by former Wisconsin governor Scott Walker himself. In 2011, Walker dealt a crushing blow to public sector unions in the state with the passage of Act 10, which among other things severely limited collective bargaining and made union dues nonmandatory. No longer able to justify their function to beleaguered members, many of the state's unions have since collapsed, hemorrhaging one-third to one-half of their membership. But not the police union, which along with firefighters was exempted from Act 10 by a carve-out from the law's provisions. Far from an isolated incident, however, the reality is that police unions have been little more than a massive carve-out from the beginning, extorting higher wages and special privileges in exchange for loyalty.

Police claim union status when it suits them, but where it benefits them to refuse the label of workers, they are the first to do so. For instance, in 1970, the New York PBA went even further than the law required to dissociate themselves from other city employees. And "in major confrontations" today, writes Matthew Cunningham-Cook of *The Intercept*, "police unions have already failed to show solidarity with other public sector unions." When Walker carved cops out of his anti-union crusade, this "depriv[ed] teachers and other public workers of the political protection that could come from a broader coalition. The police unions did not stand with the other workers."[40] When Walker floated the possibility of applying similar changes to police in 2013, moreover, police associations balked: for Milwaukee Police Association president Mike Crivello, there was "an absolute difference between public safety and general employees in this regard." Well, so be it. More recently, though, the Houston Police Officers' Union showed just how little solidarity cops feel even for other public safety workers, by spearheading the defeat of a ballot measure that would have equalized pay between police and firefighters.

This is why calls either to reform the police from within a broader labor movement, or to embrace dissident elements within cop unions, are naive nonstarters. Political scientist Cedric Johnson, for example, argues that we should engage with "reformist elements within police unions and departments," in order to "embolden internal dissent . . . and counter the most vocal, reactionary police elements." Police aren't all bad, Johnson suggests: most join the force out of "an earnest desire to serve" and are subject to the same expendability and austerity as other public sector workers.[41] However, this is a misunderstanding of the police and their power from top to bottom. Police are simply *not* subject to the same austerity and expendability as other workers—they are shielded from these by special rights and negotiated privileges—and even where austerity slows the growth of their exorbitant wages, police unions accept increased impunity in lieu of salary increases.

In fact, the entire structure and function of police and their fraternities is inimical to change. Even if it were embraced with open arms, we have seen how police reform does little more than legitimize the police. "Hoping for reform-minded police unions is also delusional," argues writer and activist Shawn Gude, adding that "the few reform organizations that do exist—such as the National Black Police Association—have failed miserably." If anything, Gude argues, dissident cops would have more room for maneuver without a reactionary and united police association keeping members in line and on message.[42] Furthermore, the AFL-CIO's proposed code of excellence is a cop-out, pun intended: such codes generally refer to professionalism and the quality of union work, not the behavior of affiliates. The AFL-CIO already has its own code of conduct that bars discrimination and harassment of all types, but police unions violate these basic precepts daily, since their job is to defend the police, and the job of the police is to harass, intimidate, and brutalize working-class people of color.

Moreover, to compare police unions to other public sector workers like teachers is fundamentally misleading, and while left-wing critiques of police and right-wing attacks on educators might share language of public accountability, the comparison is meaningless from the jump. Teachers are not violently hostile to the constituency they interact with daily. In fact, most teachers ultimately want what's best for their students, which is why their unions tend to support progressive policies across the board. Much the same could be said of health care workers like nurses—National Nurses United has endorsed Medicare for All, not petty privileges for themselves. For the police, as Kristian Williams argues, "these relationships are exactly reversed," providing "a permanent basis for the conservative orientation of police unions."[43] If teachers wrote into their contract the right to abuse students without punishment, would we be making the same excuses for their behavior that people make for police every day? And while it would be a good thing indeed to give teachers more control over schools, and workers greater self-management on the factory floor, we wouldn't argue that the police should run the streets—and yet, often they do.

To insist that there is a place for police within the labor movement is to embrace "workers" who routinely kill and brutalize their own union affiliates. This contradiction could not have been clearer when AFL-CIO president Richard Trumka said of Darren Wilson's murder of Mike Brown, "Our brother killed our sister's son." Brown's mother, Lesley McSpadden, a grocery store worker at the time of his death, was a member of United Food and Commercial Workers Local 88. As writer and organizer Kim Kelly has observed, this wasn't the first time and it wouldn't be the last: just months later, Los Angeles sheriffs gunned down eighteen-year-old Andrés Guardado. "His father, Cristobal Guardado, is a member of Unite Here Local 11. Once again, a brother had killed another brother's child."[44] This isn't simply about the killings, galling as they are: it's about the fact that collective bargaining by police is about ensuring impunity for just this kind of act. No other workers bargain for the right to murder other workers without consequence.

The right has never needed an excuse to attack unions and we provide them no new weapons by dismantling police associations, which is why to argue that targeting police associations would encourage such attacks borders on bad faith. The reality is the opposite: the future of the labor movement and its most radical base, especially when it comes to public sector unions, is low-income people of color—precisely the same demographic targeted by police violence. What message does it send to those workers when union leaders bend over backward to appease their oppressors, and what image of a labor movement does it project? For Saladin Muhammad, a founder of Black Workers for Justice and co-coordinator of the Southern Workers Assembly in North Carolina, "This killing with impunity that exists really speaks to the question of whether the working class is going to unite on a multinational, multiracial basis around conditions that affect a section of the working class."[45] If our goal is to build a larger and more vibrant labor movement in the future, the question isn't simply a quantitative one, and not all disaffiliations should be seen as a net negative.

None of this is to suggest that unions, especially large federations like the AFL-CIO, are somehow innocent. Historically, many have trafficked in the same kinds of privilege and racism in order to legitimize their own power. But it's no coincidence that it was precisely after many large unions had themselves become integrated within the capitalist system that police decided to play worker—police unions were born full-grown as a "labor" aristocracy, guns and all. Rather than worry that the expulsion of cop unions will weaken labor movements, we need to recognize that their *presence* is a liability to movements and a barrier to their growth. In the words of Clarise McCants of the Black Youth Project 100 (BYP100), "We're definitely pro-labor union" but "the Fraternal Order of Police (FOP) is not just like any union. They are a fraternity—and they are the most dangerous fraternity in America."[46] For writer Alex Press, we can glimpse an alternative in the 2016 march of Minneapolis teachers in solidarity with Philando Castile—killed by police outside of Saint Paul—which took place in defiance of local police associations. "An anti-racist labor movement," Press argues, "requires an end to collaboration with the police."[47] And she's right: it is only once police "unions" have been expelled and abolished that a vibrant and inclusive vision for labor can appear on the horizon.

Whatever quantitative loss the disaffiliation of police unions entails would be more than compensated by the qualitative impact, in ways that go well beyond anti-racism. The very presence of police unions has an overall conservatizing effect on broader federations, as Bill Fletcher himself argues:

> Having law enforcement units in other unions, whether it is AFSCME, UFCW or the Teamsters, has a very conservative impact on the union ... The law enforcement units tend to be very well organized and very conservative. They will intervene when there are union debates on anything that has to do with law enforcement, the movement for black lives or issues of immigration and detention.[48]

Police unions are not partners in the project of building a more just world—they are an albatross weighing heavily on the neck of labor and narrowing its political horizons. Moreover, the demand to defund the police and reinvest those funds in social goods would mean a redistribution of resources toward large swaths of the public sector labor movement—helping to build a broader constituency for change in the process.

For Williams, the history of police unions represents a paradox. Police have formed unions and gone on strike, while breaking strikes as well. They have fought elected authorities not in the name of greater freedom and equality, but in support of authoritarianism and hierarchy. They claim to uphold the law, but they break it all the time, and they claim to prevent violence while inflicting it on the public. But, Williams concludes, this dilemma is merely "illusory": "Working people cannot afford to extend solidarity to the police, and we cannot let the reactionary goals of police unions restrain us in our attacks on injustice."[49] Even police from working-class backgrounds are brought into the job as "part of the managerial machinery of capitalism," controlling the poor and Black people in particular for the sake of capitalist control. Police are a *part* of contemporary capitalism just as overseers were *part* of slavery; they weren't against it then, and they aren't against it today.

Moreover, disguising police as workers is a trick, part of the broader system of police magic that helps to bind the capitalist system together. We have seen how police magic transforms violent crime—ostensibly a *failure* of policing—into an argument for more police, and how it magically turns movements for police reform and change into window dressing for a violent status quo. Here, we see how, equally magically, police are transformed into "workers" and their fraternities, whose concrete function is to ensure that broader solidarity among workers is impossible, are turned into "unions." In the words of Jed Dodd of the Pennsylvania Teamsters, "I always considered police unions to be little more than organized scabs." But they are actually *worse* than that: scabs cross picket lines; cops *break* them. "There is no justification for defending police unions," Robin D.G. Kelley concludes. "They are company unions. Their job has not changed, and it will not change: to provide security for the reproduction of racial capitalism."[50] And for the sociologist Eve Ewing, there is a deeper reason still that police fraternities shouldn't be considered unions: whereas "a union is a pact, wrought among the human. Among the fallible . . . there can be no error in the brotherhood. And the brotherhood can never be reformed."[51]

The deepest irony here is that those who avoid conflict with police unions in the name of protecting labor participate in a sleight of hand that ensures police power goes unchallenged. Republicans attack unions while sparing cops, but Democrats— hamstrung by the demand to support labor—are unwilling to push back on the police "union" masquerade. Why would the left want to play into this game? Cities don't need to hand over as much power to the police as they do, but because not even liberals will put up a fight, "some of the worst police departments in the country are in cities, like Baltimore and Oakland, run by liberal mayors."[52] What if unions—and workers more broadly—refused to be blackmailed and instead played a leading role in the struggle against these violent fraternities? Their arguments lose their power as soon as we refuse to take them seriously.

Ultimately, there's no path toward police abolition—or even police reform—that doesn't involve a reckoning with police unions as the central bastion of police power. Not only are the police the enemies of workers and people of color, but from their very origin they have been *synonymous* with the racialized division of the working class that has always forestalled progress, much less revolution. Police unions today remain faithful to those origins and to that history of betrayal.

–

Our task is to break police power, and this means starting from its very foundation: police unions. On the federal level, this begins above all with an immediate *end to qualified immunity* through a modification of the federal code. On the state level, it means the *immediate repeal* of all Law Enforcement Officers' Bills of Rights and refusing the idea that police should enjoy a special layer of due process, above and beyond other citizens. On the local level, there should be a nationwide campaign to immediately *suspend binding arbitration*—even the editorial board of the *New York Times* agrees that it's long past time to "ax the arbitrators."[53] Ultimately, cities should be pressed to unilaterally cease contract negotiation with FOP, PBA, and other police unions—adjusting state law where necessary in order to achieve the latter (in Pennsylvania, for example, this means changing or repealing Act 111 from 1968).

We should immediately push to disaffiliate all police unions, prison guard unions, and border patrol unions from the AFL-CIO and other labor federations on the grounds that these are not labor organizations, that they do not represent workers, and that their presence violates the spirit and the word of the organiz-ations to which they currently belong.[54] This may mean losing some members and leverage in the short term, but in the long term it opens up the possibility of rebuilding a vision of public sector labor organizing from the grass roots, bringing together a broader majority of low-income workers, working women, and workers of color. The FOP—the worst of the worst—is not affil-iated, and stands to gain thousands of members if unions disaffiliate. Nevertheless, by isolating police organizations and denying them the legitimacy provided by the broader labor movement, we will reveal them for who they are and make them far easier to fight on the local, state, and federal level.

As Kelley has argued, we also need to simultaneously work to dismantle police *foundations*. By operating as "conduits for corporations to contribute financially to police, influence policy, and introduce hardware and technologies in which they may have a vested interest," police foundations have come to play an underrecognized role as surreptitious transmission belts between private capital and policing. As thinly veiled payoffs for the protection of property, moreover, they also underline the rela-tionship between policing and capitalism: most of America's largest corporations funnel millions into police foundations, either because they have a vested interest in equipping police with new technologies they stand to profit from, or simply because they know the police are there to protect *them*.[55] Small wonder then, as Kelley demonstrates, that the Philadelphia Police Foundation receives large donations from real estate companies and (what are effectively the same thing) local universities like Temple and University of Pennsylvania, for whom policing is essential for attracting wealthier students and guaranteeing lucrative student housing contracts.[56]

Today, police unions are on the defensive, although you wouldn't know it from their rhetoric. The leaders of police asso-ciations have become some of the most visible and aggressive critics of Black Lives Matter, Antifa, and other dangerous figments of the racist imagination, but while such belligerence is nothing new, there are signs that it might not be working today. "As their public image declines," Sam Adler-Bell writes, "police unions rely more heavily on fear tactics, singling out their political enemies for ridicule and worse."

> Their response has been to abandon any pretense of neutrality. They appeal, more explicitly than ever, to the social factions they intend to protect, while adopting a posture of unconstrained menace toward their critics and enemies. They act and speak as a class for themselves. In this way, police unions are contributing to the dissolution of the myths that might otherwise preserve their political power.[57]

Rhetorically and politically, police unions have become more firmly associated with the far right and with Donald Trump's cartoonish worldview, while on the local level they have consistently alienated potential supporters with their intransigence. Think of Minneapolis, where the union's militant opposition to minor reforms pushed the city council unwillingly to the brink of abolition. Or think of New York, where whatever sympathy police garnered when two officers were shot in 2014 was quickly squandered with an ill-conceived offensive against the mayor. Writing in the *Washington Post*, Andrew Grim suggests that the same tactics that helped expand police power, the "blue flu" in particular, "might backfire" today.[58] Stuart Schrader agrees: "They're in a process of overplaying their hand."[59]

Police associations are under increased scrutiny nationwide, and they aren't taking it well. While many city councils have been historically bought and paid for by police unions, Austin has recently seen its entire city council and mayor pledge to refuse donations from the Austin Police Association. In Philadelphia, a city where the police have been historically untouchable, the FOP was already under pressure from the 2013 Josey incident and the killing of Brandon Tate-Brown the following year, and cops seethed when voters put a sworn enemy, progressive defense attorney Larry Krasner, into the district attorney's office in 2018. In the post–George Floyd moment, blowback has only increased: in response to heavy-handed police violence against protesters, the city council banned the use of tear gas, rubber bullets, and pepper spray. A recent op-ed signed by the editorial board of the *Philadelphia Inquirer* urged City Hall to "disarm Philly's police union from the weapon of secret arbitration," and organizers are pressuring the city to break off negotiations entirely. FOP president McNesby has admitted that the once-powerful organization is increasingly politically isolated, remarking, "Some of the ones who were our friends . . . now their phone is off the hook." The blame, he insists, lies with a "couple of a-holes in Minneapolis"—the officers who killed George Floyd.[60]

Of course, it isn't just a "couple of a-holes," much less as far away as Minneapolis. On October 27, 2020, Rickia Young took a wrong turn. Just a few hours earlier and a few blocks away, Philadelphia police had shot Walter Wallace Jr. dead. Under the microscope for their use of excessive force in June and their wings clipped by city officials, that night the cops took their revenge, beating many protesters bloody. Young was in the wrong place at the wrong time: after accidentally driving toward the unfolding police riot, she was attempting a U-turn when cops swarmed her SUV, smashing the windows before tearing the passengers out and beating them brutally. Young's two-year-old son was stolen from her as she was detained. In a tweet that was quickly deleted, the national FOP shared an image of a female officer holding the kidnapped boy, who was left deeply traumatized by the events. The child, the FOP falsely claimed, "was lost during the violent riots in Philadelphia, wandering around barefoot in an area that was experiencing complete lawlessness."

Police are technicians of violence, armed specialists in the state's monopoly of force. As such, policing—*any* policing—is a community-destroying machine that dismantles and co-opts the power of solidarity, self-government, and real democracy. Reforms like "community" policing rupture the horizontal bonds of community, replacing them with vertical bonds to the police themselves. By throwing a wrench in police power, we create space to rebuild community alternatives, and as we will see, these alternatives already exist in embryonic experiments both in the United States and abroad. Abolishing so-called police unions won't solve all of the problems of policing. But just as the police are a central pillar of white supremacist capitalist power, police unions are *the* central pillar of police power.

Police associations are just the beginning—and their liquidation is a key step toward the abolition of the police more broadly. As we have seen, even the tiniest constraints on the unlimited power of the police leads to a whiny pity party and the perennial proclamation of a "war on police." But without knowing it, these complaints let us in on a secret: that anything less than absolute impunity *is* in fact a real threat to police power. And that even small changes might just unleash far larger ones.

These changes begin with breaking the power of police unions. That's the only war on police worth starting today.

5
Building Communities without Police

Deep down, we all know what a world without police looks like. We have all seen it. We have all needed help and asked, or called on friends or family in an emergency. We have all experienced moments when we worked together to resolve conflicts without calling in professional violence workers. We have all experienced, however fleeting, the warm embrace of community. We have all trusted the support and generosity of others, and without thinking twice we have been generous in turn. For Tom Joad, the protagonist of John Steinbeck's 1939 *The Grapes of Wrath*, this world is no distant fantasy:

> I been thinkin' how it was ... how our folks took care a their-selves, an' if they was a fight they fixed it theirself; an' they wasn't no cops wagglin' their guns, but they was better order than them cops ever give. I been a-wonderin' why we can't do that all over. Throw out the cops that ain't our people. All work together for our own thing.[1]

In fact, it is precisely because this is such second nature that we overlook these small moments—and their power. The world of police tells us every day that we are isolated individuals in need of protection, and while there's no doubt that abolishing the police would represent a radical break with the present state of things, the power of community already exists, and it is the basis for a very different kind of world.

So how do we get there? Struggling with the question of the transition from capitalism to communism, Vladimir Lenin

famously spoke of a transitional period known as the dictator-
ship of the proletariat, in which the workers would need to use
armed force against their old enemies. Less well known is Lenin's
argument—following Karl Marx and Friedrich Engels—about
the subsequent withering away of that workers' state, which
would disintegrate insofar as mass organizations take over its
functions. In the words of historian Salar Mohandesi, "creation
and destruction go hand in hand," and to the degree that grassroots movements "elaborate new alternatives for living," they "eat
away at the state apparatuses like termites."[2] I bring this up not
to cast the reader into age-old leftist debates, but to note that this
process sounds an awful lot like abolition. Because the state, and
the police in particular, exist to manage the social inequalities
born of capitalist exploitation and to keep the oppressed in line,
the state—and its armed foot soldiers—will only wither away
once those inequalities have been eliminated through the direct
distribution of economic and political power into the collective
hands of the people. The state withers away when it is *obsolete*.

A world without police is therefore a world in which the police
are obsolete, useless—a world where they serve literally no
purpose. Seen from this angle, we're already halfway there: the
police *are* useless. They don't do what they claim, they don't
protect and serve, much less prevent, care, or support. At the
same time, the police *do* play an essential, indeed indispensable,
role in fabricating and upholding the world we inhabit today,
premised as it is on the domination and exploitation of the
vast majority. For abolitionists, this creates a chicken-and-egg
problem. Which came first, the police or the white supremacist,
capitalist order they uphold? If the police are both a symptom of
our contemporary world and also a key mechanism for its perpetuation, both a cause and an effect, then how do we fight
them? Do we target the police or the underlying structures of
reality itself? Do we fight the storm troopers of racial capital, or
must we set our sights more broadly on social inequality and
white supremacy?

The answer is inevitably *both*, because what we are talking about is the inescapably two-sided nature of abolition itself—the need to build the new world as we fight to destroy the old from within. All struggle is ultimately concrete, however, and we can't fight white supremacy without fighting those who embody it. Moreover, the police play such a central role in upholding and recreating our world every day that by beginning to chip away at police power, we open up new and unforeseen possibilities. Since the police exist to maintain divisions among the poor, the fight against them is central to the process of overcoming those divisions, unifying the poor and working classes, and strengthening our own fighting forces. And because people without alternatives will continue to call the police, our inescapable task is to build those alternatives now—alternatives that provide the foundation for an entirely different kind of world.

Interest in police abolition has been steadily increasing for years, with every turn of the cycle of police murder and mass rebellion amplifying once-isolated calls to dismantle policing and build something different. But it was the George Floyd rebellions that blew a hole in the dam of our collective imaginations, opening up a space in Minneapolis and elsewhere for utopian alternatives. This is the alchemy of mass struggle, which can make the previously impossible suddenly possible—even unavoidable. Before us was the possibility of something else, sitting right at the intersection of *this can't continue* and *other worlds are possible*.

What was once said in a whisper is today shouted with full-throated confidence: Policing is over. What's next?

—

On June 7, 2020, a veto-proof majority of the Minneapolis City Council stood on a stage in Powderhorn Park, just blocks from where George Floyd had been killed two weeks earlier, and publicly pledged to dismantle the Minneapolis Police Department

(MPD). The grassroots Black Visions Collective and its political arm, Reclaim the Block, had been pressuring council members to embrace radical change, and at least for the moment, elected leaders answered that call. But it wasn't only the movements that had pushed council members toward abolition: it was the police themselves.

Council members like Steve Fletcher had seen police reform in action, and they had seen that it doesn't work. Even shifting resources to the city's Office of Violence Prevention had prompted not only resistance but arm-twisting extortion: police had refused to answer 911 calls, telling business owners to take it up with their council members. All the while, MPD continued to kill, and in 2017 they pressured EMTs to sedate sixty-two suspects—even those not suspected of a crime—with the tranquilizer ketamine. Reform, Fletcher now concludes, was a failure. Another council member, Phillipe Cunningham, agrees:

> We had not just national experts but global experts in police reform coming in . . . We had de-escalation training, procedural-justice training. Every one of the four officers involved in the killing of George Floyd had received this training . . . No one could say that we didn't try reform. We tried every kind of reform. And we still paid twenty-two million dollars last year in civil settlements for the police. We still have rape kits that no one is investigating. George Floyd was still killed. It just didn't work.[3]

The behavior of police officers during the George Floyd riots only confirmed what many council members already suspected. "I was realizing, Oh, my God, people are calling me because they can't get through to 911, and nobody is responding even if they do get through to the police. No one is coming," Fletcher recalls. "At a certain point, you say, they were only defending the precinct, and they left the rest of the community to fend for ourselves." Council member Cam Gordon recalls that "it was all about defending their fortress, their building," while council president Lisa Bender argues that "the police department walked away from the city" during the uprising.[4]

If the police thought that leaving the city unprotected would prove just how indispensable they were, their actions had the opposite effect. Council members already skeptical of reform were propelled toward abolition, and toward the recognition that, while people want community safety, this doesn't necessarily mean the police. What precisely this new model of community safety might look like wasn't immediately clear, however. Council members have spoken of deploying nonpolice community de-escalation teams, while others have proposed block-by-block neighborhood teams. There is broad agreement that 911 calls should be diverted to mental health, emergency, or addiction professionals, and that traffic stops and parking enforcement should not be a police matter.

But for Fletcher, the central task is one of reengaging on a community level. "We need to build the relationship networks, skills, and capacity in our communities to support each other in resolving conflicts and keeping each other safe before things escalate dangerously. Our isolation from each other has required us to outsource the management of social interactions." "The whole world is watching," he insists. "We can declare policing as we know it a thing of the past, and create a compassionate, non-violent future."[5] The most difficult questions remain unanswered, however. Several council members have hinted that police would remain necessary for enforcement, without specifying the limits of police power.

In late June, council members approved a resolution on "transforming community safety" that quoted Angela Davis and committed to centering communities of color, public health, and transformative justice, but it offered few details. Then, in a unanimous vote, the city council endorsed a proposed ballot initiative that, if approved by voters, would have removed all mention of the police from the city charter and replaced them with a new Department of Community Safety and Violence Prevention. The measure first needed to get past an unelected charter commission, however. Hours before the vote, several of the measure's sponsors sent a letter to the charter commission insisting that "City Council is not asking you to put police abolition on the ballot," and that their proposed alternative would "include law enforcement." This confusing, last-minute gambit didn't pay off: the charter commission killed the proposal on procedural grounds by extending the debate period until after the ballot deadline, voting down an alternative proposal that would have eliminated the statutory requirement that the city fund 0.0017 police per resident. Neither question made it onto the November 2020 ballot, and the council's ambitious promise to dismantle MPD was effectively stillborn.

While council members had lost their nerve at a decisive moment, this was hardly a situation of their own making—and in reality, this was never really about city council at all. Rather, it was a testament to the power of the growing movement in the streets, and while the path to abolition may be blocked from above, pressure continues to grow from below. The proposal to dismantle the MPD "was Black Visions Collective and Reclaim the Block's baby" in the words of councillor Gordon, who recalled that many of his colleagues had to be dragged, "kicking and screaming" to the cause of police abolition.[6] It took a campaign of pressure, including installing plastic gravestones on the lawns of council members, to force the city to bend to the will of the movements.

While organizers praised the bravery of the council's position, grassroots movements remain almost universally suspicious of the council's intentions. Communities United against Police Brutality (CUAPB) has spent two decades pushing for increased oversight with no help whatsoever from elected leaders. Their current proposals include a ballot measure that would require individual cops to carry liability insurance—a mechanism that they believe would weed out the worst abusers over time. While sympathetic to abolition as a long-term horizon, some CUAPB members worry that an all-or-nothing framework could hinder changes in the present while giving grandstanding council members a radical alibi. According to CUAPB member Dave Bicking, the council members are "hypocrites" who have spent years ignoring community demands that they rein in widespread police violence, and the proposal to dismantle the police "gives them the opportunity to pose as great reformers while they're doing absolutely nothing to get things done . . . They are just pandering in front of the worldwide TV cameras."[7] The Coalition for Justice 4 Jamar is similarly unimpressed by political leaders: "The new [council members] were elected on police accountability and were elected on Jamar Clark's name. But are they gonna get accountability? No, they aren't. They haven't done it for the past five years, so why would they do it now?" Drawing inspiration from the Black Panther Party, the coalition advocates a fully empowered police oversight commission, pending total abolition.

For Kandace Montgomery of the Black Visions Collective, however, police abolition is less about all-or-nothing solutions and more about a radical faith—not in city council, but in the power of community. Montgomery, who in a now-viral video challenged Mayor Jacob Frey to commit to fully defunding and eliminating MPD, insists that we need to "believe in community, because that's who got us to this point . . . We need to be hopeful and we need to believe in ourselves . . . a belief in a future in which we are not in chains. And that's what abolition means to me in this moment."[8] In the meantime, the strategy is to reduce the annual police budget as much as possible, although this strategy can only go so far before it collides with the minimum funding currently stipulated in the city charter.

Montgomery believes that in the past, as when Jamar Clark was killed, movement organizers "were clear about the problem. Now, we are clear about the solution." That solution is a world without police:

A world without police would look like safety that is controlled and is led by our community, that focuses on transformation and transformative justice. A world without police means that everybody has what they need to survive and what they need to live healthy lives. It means we have the money that we need for education, health care, housing, workers' rights. It is a total transformation away from a racist and violent system into one that truly fosters our safety and well-being.[9]

In Powderhorn Park, where the council members pledged to dismantle the police, these open questions were already being answered, and this new world was already being born. There, the Powderhorn Safety Collective was established to provide community safety without the police.[10] Volunteers with the autonomous group are divided into "surveyors" and "dispatchers," using apps like Discord and WhatsApp to connect a network of more than 1,100 community members. This is abolition of the most practical sort: the collective decides democratically, on a moment's notice, whether or not to intervene in conflicts as they develop— and as a general rule, participants insist, they are more likely to intervene to protect people than property. "We can solve our own problems," one participant insists. "We don't have to bring the police in here."

They weren't the only ones. Similar self-managed security collectives sprang up in occupied parks across the city, filling the void left where the police withdrew or were unwanted, and other self-managed spaces like the Sheraton hotel, which volunteers repurposed to house local homeless residents, formed part of a growing network of police-free zones. Amid the rioting and looting that exploded across the city after George Floyd's murder, neighbors across Minneapolis got together to keep one another safe without the police. After a Native youth center was burned down, the local American Indian Movement established unarmed guardian patrols to protect community spaces and dissuade looters—sometimes calling their parents, but not the cops.[11] In some neighborhoods, rival gangs united and multiracial coalitions emerged spontaneously, squaring off against looters but also against armed white supremacists: in the words of one impromptu patrol organizer, "There's whites, Mexicans, blacks, Somalians, Africans, everybody's out and everybody's doing their part. The rest of the community that are not on the front lines are leaving sandwiches and cookies and coffee. They're coming out saying thank you for keeping us safe."[12] Despite their role in defending the rebellions, however, these and all forms of neighborhood watch run the perennial risk of becoming the police, or worse.

This sudden surge in practical abolitionism was able to draw upon the long-standing work of local organizations like MPD150. Conceived in anticipation of the 150th anniversary of the Minneapolis Police Department in 2017, MPD150—like many abolitionist groups—sets out from the urgent task of imagining an alternative future. The group asks community members to "imagine that you were asked to help create stability in a newly-founded city. How would you try to solve the problems that your friends and neighbors encountered? How would you respond to crisis and violence? Would your *first* choice be an unaccountable army with a history of oppression and violence patrolling your neighborhood around the clock?" The group's vision for a "police-free future" looks radically different—and far more concrete—than the stalled city council proposal, and it aims above all to divert funding toward prevention rather than enforcement.[13] For MPD150, abolition looks like the Minneapolis Group Violence Intervention program, which de-escalates community conflict without involving the police. And it looks like fighting gender-based violence before it happens with fully funded and consent-based sex education in schools, and shifting school police budgets toward counselors and restorative justice workshops instead.

For MPD150, it also means raising awareness about what individuals and communities can do to make the police obsolete through simple "action ideas." These include small, concrete measures that neighbors can take themselves: avoid calling the police; if you must, go to the local precinct rather than calling them, to avoid inviting police encounters in the neighborhood; make a list of alternative services to call; get trained in de-escalation and restorative justice; and when someone has a mental health crisis, center their own needs and safety. Above all, MPD150 urges people to connect with neighbors all the time, to establish real community bonds, and to "dream bigger," always remembering that "there was a time before police, and there will be a time after."[14] While such small steps may not seem to measure up to the task of abolition, especially in the face of one of the best-funded and most-developed repressive apparatuses in human history, they nevertheless point toward broader horizons while supporting and building community alternatives.

Funding prevention will be expensive, MPD150 admits, but cities nationwide are already paying billions on the back end in the form of bloated police budgets, millions in police brutality settlements annually, and billions more toward mass incarceration. There's plenty of money to redistribute to prevention, and while this won't immediately eliminate all societal violence, MPD150 notes that the billions we currently spend on policing and prisons haven't done so either. The new world without police won't be perfect, but we need to admit to ourselves just "how imperfect the current world is," and we need to wager on radical change:

> All of the uncertainty ahead of us is still a better choice than the status quo. The status quo is a Black man calling out for his mother as a police officer kneels on his neck. The status quo is a seemingly never-ending list of names, hashtags, and lives cut short—not just by police violence, but by the ongoing violence of

a system that cages millions of people and tears apart families. The status quo is the ongoing harassment and intimidation of communities going about their daily lives and simply existing. That's the work ahead of us. A police-free future isn't something that just *happens to us*; it's something we *build*, together.[15]

The strongest antidote to the police, and to the violence that they don't prevent—because it justifies their existence—is *community*, and when it comes to community alternatives to the police, we have far more options than many realize.

These alternatives begin to emerge when we choose to call friends, family, and neighbors instead of the cops, and build outward in concentric circles. On the level of the block and the neighborhood as a whole, this means developing deeper relationships, overcoming isolation, and checking in on our neighbors more often. It means making runs to the grocery store and making sure older and disabled neighbors have what they need. More ambitiously still, it could look like going door to door to establish a neighborhood group chat, putting in the work necessary to make sure everyone is enrolled and feels welcome to message the community with concerns. When there is a conflict among family members or between neighbors, this broader fabric can provide a critical alternative to bringing in the armed guardians of the state, because community members have more of a stake than the cops do in treating others like they matter.

This is not easy work. For years, I worked with organizers in West Philadelphia to establish just these kinds of networks. We held people's courts on street corners where local community members could step up to the mic and describe their experiences with the police. We established temporary "No Cop Zones" to broaden people's horizons and invite them to think about what a world without police might look like in the longer term. And, building on strategies like Copwatch, which observes and documents police activity, we sought to develop local rapid-response and self-defense networks that would allow the community to swarm the police, preventing brutality while also laying the groundwork for a true alternative that neighbors would be able to call upon for protection or to de-escalate and resolve local disputes. This work is almost always long and slow—although as Minneapolis shows, sometimes when the moment is ripe, you can get more than a thousand neighbors involved much more quickly. This time-intensive spadework is the price of building real community, however, and it's infinitely cheaper in economic and social terms than the devastation wrought by policing.

As historian Garrett Felber has written, "The struggle to abolish the police is not new," and US history—Black history in particular—is rich with community alternatives to the police.[16] More than a century ago, in 1919, workers in Seattle declared a general strike and shut the city down. While striking workers set themselves to the task of providing supply networks to meet the basic needs of the population, they also established security patrols composed of progressive veterans of the First World War "to preserve law and order without the use of force." "No volunteer will have any police power," they stressed, "or be allowed to carry weapons of any sort, but to use persuasion only."[17] As strikers displaced the government, in other words, they provided organized alternatives that prevented violence both within communities and from the police. Contrast this to the Boston police strike of the same year: police sought to stoke chaos and, absent strong community alternatives, they were successful—albeit ultimately to their own detriment.

It's no surprise that the most ambitious alternatives to the police have emerged historically from those communities where the cops offer the least protection while causing the most harm. This has been particularly true of Black struggles in the United States, past and present, in which the theory and practice of self-defense has always played a crucial role. Under the overt white supremacy of Jim Crow, spontaneous self-defense against white terrorism by police and vigilantes was a constant presence. As Robin D.G. Kelley has shown, organizations like the Sharecroppers' Union, backed by the Communist Party, embraced armed self-defense in the 1930s.[18] In the 1950s, Robert F. Williams, president of the Monroe, North Carolina, chapter of the National Association for the Advancement of Colored People (NAACP), realized that armed self-defense was the only effective protection against Klan violence, and began to organize Black rifle clubs in response.[19] Williams would be a major influence not only on the Black Panther Party, but also on the largest Black self-defense organization in US history: the Deacons for Defense and Justice, boasting fifty chapters across the South that defended Black neighborhoods while de-escalating community conflicts.[20]

In the words of Mississippi organizer Fannie Lou Hamer, "I keep a shotgun in every corner of my bedroom, and the first cracker even looks like he wants to throw some dynamite on my porch, won't write his mama again." In the long struggle for Black freedom, self-defense has *always* gone hand in hand with community building. The community needed to be safe from external threats before its internal bonds could be strengthened, which is why the Panthers described their community service programs—from children's breakfast clubs to safe escorts for older community members—as "survival pending revolution." These were, moreover, social and economic alternatives that actually paved the way for that revolution by helping people see beyond the status quo. These kinds of alternative initiatives, prefiguring a new world controlled by poor communities themselves, proliferated across organizations like the Young Lords, Brown Berets, Red Guards, American Indian Movement, and Young Patriots—all of which joined the Panthers in a broad "Rainbow Coalition."

After the Black Panther party was decapitated as part of the US government's global counterinsurgency campaign, self-defense persisted nevertheless. Street gangs like the Bloods and Crips first emerged to protect Black communities from the informal segregationist violence of white gangs like the "Spook Hunters."[21] Black street gangs, what Mike Davis called the "bastard offspring" of the Black Panthers, were gradually and intentionally depoliticized, reduced to bloody retribution in communities for which the only alternative to unemployment and poverty was the drug trade. However, their original function was never fully eradicated. During the 1992 riots following the acquittal of the cops who brutally beat Rodney King, the Bloods and Crips signed a historic ceasefire, teaming up against the police and releasing a community reconstruction plan under the heading "Give us the hammer and the nails, we will rebuild the city."

The plan reads like a wish list for preventative abolitionist reforms: rebuilding infrastructure, fully funding public education and health care, and revitalizing recreational facilities and public spaces by empowering local residents to do the work themselves. Of course, the proposal also involved the transformation of policing through the deployment of trained teams of "buddies," unarmed local community members.[22] But the Los Angeles Police Department had no interest in rebuilding poor communities of color. They moved swiftly to sabotage the gang truce, including by picking up members of rival crews and dropping them off deep in enemy territory. In the end, the strategy worked, and the hopes of a city free of gang violence faded.

—

Alternatives to the police have been flourishing in recent years. On every level that policing fails—from community safety to mental health care to sexual and gendered violence—grassroots community organizations already have a hard-won track record of success, doing with fewer resources, and a far less destructive impact on poor neighborhoods, what the state and the police can't or don't want to. Although some restorative and non-carceral alternatives to the police and prisons have used government and nonprofit support to expand their scope, the price has often been high: the cooptation of grassroots movements and the watering-down of the alternatives they provide to policing and the state.

In 1972, residents of West Philadelphia developed a network of block associations under the umbrella of the Citizen's Local Alliance for a Safer Philadelphia (CLASP). Their goal was to make communities safer without the police through participatory patrols staffed by neighbors armed only with flashlights and air horns. The result by 1976 was 600 organized blocks and a 75 percent reduction in crime.[23] The Achilles' heel of all neighborhood watch organizations, however, is that in the name of security they often reproduce the surveillance and inequality of the world around them. In richer and whiter areas, such organizations are adjuncts of the police, surveilling segregated wealthy neighborhoods to keep the rabble out. In Philadelphia, for example, some block captains functioned as self-appointed deputies of racist leaders like Frank Rizzo, mobilizing and transporting white voters to the polls. Even in poorer neighborhoods, street patrols can reinforce inequality by targeting the poorest of the poor, homeless people, and drug users for scrutiny and ostracism. Groups like New York City's Guardian Angels are essentially police by another name, as they make demonstrably clear every time they scuffle with protesters. And lest we forget, George Zimmerman was a neighborhood watch captain.

At their best, however, democratic and inclusive community organizations that are independent of the city, the police, and the wealthy can help to protect communities without reinforcing inequality. In Chicago, organizations like MASK (Mothers/Men against Senseless Killings) are confronting violence through a constant neighborhood presence that helps build community and intervene before violent conflicts arise. After a young mother was killed in 2015, MASK symbolically took over the corner "to simply hang out on the block, cook food, and emanate love. Our presence was felt. People began to notice neighbors were watching out for each other, and it was contagious."[24] The neighborhood where MASK operates saw homicides and shootings decline at twice the rate of Chicago as a whole, reaching historically low levels in 2017.[25] This contagious abolition has spread to half a dozen other cities, but the work remains difficult and dangerous: in 2019, two MASK mothers were killed while on a patrol. A year later, MASK founder Tamar Manasseh was so worried about violence at a local funeral that she even warned the police. Despite a police presence, fifteen were injured in a shootout. For Manasseh, these and other tragedies simply drove home the basic reality: "They still let this happen ... If the police won't protect us, then what?"[26] While Chicago mayor Lori Lightfoot was elected on the promise to shift away from a reliance on the police, the $11.5 million she has dedicated to community intervention organizations like MASK represents less than 1 percent of a staggering $1.7 billion police budget.[27]

Mental health crisis intervention hotlines exist nationwide, but because most people continue to call 911 in an emergency, 911 diversion to community alternatives is crucial. Created in Eugene, Oregon, more than three decades ago, the CAHOOTS (Crisis Assistance Helping Out on the Streets) model sends out two-person teams—one first responder and one crisis worker trained in mental health care—to de-escalate crises and connect people to the support they need. With an operating budget of scarcely 2 percent of the local police budget, CAHOOTS responds to nearly 20 percent of all emergency calls. The impact has been undeniable: in 2019, CAHOOTS received 24,000 calls, and only 150 of those calls resulted in police presence—saving millions of dollars and countless lives annually.[28] Cities nationwide are currently weighing the potential of the CAHOOTS model, and organizations like the Anti Police-Terror Project in Oakland have established similar hotlines for non-police response to mental health emergencies.[29]

Grassroots alternatives have been particularly important for confronting sexual violence. This is no surprise, given how little the state does to prevent sexual assault—and given how many police are themselves perpetrators. Rape crisis centers first emerged in the early 1970s as a community alternative in the face of state indifference, in which "women were taking care of women instead of depending on the patriarchal state," alongside other grassroots organizations like Bay Area Women against Rape and Women Organized against Rape in Philadelphia.[30] While public and nonprofit funding has seen rape crisis centers become more widespread, the institutionalization of these efforts has also taken the edge off their radicalism. Sex workers, moreover, unable to count on protection from a system of policing that criminalizes them as police sexually extort and assault them, have also developed their own alternatives in the form of collective organizations and safe spaces. Others have established what are known as bad date lines, publicly naming abusive or dangerous clients like the Black Panther Party once named abusive police.[31] Cities in the United States and across Canada have embraced bad date lines, which are now sometimes operated in conjunction with the police.

On the back end, organizations like the Communities against Rape and Abuse do the difficult work of restorative justice in the aftermath of gendered, domestic, and partner violence, providing transformative alternatives to policing and incarceration. CARA was formed after one of the first rape crisis centers in the country, Seattle Rape Relief, which had by then morphed into an institutionalized nonprofit, was shuttered by its board of directors. CARA sought to remain faithful to the original grassroots mission of much anti-violence work by shifting away from crisis intervention and embracing a community organizing model with a longer view, rooted specifically in poor neighborhoods of color.[32] CARA provides guidelines for community-based accountability that includes survivors, perpetrators, and the broader community. By equipping people with the skills necessary to pursue accountability, it rejects the idea that sexual assault can be dealt with only by trained professionals or police.[33]

Many grassroots organizations have sought to confront the intersections of community safety and gendered and sexual violence directly, by simultaneously struggling against violence by the police *and* violence within communities, families, and households. This was the case, for instance, with two groups led by women of color in Brooklyn, both of which were affiliated with the feminist anti-violence organization INCITE! In the 2000s, Sista II Sista established Sistas' Liberated Ground, a series of community circles through which "women turn to each other instead of the police to address the violence in their lives." And the Safe OUTside the System (SOS) Collective emerged in 1997 from the Audre Lorde Project to end violence against queer people of color while pushing back against broken windows policing as part of the Coalition against Police Brutality. In 2007, the SOS Collective launched a Safe Neighborhood Campaign to proactively prevent anti-LGBTQ violence and create safe community spaces. For both organizations, the fundamental goal has been to transform every community space and every block into liberated territory—free not only from the police but also from all forms of intra-community violence.

In Baltimore, the Community Conferencing Center, now known as Restorative Response Baltimore, was established in 2000 to provide a restorative and transformative alternative to policing and prisons. Through early intervention in community conflict, educational programs, reintegration counseling for those returning from prison and the military, and juvenile court diversion programs, Restorative Response has sought to address conflict before the police get involved, and even *use* this conflict as a stepping-stone to stronger communities by building relationships and developing collective confidence to intervene. Through Indigenous-inspired principles of mediation that allow people's voices to be heard and encourage perpetrators to understand the consequences of their actions, mediators craft agreements that have achieved a compliance rate of over 95 percent. In the past two decades, CCC-RR has helped 18,000 Baltimore residents resolve conflicts without the police, and because 97 percent of juveniles diverted to mediation are youth of color, the organization has also helped to counteract the dramatic racial disparities of mass incarceration.[34]

Taken together, these and countless other local grassroots alternatives serve as powerful anchors for a broader and expanding fabric of community—a loosely organized network of territories liberated from the police insofar as they overcome the intra-community violence so often used to justify the violence of the state. Recent years have seen periodic outrage over a spate of videos documenting abuse by school resource officers, and, particularly after the rebellions in Minneapolis, school districts nationwide have begun to scrutinize the presence of police, even cutting SRO contracts. Efforts to abolish campus police, which escalated after images of police pepper-spraying students at the University of California, Davis, went viral in 2011, have recently found new momentum, as coalitions have formed on UC campuses with the support of the nationwide Campus Antifascist Network (CAN). Even public libraries, overlooked catchall spaces for the most excluded members of society with nowhere else to go, are today witnessing a nationwide push to replace library police with unarmed community liaisons.[35]

This liberated territory, this embryonic world without police, continues to grow today as more communities come together collectively and as the police are pushed out of ever-larger spaces of our society. This is how the world without police will be born—not from above, but from below.

—

The systems we confront are resilient and deeply entrenched, however, and especially in light of the stalled effort to dismantle the Minneapolis Police Department, we need to remain acutely aware of the many pitfalls that surround and beset the abolitionist project. Just as minor reforms have only increased the legitimacy of the police and made policing more effective, every small and partial move toward abolition can easily become a new part of the system if we are not on guard. Efforts to abolish the death penalty, for example, have ended up strengthening life without parole, or what organizers increasingly refer to as "death by incarceration." For example, California's Proposition 34, which was narrowly defeated by voters in 2012, was couched in language that, in the words of political theorist Andrew Dilts, reinforced and legitimized "permanent exclusion, forced labor, more police, more punishment, and more prisons," thereby "reconfiguring and intensifying the carceral system" rather than weakening or dismantling it.[36]

Similarly, Critical Resistance and INCITE! were among the first organizations to diagnose the ways anti-violence advocacy, especially when taken over and professionalized by state intervention, contributed to what would come to be known as "carceral feminism." By separating anti-violence work from its grassroots origins and handing power to the state, this carceral turn isolated the fight against interpersonal violence from the struggle against state violence. The result was movements against policing and prisons that marginalize women of color and demands around gendered and sexual violence, and movements against interpersonal violence that see police and prisons as the only possible protection for women, children, and sexual minorities.[37] Debates around sex work have followed a similar trajectory, with carceral feminism manifesting as a vociferous movement against so-called human trafficking. While trafficking is very real, mainstream advocacy often leverages concern for vulnerable populations in a way that reduces all sex workers to victims, or even slaves. Rather than embrace the complex realities of sex workers and their movements, police, governments, Border Patrol and immigration enforcement, and international organizations have embraced the language of human trafficking to increase surveillance and criminalize sex work in ways that only endanger its practitioners.

The George Floyd rebellions sparked nationwide calls to defund the police, and for many, this naturally means redirecting those funds toward social workers, mental health professionals, and schools. As we have seen, however, each of these institutions is increasingly complicit in the broader carceral system, functioning more like the police and handing more people over to prisons every day. As a result, abolitionists today remind us that we must also *reimagine* welfare institutions as part of a broader abolitionist project. For legal scholar Dorothy Roberts, simply pouring money into social work runs the risk of substituting one punitive system with another. This is especially true of child protective services, which represents not an alternative to the police but an "integral part of the U.S. carceral regime" that is "designed to regulate and punish black and other marginalized people." More money to CPS, in other words, means more surveillance of poor communities of color, more families torn apart, and more parents in prison. "Rather than divesting one oppressive system to invest in another"—a sort of elaborate carceral shell game—Roberts encourages us to keep our eyes on the abolitionist horizon: "abolishing all carceral institutions and creating radically different ways of meeting families' needs."[38]

Much the same can be said for mental health care, and calls to defund the police have often gone hand in hand with calls to fund mental health services and to divert 911 response away from the police and toward crisis intervention. Since police kill those suffering mental health crises at a rate sixteen times higher than the national average, it would be better to call literally anyone other than a cop—a trained killer with only one tool to offer. At the same time, however, we should be wary of simply diverting funds to any and all "experts." Given the deep historic entanglement of mental health care with punishment and confinement, we need to ask *which* experts should be called. Are they independent of the police and the state, or are they an extension of them? Do they really have in mind the best interests of the person in crisis, or do they exist simply to manage a "problem" population? The stakes of these questions became starkly clear when a controversial photo went viral in September 2020. The image shows Hector Estrada, an employee of California's Riverside Police Department, dressed in all black with a police-issued Covid mask and a military-style tactical vest. The vest, which also bears a Blue Lives Matter flag, is emblazoned with the words "CLINICAL THERAPIST."

Even schooling, long touted as both the opposite of prison and its antidote, must be critically interrogated. While schools have always functioned in part as disciplinary institutions that both manage a potential workforce and reproduce social inequalities, the struggle to desegregate schools was also a touchstone of the civil rights movement. Racial segregation and discipline are not separable, however, as the recent resegregation of schools has corresponded to a sharpening of their disciplinary function in poor communities of color. To simply decry the "school-to-prison pipeline" or lobby for increased funding is therefore not enough, because the schools feeding the prisons are the schools that look and function most like prisons themselves. We need to fight *for* schools as we fight to transform them into spaces free of policing and other forms of repressive discipline.

Whether we're talking about defunding the police to fund social work, mental health, or schools, in the words of sociologist Ruha Benjamin, "It's not about shifting money around, it's about *reimagining*." We have to rethink the role of these institutions within liberated communities and their function in fostering a truly human life.[39]

—

Even police abolition today risks being co-opted, diverted, and repackaged as its opposite. No sooner had calls to defund and abolish the police begun to gain steam than desperate political elites nationwide started to flail about for any alternative to the project of full abolition. Suddenly, the "Camden model" was on everyone's lips. In 2012, Camden, New Jersey, had been reeling under what was by far the nation's highest murder rate. In 2013, the Camden Police Department was formally disbanded, and what has followed has been the miraculous rebirth of the city—so goes the press narrative. When the final report from Obama's Twenty-First Century Policing task force was released, the president himself even lauded Camden as a model for police departments nationwide.

For Brendan McQuade, author of *Pacifying the Homeland*, the so-called Camden model is no model at all, but a dystopian glimpse of the future. This is because in Camden, the police were not abolished at all, but immediately replaced with a county police force that was larger, better funded, more technologically advanced, and whiter:

> Fawning media profiles describe barbecues, ice cream trucks, and basketball games. They don't mention surveillance systems: 121 cameras that monitor the entire city; 35 ShotSpotter microphones to detect gunshots; automated scanners that read license plates; and SkyPatrol, a mobile observation post that can scan six square blocks with thermal-imaging equipment. They don't mention the Real Time Tactical Operational Intelligence Center (RT-TOIC), which produces the intelligence to direct police operations.[40]

These new county police have taken algorithmic targeting and broken windows enforcement to the next level, all under the watchful eye of a system of total surveillance with little to no oversight as to how the gathered data is used. This is "community policing" on steroids, in which the police recruit a network of "neighborhood sentinels" to feed information to authorities— not a world without police, but a community of snitches.

The origins of the Camden model are even more worrying than its everyday reality. There are good reasons to believe

Governor Chris Christie's austerity budget triggered the Camden crime wave in an intentional ploy to restructure the city through corrupt privatization schemes. George Norcross, an insurance magnate described in a ProPublica exposé as "the most powerful unelected official in New Jersey," was at the center of the scheme, which saw $1.1 billion in tax breaks funneled into "his own company, business partners, political allies and clients of his brother."[41] The radical restructuring of the police was only one part of a broader shock doctrine, "a comprehensive pacification project, carried out to benefit business interests."[42]

Most ominously, McQuade sees this strategy as a response to decarceration itself. As sectors of the neoliberal ruling class opportunistically embraced the long-standing abolitionist call to reduce prison populations, New Jersey has seen a staggering one-third decline in its prison population. But being released from prison isn't the same as being free. This decline has been matched by an increase in electronic monitoring, or "e-carceration," and with no jobs for those who have been released, the drug trade continues to fill the vacuum—to the tune of $250 million annually in Camden alone. Rather than abolition in practice, Camden today is an "open-air prison" for storing the human refuse of late racial capitalism, and "ubiquitous surveillance and aggressive policing now manage a surplus population that is too costly to cage." Decarceration and e-carceration go hand in hand, both accelerated dramatically by the Covid-19 pandemic, and as mass incarceration recedes, its cheaper, neoliberal variant looms menacingly on the horizon as America's next peculiar institution: "mass supervision."[43]

For McQuade, the current "Camden fetish" seeks to skirt the abolitionist challenge and the failures of racial capitalism by instead "recalibrate[ing] state violence in the guise of progressive reform." "Camden is not a model," he writes. "It's an obstacle to real change," a misleading sleight of hand that represents "the most dangerous idea circulating in liberal elite circles at the moment."[44] This is precisely why the model is being touted today in the aftermath of the George Floyd rebellions. Despite the fact that grassroots organizers in Minneapolis have rejected Camden as a model, without organized and sustained resistance, the Camden nightmare represents one possible future for Minneapolis and for abandoned communities of color nationwide: mass technological supervision masquerading as abolition.

—

Abolition isn't reform. It isn't social policy, lobbying, progressive think tanks, or progressive legislation to cushion the blows of a violent status quo. Abolition isn't mandatory diversity training, new university hiring lines, or harm reduction—no matter how necessary and welcome these may be.[45] It's a horizon for the total rebuilding of society from the bottom up: a society with no police or prisons because there's nothing that needs policing and no one who needs to be in prison. Abolition means dismantling *all* systems of inequality, oppression, and institutional inhumanity at the same time that we build new, more emancipatory alternatives that put power directly in the hands of poor communities.

Abolition is not a policy platform, either. Commenting on the undeniable importance of the policy platform released by the Movement for Black Lives, Keeanga-Yamahtta Taylor offers an essential caveat: "After demands have been delivered and promises have been made, someone has got to fight to make them a reality ... Without a social movement on the ground to create the muscle necessary to coerce the political establishment," Taylor wonders, "how would any of it become achievable?"[46] While we need to fight on many levels to break the power of the police—in city councils, state legislatures, the courts, and even Congress—the new world won't come from the halls of power or from changes to the law. No government willingly abolishes its own armed enforcement wing, and we know full well that the police break and remake the law in their own image every day of the week.

But just because we don't control the levers of official power doesn't mean we don't have *real* power. While abolishing the police can seem daunting, we can't forget that for many, it seemed utterly impossible before Minneapolis and the nation rose up to demand change. Radical possibilities are on the table today only thanks to mass rebellion, so we can't let the cop in our heads tell us it's impossible. We move forward by remaining faithful to these struggles, by keeping up the pressure, and by making police abolition common sense, an unstoppable idea whose time has come. This means constant mobilization around *every* case, ensuring footage is public, fighting to know the identities—and home addresses—of killer cops, and demanding the release of their full and unredacted disciplinary records. It means showing up to shame any city officials who stonewall the people's demands for answers, and driving a wedge between mayors (and even police chiefs) and the aspiring fascists at the fraternal orders or police benevolent associations.

It absolutely means encouraging and facilitating leaks and defectors from the blue wall of silence, while remaining cognizant that the goal is to abolish police and their unions, not to legitimize the so-called good apples by picking out the bad. And it means taking advantage of a peculiar Achilles' heel of policing: a white supremacist institution that relies increasingly on officers of color. According to a recent Pew survey, in private, Black officers differ from their white colleagues dramatically when it comes to their positions on racial equality and the legitimacy of movements against police murder.[47] While data shows that Black cops engage in the same brutality on the job, these disagreements can provide a useful wedge for dividing police forces and encouraging fractures and whistleblowers.[48] Policing today needs to tread carefully around this fault line—we should do whatever we can to raise the pressure.

If abolition begins with breaking police power, however, pushing back on police power means prying open new possibilities and allowing these to spiral forth toward an unknown future. It means creating breathing room for over-policed communities to regenerate a lost social fabric and to build real alternatives. It means working to build local alternatives while coordinating to make more ambitious demands, and leveraging moments of heightened struggle to stake out broader ideological and practical claims. It means building ever-expanding liberated territories, free from the police but also free from everyday insecurity, poverty, and violence. It means developing new ways of caring for ourselves and others, new forms of being-together—the reconstitution of a collective alternative that embodies a new world as it makes the world of police obsolete, and indeed impossible to sustain.

This is how we break police power and build a world without police—not through policy papers, lobbying, or legal briefs but by helping communities recognize how much power they already have.

———

The risks of partial abolition point toward a paradox built right into abolitionist struggles. Abolition is a horizon for the total transformation of society, but our struggles only become concrete when they target specific institutions—the death penalty, prisons, the police, immigration enforcement. We cannot avoid taking aim at particular pieces of the massive and expanding carceral apparatus, but to do so is never enough, and immediately invites co-optation: recycling abolitionist energies into support for the status quo and the creation of new targets for abolition in the process. By a sort of perverse dialectics, moreover, our own struggles often serve as a sort of vulnerability test that can make systems of domination more refined, more effective, more impenetrable, and harder to fight in the future.

Writ large, this could even be seen as the central dynamic of US history: the abolition of slavery, the loophole of the Thirteenth

Amendment, convict leasing, the criminalization of Blackness, and mass incarceration. Indeed, the past century has seen at least as much continuity as change. One peculiar institution was replaced with another, and while we must find some progress here—after all, these concessions would not have been granted but for the power of Black freedom struggles—it's also true that every new institution emerges more legitimate than the last. One could oppose slavery but support Jim Crow, just as one could oppose Jim Crow but continue to support the unrestrained policing and mass incarceration of "criminals" today—as even some civil rights leaders do.

Abolishing slavery without abolishing capitalism and whiteness was certainly a perilous endeavor, but this was not the sole reason for its failure. It was also fundamentally a question of alternatives, of building new institutions to underwrite a newly emancipated world of social and economic equality, and a substantive democracy with healthy and educated citizens. The true meaning of full equality and education, and of the demand for forty acres and a mule, was this: that a displaced workforce without self-sufficient alternatives would be easily corralled into a new system of domination. What might have been possible if emancipated slaves were integrated into self-sustaining and democratic communities as equals, rather than abandoned to the whims of landowners and sharecropping? When we set ourselves the task of building alternatives, of building a world without police or prisons, our strategic horizons expand by necessity.

To abolish the police without confronting this deeper structure is to invite a world of white vigilantes and private security guards—glorified slave catchers of late capitalism. Just as we can't abolish the police without abolishing the white power structure, police abolition will fall flat if we don't also dismantle the dungeons they fill or the capitalist inequalities that are their raison d'être. Where there is economic and racial inequality, there will be police. And to abolish police and prisons without confronting racism and patriarchy is to produce communities unworthy of the name, mere facades for continued racial and sexual domination. It seems like a tall order to fight against the entire world all at once while also laying the foundations for a new one. But the reality is that to do the latter is already to do the former. The only antidote to the police is community, community, and more community.

To build community is to make the police unnecessary, irrelevant: obsolete. It is to create sanctuaries for all, where women, children, and the elderly are not abused; where disagreements and mental health crises don't become deadly; where security doesn't mean the exclusion and surveillance of the poorest and most precarious. It is to build educational institutions and care facilities that are expressions of those communities and the equality they embody. And it is to do all of these at once. It means the establishment of liberated territories that are free from police violence because they are free from *all* violence. It means starting from each and every corner and block, but also refusing to be content with that—expanding across neighborhoods and cities and creating support networks that can intervene in ever-broader struggles for territory.

If abolition is all of these things at once, bringing the pieces together in practice is not always easy. During the Oscar Grant rebellions in Oakland over a decade ago, sharp debates emerged among prison abolitionists around the unambiguous community demand to jail Grant's killer—debates that resurface around every wave of rebellion. Does jailing a cop reinforce the punitive solutions offered by the prison-industrial complex, or undermine them? At the time, I was among those insisting that "to send a cop to jail is to support abolition, especially when this results from popular mobilization," that jails weren't built for cops, and that ultimately, "we cannot reach the horizon that is abolition without the bridge of popular action."[49] I still believe the same today. We can't allow the abolitionist horizon to become an abstract moralism that divides struggles from one another and, more importantly, cuts organizers off from communities in struggle. Abolition is a mass struggle or nothing at all.

Moments of mass upsurge throw people into the air, destabilizing even long-held beliefs about what is right and what is possible. How and where they land depends on how well the momentum of rebellion is organized, and whether its participants remain faithful to its lessons—that the state and the police won't save us, that there is no capitalism without racism and the police, and that there is no abolition without community. These are debates to be hashed out within movements: abolition is a road we make by walking it. But while there is no roadmap for abolition, this doesn't mean we don't know which way to walk or how to take our first steps. We know what it means to take care of ourselves and one another. We know how to begin to manage conflict without involving the cops. We know that there are hundreds of organizations across the country chipping away at the carceral society and tugging on the loose threads of the police state. Our first task is to learn from what people are already doing, to connect these disparate experiences, and to weave from them an ever-expanding fabric of community.

This is how the world without police will be born, *is being born*. Weaving the abolitionist horizon from a thousand small acts of revolt and care doesn't mean embracing gradualism, however, but that, in the words of Mariame Kaba, that "we have to act with the urgency of the moment and the patience of a thousand years."

6

Self-Defense and Abolition

The barricades were burning when my plane landed in Caracas. Hundreds of residents, armed with everything from automatic weapons to rickety old shotguns, had built makeshift blockades of burning wood and tires to block all access to the radical neighborhood of 23 de Enero (January 23), in the city's western foothills. Faces shrouded in bandanas and ski masks, they stood in formation to address the media, denouncing a recent police incursion. A few days earlier, a left-wing militant had been killed when the bomb he was planting at the right-wing chamber of commerce preemptively exploded. In response, heavily armed police had stormed this community he called home. Not only was the raid unwelcome—it was unheard of. The year was 2008, and President Hugo Chávez's election a decade earlier had counted on the direct support of these same revolutionary movements. Their support didn't extend to violent and corrupt police, however, and many parts of this neighborhood hadn't seen the police in years.

As the guerrilla struggle of the 1960s wound down, radicals had moved into the barrios ringing Venezuelan cities, which were swelling as many fled the countryside for the oil wealth of the capital city in particular. Sinking their roots deeply into these abandoned zones full of abandoned people, militants contributed to the emergence of new movements that demanded one thing above all: community control. They established assemblies to make local decisions democratically. If the garbage wasn't getting picked up, they hijacked the trucks and did it themselves, and when they wanted secure streets, they started their own armed patrols.¹ As economic crisis hit hard in the 1980s, Caracas became one of the most dangerous cities on earth, and the drug trade flourished. Rather than preventing drug violence, however, police played an active role in it—bringing in the drugs themselves, and brutalizing anyone who stood in their way. Thus, local movements needed to recover their communities not only from drug dealers, but from the police as well.

Bit by bit, neighbors reclaimed this territory as their own, expelling the drug trade and the police in one fell swoop and building local self-defense networks that provided safety *without* the police. One of the best known, the Coordinadora Simón Bolívar, today operates out of a former police station where its members had once been tortured before neighbors got together to drive the cops out. While these organizations are far from perfect—some are fully democratic, some less so—the neighborhoods they protect are far safer for their presence, with neighbors and even children participating in community security as a collective task. I always felt safer living under the watchful eye of these grassroots militias than I ever did in the wealthiest districts of the city, with their checkpoints and private guards, where the rich live as isolated individuals rather than as communities.

Whenever I tried to explain these grassroots militias to friends in the United States, the best comparison was always the Black Panthers who, lest we forget, had "self-defense" in their very name. Indeed, the struggle for Black self-defense from racist vigilantes and the police—from Robert F. Williams and the Deacons for Defense to Malcolm X to the Black Panthers—runs in striking parallel to struggles in Venezuela and elsewhere. Like the Panthers, Venezuelan movements built survival programs to keep their communities safe and strong. Like the Panthers, they denounced their government for covertly flooding poor communities with drugs. And like the Panthers, movements in Venezuela and elsewhere were targeted by a global counterinsurgency program headquartered in Washington, DC. In 2006, I had moved to Caracas from Oakland, the birthplace of the Panthers, to study the history of these movements. Flying back and forth between California and Caracas, however, it became clear to me that these were movements in a single, shared struggle. After all, capitalism is a global system, and the police are its most indispensable foot soldiers—so why wouldn't resistance to that system and those police also occur on a global scale?

Then, on New Year's Day 2009, Oscar Grant was shot dead by police in Oakland, setting off a wave of rebellions that irreversibly transformed the city and the nation. Between moments of open rebellion, a group of comrades known as the Raider Nation Collective turned to examples from Venezuela, Oaxaca, Mexico, and the history of Third World struggles in California. We helped establish the Oakland Assembly, a democratic space that came together weekly to coordinate strategy and tactics while embodying the demand for community control against the police. In the process, we learned how profoundly similar these struggles were. Poor people everywhere—suffering the brunt of global white supremacy, poverty, segregation, and the police oppression that these invariably bring—were finally standing up collectively and saying, in the words of Mexico's Zapatista rebels, "*¡Ya Basta!*" Enough!

The demand for community control knows no borders, and it is from such basic demands for community self-defense that ambitious experiments in police abolition have emerged worldwide, providing important lessons for those of us in the US as well.

—

When challenged in June 2020 about what defunding the police would look like in practice, congresswoman Alexandria Ocasio-Cortez replied, "It looks like a suburb." Her point was clear: wealthy neighborhoods are safe not because they are heavily policed, but because they are well funded, and therefore, resources can be shifted away from policing and toward education without sacrificing community safety. By giving Middle America a ready-made image of community without the overwhelming presence of the police, comparing defunding to the suburbs can make it seem like a less frightening prospect. But this kind of rhetorical strategy for smuggling defunding into mainstream consciousness through the back door risks further naturalizing the very world that the police uphold. It tacitly upholds the myth that the police protect the community by preventing violent crime. It reinforces a model of false scarcity in which we must choose to fund either the schools or the police. And more than anything, it neglects the underlying fact that, rather than a solution to the problem of policing, the suburbs *are* the problem—because, historically speaking, the suburbs and the police are fundamentally inseparable.

As historian Jacquelyn Dowd Hall has demonstrated, the "long civil rights movement" was the product of not one great migration but two, as Black Southerners trudged northward and white urbanites fled to the suburbs. Not only did suburbanization fuel what would become the petty conservativism of small property owners, but it did so by reproducing the segregation many had sought to escape—generating a "long backlash" that predated even the civil rights movement proper.[2] In the North as in the South, this segregation was—as in Frantz Fanon's description of a colonial world cut in two—upheld "by the police and the military . . . by rifle butts and napalm," a description that rings as true in Chicago and Philadelphia as it did in Algeria and Soweto.[3] In their original form, the American suburbs were therefore born of those who fled toward the police rather than away from them, territories carved out *by* the police whose function was to uphold their segregated boundaries and maintain their borders.

For sociologist Tamara Nopper, Ocasio-Cortez's appeal to the suburbs as a metaphor risks cutting abolition off at the knees, glorifying white segregation, and reducing the call to defund the police to a budget shuffle—social democracy with the police, as it were. Abolition, Nopper rightly insists, "is not a suburb," and rather than choose between earmarking resources for schools or police, the abolitionist demand is to "*never* fund the police, regardless of the budget."⁴ Strategically, too, this misdiagnosis of the problem becomes a liability, especially on a global level. The suburban metaphor might be a useful ploy to argue for redistribution, but it will never furnish a political force capable of demanding abolition, much less of making it a reality. White, middle-class, suburban Americans would be the last to support police abolition, lest the imaginary urban rabble soon appear on their well-manicured doorsteps. In fact, it is revealing that the "suburbs" only enter history as a radical force where they stand for exactly the opposite: as in Ferguson, where the poor were pushed from the city to impoverished suburban areas, or in the French banlieue, which shares more with the semi-urban Venezuelan barrio than with the suburbs in the classically American sense.⁵

The same goes for the colonial enclaves of the global suburbs and the global police that patrol their boundaries. Liberation doesn't come from above, from the rich or the powerful in their privileged citadels; it comes from the direct struggles of the wretched of the earth, those promised little but given even less. It comes from those on whose shoulders the entirety of the system rests, and who simply need to rise up to shake it off. It comes from turning neglect into revolt and liberation—demanding not *more* policing but *less*, in proportion to the establishment of grassroots alternatives to secure the streets, mediate conflict, and weave more tightly the threads of community. Globally, as we will see, movements for abolition grow not from comfort and privilege but from poverty, insecurity, devastation, and war—not from the suburbs but from the burning barricades and armed self-defense movements of Caracas and elsewhere.

—

Like all abusers, the police claim to protect their victims. We are told that those communities that suffer the most, and where the police do their worst, are the same communities where police are most needed. By virtue of the direness of their circumstances—the poverty and everyday violence they experience—abolition is simply too risky, a luxury too costly for the most vulnerable. There is a kernel of truth here: capitalism abandons poor communities of color to radical vulnerability and early death—what Ruth Wilson Gilmore calls "organized abandonment." But it is precisely these same vulnerabilities that the police themselves prey upon—targeting, stalking, sexually assaulting, and murdering the vulnerable with impunity because, from the perspective of the system, they don't matter.

The idea that the police protect the vulnerable—poor communities of color, those struggling with mental health crises, women, queer and trans people—and, moreover, that there's nothing the vulnerable can do to break the cycle of abuse, is a patent lie. And it is this lie more than any other that collapses once we look at policing, and police abolition, in global context. The most ambitious experiments in police abolition have emerged not from wealthy areas where safety is taken for granted, but from some of the most dangerous patches of earth—where communities at a breaking point have turned to radical alternatives. In war zones, revolutions, or the carnage of the drug war, from the manufactured disaster of neoliberalism, or amid the apparently natural wreckage of earthquakes, hurricanes, and floods, communities in struggle give us powerful examples of how to rethink our collective security from the bottom up, without the police as we know them.

This was certainly true in Northern Ireland's long war against British colonialism and South Africa's struggle to overthrow the apartheid regime. When British-backed police withdrew from heavily Catholic neighborhoods in occupied Northern Ireland in the 1970s, the security of residents initially fell to the Irish Republican Army (IRA). In the words of one local resident, the police "are not there to help. In this area police are not people that you normally go to. I mean, to walk out and stop them in the street, they would laugh at you . . . they don't have any contact with this community whatsoever."[6] As an underground combat organization, however, the IRA was ill-suited to providing basic community justice, and often opted for kneecapping and other punitive measures to deter drug dealing and sexual assault. As a result, in the 1990s, organizers and researchers convinced the IRA and its political front, Sinn Féin, to abandon punitive justice in favor of what are called community restorative justice centers.

Often staffed by former militants, CRJ centers refused to work with the police—who at the time were only 8 percent Catholic. Instead, they brought all parties involved in a particular conflict together for a mediated resolution. Over the course of more than two decades, CRJ centers have responded to 25,000 cases involving nearly 100,000 people, closing over 90 percent of those cases.[7] Under pressure from London, however, in 2007 Sinn Féin reversed course, embracing collaboration with the police and accepting positions on policing boards, prompting some high-ranking members to resign in disgust. No longer independent of the police, CRJ centers have become a palliative rather than a true alternative, and as in the United States, talk of reform today centers not on transforming the function of the police but improving their image and diversifying recruitment of underrepresented minorities, Catholics in this case.

A similar experiment emerged in South Africa, where apartheid police represented an enemy regime and provided little in the way of security in poor townships. In the 1960s and '70s, community courts known as *makgotla*, though periodically outlawed, were called upon to resolve local conflicts. These courts tended to be controlled by older and more conservative community members, however, and verdicts were often punitive. But in the 1980s, younger anti-apartheid activists reinvigorated the *makgotla*, creating new people's courts and street committees that "took over the functions of local government, especially in ungovernable areas." In areas governed by the committees, "the distinction between the people and their organizations disappeared. All the people young and old participated in committees from street level upwards."[8] By the end of apartheid, 400 street committees were operating as an effective alternative to the police, mediating and resolving conflict within and between communities.

Punitive measures were not fully abolished, but the overarching goal of the committees and courts was to reintegrate perpetrators into a collective revolutionary struggle, and so rather than simply uphold tradition, "people's courts took action against elders, and against men on behalf of women."[9] As with Northern Ireland, however, the committees faced the same fate as many other institutions of popular power when the state gets involved. While the African National Congress saw the committees as useful weapons against apartheid, they often viewed grassroots protest as either threatening to "rock the boat" of a negotiated settlement or as a useful resource that could be "turned on and off like a tap."[10] And once the ANC came to power, their directly democratic structure became a liability: many popular organizations were dismantled in 1994, and most remaining committees have since been incorporated into a system that has scarcely changed. The lesson is clear: wherever popular struggles recede to accommodate the capitalist state, the police return with a vengeance.

More recently, amid the carnage of the Syrian Civil War that began in 2011, the heavily Kurdish autonomous region of Rojava has seen similar experiments in building communities from the bottom up without the police. From a Turkish prison, Abdullah Öcalan, founding head of the Kurdistan Workers' Party (PKK), developed an ideology, now known as democratic confederalism, rooted in direct democracy, community autonomy, and feminist principles. In terms of local security, this has meant maintaining a strict division between the Asayish (Internal Security Forces) and community-based Civil Defense Forces (HPC). According to Kurdish scholar Hawzhin Azeez:

It is always the HPC that protects a neighborhood, never the Asayish ... Through this alternative method, the possibility of instituting hierarchies of power and authority are considerably reduced. The people are protecting themselves. Security forces protect those who they live with and interact with daily in the neighborhood. This proximity ensures that violations occur only rarely. When they do occur, the neighborhood communes immediately activate community mechanisms of justice, honor and restoration.

The HPC are required to be at least 40 percent women, although the number tends to be higher in practice, including even many older women. With "the matriarchs of a neighborhood stand[ing] confidently at street corners wielding AK-47 rifles for the people's protection," there is no need for police. For abolitionists in the United States, Azeez argues, Rojava provides a hopeful example of what is possible: "Although our chains may appear different, Kurds and Black Americans ultimately face the same oppressive system that continues to kill us and impose countless forms of violence upon us. With Rojava, we are trying to show that an alternative world is possible."[11]

These experiences may seem a world away from our concerns. After all, most of this book—like many US-based abolitionist movements—has focused on the historical contours of policing and anti-Black racism in the United States. And yet, these experiments share more than we might think with struggles for community control closer to home. Of course, not all police function exactly the same, but capitalism is nothing if not a global system, and private property its precondition. Where labor is extracted as profit and accumulates as capital, you will find police to protect that accumulated wealth and attend to the divisions of labor that create it. And in a global capitalist system born of colonialism and chattel slavery, the police uphold and reproduce the rule of whiteness as well. While police in the global South tend to be poorer and rulers tend to govern more through abandonment and neglect, the US experience shows that this is the ultimate tendency of *all* policing. In rich countries, the police simply clamor for more resources for themselves, while politicians earmark millions for flashy reform efforts. And for the most part, even poor police are still police—if anything, low salaries stoke corruption and abuse.

In fact, the abusive blackmail of police protection originates in a deeper lie that provided the backbone for the colonial system: that colonized people were incapable of governing themselves, and that they consequently *needed* colonial rule. If policing enforces territorial segregation along racial lines to ensure the easy extraction of labor and resources, it isn't much of a stretch to view colonialism as a form of policing. And policing—from upholding segregation to facilitating gentrification—is undeniably colonial to its very core. Police forces in the US and the UK drew recruits and inspiration from colonial occupations in Ireland, Haiti, Texas, Nicaragua, and the Philippines. Moreover, the colonial constabularies they left in place were often taken over directly in the service of settler colonial domination. The case of Israel is particularly instructive here: Israeli police were modeled on Britain's colonial Palestine Police Force, which itself drew heavily from the Royal Irish Constabulary, veterans of which would be deeply embedded in counterinsurgency worldwide.[12]

Little surprise, then, that the US invasion of Vietnam was described by its perpetrators as a "police action," or that Black and Chicano militants of the 1960s began to understand their communities—oppressed, exploited, excluded from democratic rights, and segregated—as an internal colony and therefore as part of a broader international, anti-colonial revolutionary movement. Or that US interventions in Latin America today fly under the cover of regional policing strategies—like Plan Colombia and the Mérida Initiative—while pouring millions into strengthening domestic police forces that torture and kill with impunity. And little surprise that those on the receiving end of carpet-bombing or drug eradication campaigns rarely buy the narrative that this is all being done for their own good. For many in the global South, there is no illusion that either the global imperial police or their brutal local surrogates are truly there for the benefit of the community. From the 2005 riots against policing in the heavily Arab and North African banlieues outside Paris, to the policing of the southern US border, global North and South are far from separate spheres; they are interlocking realities marked by colonialism, segregation, racial discrimination, migration, and deportation.

Policing is global—and so is resistance.

—

Latin America has a long history of filling the space left by neoliberal abandonment with organized communities, and grassroots social movements were the overlooked motor force behind the region's wave of progressive governments known as the Pink Tide. The economic crisis of the 1980s unleashed neoliberal reforms and austerity, which in turn provoked more crisis. By both accident and design, force and fraud, the neoliberal ideal of a "minimal state" became a reality across the continent. But while public services and education were decimated, the same couldn't be said for cops, who became even more indispensable for wealthy Latin American elites. Policing strategies instead shifted toward the cheaper but even more heavy-handed approach known as *mano dura*, in which entire populations were targeted for repression and poor communities sealed off by police checkpoints and left to fend for themselves.

As a result, the 1990s were marked by a wave of self-organized experiments across the region: building roads and housing, digging wells and managing water access, and developing community sporting and cultural events. In every poor neighborhood racked by neoliberal austerity, moreover, safety was a central concern. This was as true in Mexico as it had been in Venezuela, although as elsewhere, the roots of community self-defense ran far deeper, going back to the guerrilla struggles of the 1960s and beyond. But during the "lost decade" of the 1980s, as the Mexican state withdrew from even its most basic functions—security included—grassroots movements stepped in to fill the vacuum. When a massive earthquake decimated the capital in 1985, it shook the very foundations of one-party rule by the Institutional Revolutionary Party (PRI) as well, revealing the craven neglect of a corrupt ruling class. As the wreckage of the earthquake piled on top of the wreckage of neoliberalism, a powerful new wave of community movements emerged with equally seismic effects, to fashion a future from the ruins.

On New Year's Day 1994, armed Zapatista rebels stormed into San Cristóbal de las Casas in southern Chiapas state, seizing the police station and emptying the local jail before retreating into the jungle. There, they have since established a massive self-governed territory without any police at all. In Zapatista territory, security patrols are popularly elected and recallable—they are unpaid and wear no uniforms to distinguish them from those they serve. Zapatista principles of justice are famously reparative and restorative, revealing in concrete practice the fundamental absurdity of our own punitive system. If a murderer is locked up for life, then it is not one but *two* families that have lost a way to support themselves, since "the guilty just rest all day in jail and gain weight, but their families are the ones who have to work the cornfield and figure out how to survive."[13] Perpetrators, who after all are still members of the community, must instead do double labor under Zapatista law—supporting their own family as well as the family they have harmed.

However, the Zapatistas represent only one part of a broader patchwork of Mexican experiments in armed self-defense and community security. For instance, rescue and cleanup efforts after the 1985 earthquake spawned a distinct wave of urban social movements. In the shadow of the Xaltepec volcano in the eastern part of Mexico City, 500 families took over an empty terrain known popularly—and prophetically—as La Polvorilla

(Spitfire), where they have since built a collectively managed community from the ground up. The families were members of the Francisco Villa Popular Front, a militant organization representing those left homeless and displaced with all the audacity of its namesake: revolutionary leader Pancho Villa. Today, La Polvorilla represents "an alternative order" to the *dis*order reigning across much of the Mexico City megalopolis, an "oasis amid a desert of poverty and gray houses."[14] Entry is limited, with checkpoints staffed by local women. Gardens and homes are well kept, cars drive slowly as children play in the streets, and the walls bear announcements for local events and workshops.

For César Enrique Pineda, a sociologist at the Universidád Nacional Autónoma de México, this is a *community*, in contrast to what so often goes by the name:

> While you might not find opulence in this self-organized neighborhood, perhaps you will be able to find another kind of wealth, one based on cooperation, collaboration, reciprocity, and the organization of the poorest who have been able to build a new community from nothing, making decisions by assembly, with its own radio station and internal security system, its collective vegetable gardens and common spaces built in a largely self-managed way, all in the middle of a precarious marginalized slum.[15]

The police have no place here, because there is no *need* for them—they have been displaced and rendered obsolete by the fabric of the community itself. In the words of Rosario Hernández, one of the many women working the gates, "We don't have any confidence in them, so we take care of security ourselves." Whether it's a conflict between community members, domestic violence, or a robbery—a rarity these days, unlike those areas beyond the walls—an elected vigilance committee resolves the dispute. La Polvorilla's feminist praxis goes beyond addressing gendered violence, moreover: Hernández insists that her participation in community organizing has helped her overcome her own internalized patriarchal limits, and to become a "total woman" in the process.[16]

In 2006, police attacked a sprawling occupation that striking teachers had set up around the sprawling zocalo at the center of Oaxaca City, in southwestern Mexico. The attack galvanized mass resistance, giving birth to what many would come to call the Oaxaca Commune. Thousands of barricades went up, and the entire city was taken over, with the directly democratic Popular Assembly of the Peoples of Oaxaca (APPO) serving as its de facto government. Assuming political control of the city meant keeping people safe, so residents created the Honorable Cuerpo de Topiles. Named for the sticks carried by its deputies, this was "a group of civilians appointed by communal authority to enforce APPO resolutions, modeled on indigenous traditions of community policing." "Neighbors and merchants organized block committees and patrols," and the very same barricades built out of an urgent need to protect the community from repression also created a permanent network of relay points for political discussion, debate, and the further consolidation of communal bonds.[17] For nearly six months, "there were no police in Oaxaca City."[18]

It was in part to distract attention from this revolt in Oaxaca that the newly inaugurated president, Felipe Calderón, declared an ill-fated 'war' on narcotraffickers in December 2006. If anything, the narcos had a better record of defending and financially supporting local communities than the government did, even earning the nickname *los valientes* in some cases. But this is hardly a testament to the benevolence of the cartels; that same government was busy destroying communities and displacing their inhabitants under the guise of US-sponsored eradication campaigns, all while turning a blind eye to the main players in the drug game. Regardless, those days are long gone. In the end, narco-capitalism is still capitalism, and no matter who's in charge it's still poor, heavily Indigenous communities that bear the brunt of its costs.[19] The result of Calderón's war has been predictably horrendous: more than 120,000 dead and many more disappeared, as cartels battle one another and the Mexican state for control of lucrative markets and transit routes.

Amid and increasingly *against* this carnage, however, new experiments in grassroots power have materialized. In the 1990s, a police massacre in Guerrero state, just up the Pacific coast from Oaxaca, led to the creation of what are called, somewhat misleadingly, "community police." In reality, the local grassroots vigilance networks that coalesced as the Regional Coordinator of Community Authorities (CRAC) were part of a broader system of alternative justice grounded in Indigenous law and principles. Its elected coordinators prioritize reconciliation among all parties involved, and offenders participate in "reeducation" or rotating community service among nearby towns. Even the "police"—if you can call them that—are elected from their own communities and are unpaid, calling upon grassroots knowledge to ensure local security. In reality, community members empowered to safeguard their *own* streets have nothing in common with armed professionals sent in from afar to protect property and privilege. The CRAC, which quickly spread to more than a hundred local communities, "was able to significantly reduce local violence and insecurity . . . demonstrating the possibility of addressing crime, confronting insecurity, and working for peace when the force of a community and its cultural identities are mobilized to weave the social fabric."[20]

Further north in Cherán, a municipality in Michoacán state, a 2011 dispute with narcos over illegal logging led the largely Purépecha Indigenous community to rise up, chasing the loggers out with sticks and fireworks before replacing the local police and government entirely. According to the anthropologist Gilberto López y Rivas, Cherán's new government and security force has since reinvigorated and transformed traditional Indigenous principles: "There has been a renovation of neighborhood organizing, mutual aid (*Jarhojperakua*) and collective work [*tequio*]; the collective fire (*Parhangua*) has becomes an extension of the kitchen on the communal barricades; and patrols [*la ronda*] by community members themselves, mostly the youth, have become an effective form of territorial defense and citizen security."[21] While the Mexican government has sought to divide-and-conquer the CRAC, persecuting its more radical elements, Chéran has taken advantage of what little legal protections exist for Indigenous autonomy to establish a sort of détente with the state, staving off government aggression while avoiding many of the pitfalls of state incorporation. A microcosm of a world without police, Chéran remains today an "oasis of hope," as a BBC report put it, "its peace and security a stark contrast to the fear that still dominates neighboring communities," despite—or often due to—the police.[22]

As the catastrophic violence of the drug war reached its apex, the most devastating symbol of which was the 2014 disappearance in Iguala, Guerrero, of forty-three student teachers from the Ayotzinapa Rural Teachers' College, more Mexican communities would be pushed to the brink. This was the case most spectacularly in the Tierra Caliente region of Michoacán, not far from Chéran. There, entire towns fed up with extortion and violence took up arms and drove the brutal Knights Templar cartel out of broad swaths of the state—doing in mere weeks what the entire force of the Mexican state couldn't accomplish over eight years of counterinsurgent warfare. Membership in these *autodefensas* quickly surged to 20,000, but it was never clear whether they represented poor communities or the local landholders who supplied most of their weapons. Lacking the solid anchor of Indigenous tradition like Cherán, the autodefensas were politically vulnerable from the outset. When the state pressured participants to join the official state police or lay down their arms, the movement fractured, and those who tried to chart a more radical course were jailed.

All across Mexico, communities have—by will or out of urgent necessity—taken security and justice into their own collective hands. But while Indigenous customary law, understood across much of Latin America under the heading of *usos y costumbres*, is often based on restorative principles, it isn't always egalitarian, and it can reinforce hierarchies of age and gender. Moreover, customary law and popular justice have been linked to a spate of mob lynchings in Mexico as elsewhere, most famously in 2004 when two undercover police were burned alive in San Juan Ixtayopan, on the southwestern outskirts of Mexico City, after neighbors observed them taking photos of children. While the connection between Indigenous tradition and mob violence is often mobilized by the racist right and has been used to discredit progressive president Andrés Manuel López Obrador, it nevertheless raises important challenges for the left across the region and beyond.

For the Uruguayan intellectual Raúl Zibechi, the experience of El Alto, Bolivia, offers not only inspiration but also some important caveats about Indigenous democracy and community self-defense. Here, perched above La Paz at 13,000 feet, a million heavily Indigenous Bolivians persist at the intersection of abandonment and tradition. Since "the police do not exist or are an accomplice to the thieves, rapists, and those who attack the residents, and state justice is a bad joke," local residents have turned to traditional councils to resolve local conflicts. But community reactions to "extreme conditions of state abandonment" often take the more immediate and brutal form of mob justice in the streets, in the beating and even lynching of thieves—or those wrongly identified as such.

For Indigenous feminist Silvia Rivera Cusicanqui, however, community justice and mob violence could not be more different. The spate of lynchings, she argues, is a direct reaction to and cathartic expression of neoliberal powerlessness. Community justice, by contrast, is "a form of reintegrating the person who had violated the rules. On a third offense, they can kill you . . . But there is always a long, considered, and deep period of deliberation. The decision is not taken in the heat of anger. The defendant is allowed to speak; everyone has their say, and that is community justice."[23]

The power of community, in short, is an *organized* power.

—

Straddling the artificial dividing line between First and Third Worlds in the still-colonized territory of Puerto Rico, a century-long denial of self-determination has given rise to what University of Texas professor Marisol LeBrón has described as a form of "punitive governance" that relies increasingly on the policing of life and death. Here, policing is quite literally a colonial project, but one that is never fully victorious, and LeBrón has documented the stubborn persistence of "alternative understandings of justice, safety and accountability," efforts to "imagine new ways of living" by forging "local solutions to violence that decenter policing."[24]

The town of Loíza, LeBrón notes, was a former destination for the slave trade and today remains "synonymous with Blackness." It has seen some of the worst police brutality on the island, at the same time that a "near-constant police presence" has done little to make communities safer, leading local residents to develop alternatives.[25] In 2012, a local feminist organization called Taller Salud adapted what is known as the Cure Violence model in an attempt to build what LeBrón calls "security from below." First developed in Chicago in the 1990s, Cure Violence takes an epidemiological approach to community violence—as a disease to be cured—training community members to "interrupt" conflicts before they become deadly. In Loíza, this took the form of interventions that were explicitly feminist, and not only for their restorative nature. Taller Salud taught participants how violence between young men was also gendered violence, and that ultimately, "women will never feel safe if the territorial battles between young men in the community are allowed to continue claiming lives."[26]

By intervening in community disputes, Cure Violence mediators were able to empower local activists and dramatically reduce violence over the course of several years. But the program's shortcomings are just as important as its accomplishments. Cure Violence—with its reliance on metaphors of disease and targeting of "high risk" individuals and communities— threatens to distract from the social inequality that drives violence while pathologizing those same communities already subject to colonial domination—seeing the community as the disease rather than the cure. This danger seems to have been confirmed in the most obvious of ways: US occupiers have deployed the Cure Violence model as part of imperial pacification campaigns in Iraq and Syria—evidence that even restorative justice can play handmaiden to a global police state if not supplemented with genuine grassroots power. In the end, the Cure Violence model in Loíza collided with the fiscal and political contradictions of alternatives to policing that rely on state support. Amid the 2014 Puerto Rican financial crisis, funding for the intervention program in Loíza was cut. But if financial disaster revealed the weakness of the Cure Violence model, a different kind of disaster soon revealed other possibilities.

In Nicaragua, a 1972 earthquake set into motion the long march of the Sandinista Revolution; the 1985 temblor in Mexico spawned a wave of community organizing; and the devastation of New Orleans by Hurricane Katrina inspired the creation of organizations like the Common Ground Collective, which rescued people from the storm, patrolled communities, and even engaged in armed standoffs with roving white vigilantes.[27] In Puerto Rico, it was Hurricane Maria in 2017 that revealed the utter ineptitude of the local government while reinforcing the idea that "only the people will save the people." When the state fails, people often step up to establish grassroots mutual aid and self-defense networks—what LeBrón revealingly calls "survival programs," echoing the Black Panthers.[28] In *The Shock Doctrine*, Naomi Klein rightly warns that natural disasters provide dangerous shocks that well-prepared right-wing forces can leverage to advance a radical neoliberal agenda.²⁹ This dynamic is undeniable: if the police withdrew after Katrina, they returned with a vengeance in its aftermath as the foot soldiers of a post-disaster land grab that can only be understood as ethnic cleansing. In the end, New Orleans lost 100,000 Black residents and the public school system was gutted.

But when all that is solid melts into air, new possibilities can also emerge in the form of the stubbornly resilient fabric of community. From the beginning, the state has been a kind of organized blackmail: without it, we are told over and over again, things would be so much worse. Every outburst of violence, every act of human cruelty, serves to bolster the otherwise-absurd argument that we need far crueler a power to keep us in line. This blackmail is doubly true for the police, the curators of that organized cruelty. As with the state, however, the question is always this: How bad do things need to get before the argument breaks down and we see policing for what it is? Before we realize that the "protection" offered is illusory, and far less than the devastation wrought? Sometimes, when the state withdraws or collapses, the promised catastrophe fails to materialize.

While we don't wish for disaster, the simple fact is that racial capitalism—and the policing it inevitably brings—is the real disaster. It is this perpetual, slow-moving catastrophe, what historian Gerald Horne deems the "apocalypse of settler colonialism," that determines who lives and dies every day, and this is only more true when a storm hits.³⁰ Real demands for police abolition often emerge from the depths of disaster and catastrophe, from those communities all too intimately familiar with both the danger of social violence and the equally dangerous devil's bargain of policing. If South Africa and Northern Ireland can develop alternatives to the police amid armed struggle and revolution, if Puerto Ricans can do so during and after a hurricane, if Mexicans living through the automatic cross fire of a drug war with no end can turn to the organized community as an alternative, then we can too. The difference isn't danger or insecurity, and it isn't that police in the United States provide safety and security—they don't.

It's that extreme circumstances can tear away the mythical veil of policing and force people to see what was already in front of their faces: that the police don't protect us. Only we protect us.

—

More than a half century ago, James Baldwin famously described Harlem as "occupied territory" where every rooftop was suspected of harboring a treacherous "guerrilla outpost"—think of the militarized occupation of Ferguson. In occupied territory, Baldwin wrote, "any act of resistance, even though it be executed by a child" provokes a response from "the full weight of the occupying forces"—think of Aiyana Stanley-Jones, or Tamir Rice. Communities of color, and Black communities in particular, have always been subject to the brutal military force ostensibly reserved for the colonized, and have always been deprived of due process and the right to self-defense, because they are insurgents by definition. "Occupied territory is occupied territory," Baldwin wrote, "even though it be found in that New World which the Europeans conquered."[31]

For wealthier and whiter communities, and the suburbs in particular, the line between the military and the police is stark: they have never seen occupation and will never know what it feels like to be labeled an insurgent. But for the rest, this line is as elusive as it is illusory. In moments of calm, the police act like police, which is to say they harass, belittle, stop and frisk, and often resort to the kind of brutal individual discretion that is the divine right of occupation. When things get out of hand—too much humanity, too much dignity, too much faith in rights— things shift unpredictably and dramatically: the police become soldiers, and when that isn't enough, they call in the National Guard.

This is a global reality. From Northern Ireland to South Africa, across Latin America and beyond, capitalist exploitation, colonial occupation, and white supremacist rule terrorize local populations, forcing communities to seek out radical alternatives that can provide an everyday level of security the occupier never will. In fact, the poorer communities get, the more obviously the police are reduced to their fundamental role. With no surplus funding for community barbecues and basketball tournaments, cops do the bare minimum required: protecting property, whiteness, and colonial, capitalist power.

Between the British armored vehicle used to brutalize Irish nationalists during the "troubles" (nicknamed the Humber Pig) and the mine-resistant Casspir designed to patrol South African townships, the differences are cosmetic. But so too the differences between these and the armored vehicles deployed by Bull Connor in Birmingham, Alabama, by the Missouri National Guard in Ferguson, by local, county, state, federal, and private forces at Standing Rock, or the MRAP (mine-resistant ambush protected) vehicle that rolled through my neighborhood of West Philadelphia during the George Floyd rebellions, tear-gassing my neighbors in their own homes. But if the line between the police and the military, between domestic white supremacy and global imperialism, is illusory, this also points toward the task of stitching together broader solidarities in a broader fabric of struggle against the global police state.

As with all abolition, however, to be against the police is to be *for* a very different kind of community and world. Poverty, inequality, and violence so often go hand in hand for a reason. Organizers in Venezuela, for example, knew that it wasn't enough to simply expel the police if they didn't also work to rebuild their communities on new, collective foundations. Spontaneous grassroots assemblies provided the model for the establishment, in 2006, of communal councils—neighborhood organs of directly democratic participation that interfaced with the Chávez government to fund local development projects and build an alternative, socialist economy. In 2009, this project became more ambitious still with the establishment of larger units called "communes" that brought the communal councils together with socialist producers in an expansive and democratically managed socialist project. Moreover, these organized communities do more than simply provide local security: strong collective structures have become central to defending Venezuelan socialism from infiltration by Colombian paramilitaries and global imperial aggression from the United States.

It may seem strange to some to speak of police abolition and armed self-defense in the same breath, but this is exactly the point. Especially as abolitionist discourse enters the political mainstream, we need to be clear that just as abolition is not a suburb, nor is it an abstract ethical critique of violence or a purely prefigurative gesture—building the new world *without* fighting the old. Abolition is a material struggle, one that entails destroying the old *and* building the new. And for those most vulnerable to the many interlocking violences of our world, this means securing the community in order to rebuild it. This doesn't mean the police, of course: self-defense by and for the community has nothing at all in common with those professional armed outsiders sent by the state. It's about new, community institutions born of the struggle against policing.

When London's Metropolitan Police targeted the Mangrove restaurant in 1970, these racist attacks only cemented the space's importance as a center for Black organizing. In the words of the Trinidadian radical Darcus Howe, recently dramatized in Steve McQueen's film about the Mangrove Nine trial: "In defending themselves against attack a community is born, and wherever a community is born it creates institutions that it needs." Of course, we should always remain alert to how community alternatives can reproduce carceral logics, but these logics emerge most clearly through collaboration with the state. If we can't abolish the police without building alternatives, the opposite is true as well. And for those communities most besieged globally, there can be no abolition without self-defense.

Seen from an international perspective, police abolition becomes even more urgent and the constituency of abolitionist struggles even larger. But the global imbrication of policing with imperialism and counterinsurgency poses challenges for abolitionists as well. When Venezuela sought to "humanize" policing, it soon became clear that even as part of a revolutionary project, reforming the police under capitalism remains an elusive if not impossible task. Moreover, when the government purged police forces of corrupt and violent officers, they simply joined the organized crime networks with which they had already become enmeshed. This challenge becomes even more daunting in countries like Colombia and Mexico, where US-backed counterinsurgency wars created a reservoir of hundreds of thousands of available mercenaries—trained killers walking the streets in search of work suited to their particular brutal skillset.

Most infamously, the Mexican cartel known as the Zetas was formed when dozens of elite soldiers defected from the Mexican military to join the Gulf Cartel. Their tactics, learned from Israeli and US special forces (one-third of the original Zetas were trained at the infamous School of the Americas in Fort Benning, Georgia) have led to a reciprocal escalation of carnage on all sides of the drug war. As we have seen, the problem of violence workers goes beyond the police, and even if the police were to be abolished, professional violence workers won't simply disappear. But the solution to both is, once again, stronger communities. The struggle for community control against the police is a global struggle that seeks to establish ever-expanding liberated territories, insurgent zones where occupiers—domestic or imperial—dare not set foot without always glancing fearfully toward the rooftops.

What would this global solidarity against the police look like? How would it remain faithful to the amplitude of the George

Floyd revolt, in which police chiefs—like statues to slave traders and colonizers—began to fall like dominoes? How to demand not only an end to the police as a specific institution, but to the global white supremacist, capitalist order that sees police as its only line of defense? It looks like radical organizers from Cooperation Jackson who, in their attempt to build a communal economy in Mississippi, looked consciously to Venezuela's communes, alongside other experiments in grassroots democracy. Of course, this entailed confronting police power, through the proposed establishment of a "police control board," elected by the people with the "right to monitor, subpoena, and indict police officers for gross misconduct."[32] Or inversely, it looks like Afro-Venezuelan organizers who put this global solidarity into practice when former NYPD commissioner and "broken windows" guru Bill Bratton was invited to Caracas to advise the historically brutal Metropolitan Police—graffiti reading "Bratton go home" quickly appeared, and amid an overall atmosphere of grassroots resistance, Bratton beat a hasty retreat.

Police abolition is a global task, in part because the police are synonymous with the white supremacy that has always sought to divide the poor and legitimize their oppression in the name of capitalist accumulation on a world scale. If the self-defense movements that we have seen in Mexico, Venezuela, and elsewhere share many of their objectives with the Black Panther Party, we would do well to embrace the Panthers' radically expansive, transnational vision of struggle as well. As the New York City Panther 21 put it in a 1971 open letter to the Weather Underground: "We don't accept the pig's boundaries—thus when we talk of an American revolution—we are speaking of America—north, south, and Latin—ALL of America."

And all of the world, in fact.

7

Abolish ICE, Abolish the Border

Rigoberto Ortiz's bones were found on the Barry Goldwater bombing range, alongside those of his cousin, Carmelo. They weren't the first to lose their lives faltering deliriously across this barren stretch of desert, their skin cold and clammy under a raging sun, and they would be far from the last. A massive swath stretching seventy miles eastward from Yuma, the Goldwater range spans nearly a third of the state of Arizona. It's a poetic injustice, to say the least, that Rigoberto and Carmelo would take their last, hurried breaths on O'odham Indigenous land, later Mexico, now named for an arch-nativist and father of the "law and order" politics that came to criminalize this border and its inhabitants. If the desert is a trap, the Goldwater range is even more treacherous. It's nearly impossible to travel north without crossing it, and many only reach it after they have been on their feet for a week. They are invariably running low on water—it's physically impossible to carry enough to make the trip safely—but the federal government bars access to the aid workers who would provide it or, failing that, search for remains. Many a disoriented migrant has likely stumbled upon a more surreal scene still: one of several mockups of Iraqi villages designed like movie sets to be strafed by military aircraft from the air.

Rigoberto's brother, Ely Ortiz, lost cell phone contact with the pair as they crossed the border. "Their guide [*coyote*] abandoned them," he recounted. "I asked immigration for help and they refused. I asked the consulate for help and they refused. I asked the police for help and they refused too." Days later, Ortiz got an unexpected call from his own home state of Oaxaca. The voice on the other end of the line was a migrant from the larger group that had left the two behind. After being detained by Border Patrol, the caller said, he alerted agents to Rigoberto and Carmelo's location. Border Patrol helicopters scanned the area a couple of times before deporting the man back to Mexico. "I think my brother was still alive," Ortiz said. "They could have sent people to look on foot. I think if they would have looked, they would have found him alive."[1] With no other option, he got some friends together and went to search himself.

It would be nearly five months before they found Rigoberto and Carmelo, or what was left of them.

> When I walked to where the bodies were, one of the young men went ahead and said, "Don't look at them." I said, "I'm psychologically prepared for how I'll find them." But I never imagined in that moment seeing them that way. It was really traumatic for me to see the condition my brother was in, to see the condition my cousin was in, and to smell the smell in that moment, in the middle of nowhere. A million things came to my head. I started to think about his last moments, the desperation he was experiencing, that he needed water, that he shouted for water. How his body was fading, how the animals had eaten him, seeing where my brother had died.[2]

It was there and at that moment that the Águilas del Desierto—the Desert Eagles—were born of Ely Ortiz's grief. The Águilas answer calls from families of migrants, sometimes even those crossing themselves, using Google Earth to narrow down a search area before trekking out into the unforgiving heat to do the impossible. Before every search, Ortiz pauses briefly, praying to a picture of his brother Rigoberto.

Ricardo Esquivias, a volunteer with the Águilas, penned a corrido dedicated to the organization's founders and the loved ones they have lost:

Today I say goodbye to family and to friends
I'm going to the other side to change my destiny
I go disillusioned, my money isn't enough
I feel marginalized, I'm going there with *La Raza*.
Today I will try at Altar, since there's no surveillance there
and I already feel my longing to arrive in Arizona.
Five days have already passed, with their moons and suns,
my body is already very tired, I feel only pain.
Under this merciless sun my dream has come to an end,
forgotten here by the American people.

In Esquivias's ballad, however, it's a happy ending—the Águilas swoop in to save the day. But to call what they do a rescue operation is naive, even Pollyannaish. The reality is that the Sonoran Desert—Mexico's hottest—is far too large, its identifiable landmarks too few and far between. While the Águilas have located and rescued migrants, more often they provide families the same kind of agonizing closure that Ely himself experienced a decade ago. Once, they recovered the remains of eleven migrants in a single day.

Years later, when the Águilas were granted permission to search a small corner of the Goldwater range, they found twelve bodies, leading researchers from the Marshall Project to speculate that the base likely holds hundreds more. The federal government has blocked any further access.[3]

—

Donald Trump wasn't responsible for the deaths of Rigoberto and Carmelo Ortiz. They died in 2010, as Trump was charting a dizzying path from Obama supporter to conspiratorial "birther." But for that matter, Obama wasn't really directly to blame, either. Their blood wasn't on the hands of Immigration and Customs Enforcement (ICE)—which leaves border issues largely to Customs and Border Protection (CBP)—or those of George W. Bush, who oversaw ICE's creation. The problem is far bigger than ICE, and its origins more distant. According to Ely Ortiz, the blame instead falls squarely at the feet of Bill Clinton: "It was the policy of closing off the border and forcing them to cross in the most dangerous areas" that killed his brother and cousin.[4]

Ortiz is referring to Clinton's 1994 Operation Gatekeeper, the real predecessor to Trump's vaunted border wall. By building a wall eastward from the Pacific and upping enforcement, Gatekeeper sought to eliminate unauthorized entries in and around San Diego. The predictable consequence has been to drive migrant routes east toward Arizona and the sweltering "funnel" of the Sonoran Desert, "one of the most inhospitable and arid areas of the world."[5] Fewer people crossed—that much is true. But far more died in the attempt. Even according to official sources, annual deaths on the border increased tenfold to more than 800 by 2007, and this was only the bodies that were found and counted.[6] Conservative estimates place the number of border deaths since Gatekeeper at 10,000—others, like the humanitarian organization No More Deaths, put that number in the tens of thousands.[7]

The border wall was born in an era marked by lofty rhetoric about global integration and free trade—a fact that was less ironic than it was cynically sadistic. In January 1994, the North American Free Trade Agreement came into effect, freeing capital to hop effortlessly over the border and glide through bank accounts, but unlimited mobility for the poor was never part of the deal. Clinton knew perfectly well what devastation NAFTA would wreak on the Mexican economy, and how it would dislocate the poorest of the poor.[8] Subsidized corn from the United States flooded the Mexican market, decimating small producers and forcing millions off the land, in a historic exodus from the countryside. As the Zapatistas revolted against NAFTA in the south, millions rebelled northward with their feet. Clinton had driven hundreds of thousands of Mexicans to the gates of hell and then turned up the heat.

When it came to Clinton's strategy for stopping these displaced workers from entering the country, dubbed "prevention by deterrence," death was all part of the plan—a message to others who might try to cross. However, Operation Gatekeeper also responded to NAFTA in a different way. As author and activist Joseph Nevins has shown, Gatekeeper was a "trade-off," a bribe to buy off the increasingly vocal anti-migrant backlash that NAFTA itself fueled. "Neoliberalism and globalization," Nevins concludes, "go hand in hand with the buildup of national boundaries," leveraging borders for profit rather than seeing them vanish.[9] The "nativist revolt" would not go quietly, however, and instead Operation Gatekeeper opened the floodgates to a process of criminalizing migrants that has played into the hands of the nativist far right ever since.[10]

Operation Gatekeeper was soon followed by the Illegal Immigration Reform and Immigrant Responsibility Act of 1996 (IIRIRA), an overlooked piece of legislation that essentially gave us the immigration system—and the deportation apparatus—that we have today. Those convicted of nonviolent crimes, even long ago, were now "criminal aliens," an intentionally misleading category that sought to permanently fuse "criminal" to "alien." Clinton himself pressed this conflation even further, describing migrants as an inherently criminal class, "people whose first act is to break the law as they enter our country." Those with minor convictions, as well as any picked up within one hundred miles of the border, were now fast-tracked for expedited removal, making immigration agents judge, jury, and executioner. On top of all this, IIRIRA made the already-difficult task of gaining legal status downright impossible for many. In the words of one legal scholar, "IIRIRA's unprecedented crackdown on non-citizens who commit crimes, then, did not arise from an identified harm . . . it was merely craven politics."[11]

The impact has been devastating. Immigration enforcement was no longer an administrative affair, but a squarely criminal one, and Clinton's criminalization of migrants was part and parcel of a larger strategy. After all, 1994 was not only the year of NAFTA and Operation Gatekeeper, but also his draconian crime bill—which, lest we forget, also plowed billions into border policing and detention. Clinton had been steering the Democratic Party to the right and appeasing white supremacy for years. In 1992, he compared Black nationalist rapper Sister Souljah to KKK grand wizard David Duke, just months after hosting a press conference at Stone Mountain (the birthplace of the Klan), against a backdrop of Black prisoners. For Clinton, the criminalization of Black Americans and predominantly Latinx migrants went hand in hand, and in both cases, criminality became a convenient pretext to mobilize racism.

"In the era of colorblindness," Michelle Alexander reminds us, "it is no longer permissible to hate blacks, but we can hate criminals" and are even "encouraged to do so."[12] Long before Trump was demonizing migrants as "rapists" and the Mara Salvatrucha gang (MS-13) as "animals," the Clintons—Bill *and* Hillary—were busy pioneering the same dehumanizing rhetoric under the guise of "criminal aliens." This is not hyperbole but a matter of historical fact: among the first "criminal aliens" that Clinton deported en masse were those inmates in California prisons who, upon arriving in El Salvador, would cement MS-13 as a hemispheric force. For Black and Brown "superpredators" in American cities and south of the border, Clinton's answer was one and the same: the police.

For Stephanie Ortiz, Ely's daughter and Rigoberto's niece as well as an organizer with the Águilas, Operation Gatekeeper and the flood of anti-migrant legislation it unleashed since have "normalize[d] the psychological and physical violence" meted out on those who dare to cross: "We have an obligation to ask, and the U.S. government to respond and be accountable for, the humanitarian crisis taking place along the border by rejecting policies that violate human lives. We deserve to live in a dignified way and not be asked to walk along countless graveyards along the U.S.-Mexico border to find our relatives."[13]

—

While the scale of Bill Clinton's expansion of the US immigration enforcement apparatus was unprecedented, the criminalization of migrants didn't begin, and wouldn't end, with him. As historian Kelly Lytle Hernández has shown in *Migra!*, when the Border Patrol was first established a century ago, it policed people more than the border, introducing in the process a new "axis of racial division" grounded in illegality. "Border Patrol officers linked being Mexican in the U.S.-Mexico borderlands with being illegal in the United States," setting into motion the long chain of events that would lead to 1996 and beyond.[14]

ICE was established in 2003 under the aegis of the newly established Department of Homeland Security (DHS), weaponizing the fear of the post-9/11 context and painting the border as an inherent threat. The 2005 Real ID Act helped speed the construction of the border wall at the same time that ICE upped the ante with Operation Streamline, requiring that migrants who crossed the border, even for the first time, be subjected to federal criminal prosecution—a step previously reserved for more serious immigration "crimes." Like Clinton, Obama sought to placate the right by continuing—indeed, radically expanding—these policies, prosecuting record numbers and deporting millions, while leaning on Mexico to harden its southern border against Central American migrants displaced by US-backed coups and gang violence. In 2003, 4,000 migrants were prosecuted for crossing the border; a decade later, that number had reached 97,000 through mass hearings and blatant violations of due process.[15] "By the end of Obama's first term," journalist Daniel Denvir writes, "immigration enforcement and criminal justice institutions would be almost seamlessly linked."[16]

From Clinton to Bush and from Obama to Trump and Biden, Natascha Elena Uhlmann argues, "the cruelty of US immigration policy is a bipartisan affair," and Trump "inherited a well-oiled machinery of death."[17] Trump made the most of this machinery, of course: in his first eight months, ICE arrests shot up 42 percent, with intimidation tactics like courthouse arrests jumping 1,700 percent.[18] Deportations from the interior—ICE territory—immediately increased 34 percent.[19] Trump sought to intentionally criminalize migration, linking it to fears of religious terrorism with the short-lived 2017 Muslim Ban and to violence along the southern border by exaggerating the threat of MS-13. History shows that it takes a lot to shock the American conscience, but shocked many were when, in May 2018, the Trump administration announced a "zero tolerance" policy that entailed prosecuting all unauthorized migrants and—most shocking of all—the mass separation of children from their families. In reality, CBP had already been separating families for months, and prosecutions had been increasing exponentially for years, but the sadistic glee with which the Trump administration did so sparked widespread outcry and calls to abolish ICE entirely.

Beginning in Portland, Oregon, anti-ICE protests morphed into encampments, which in turn inspired blockades nationwide, combining the ethos of Occupy Wall Street with the ethical vision of Black Lives Matter, all within a transnational framework that sought to break the prevailing mold of US movement politics. The encampments, which oscillated between the monikers #OccupyICE and #AbolishICE, embraced direct action, surrounding ICE offices and blocking vehicles in a direct attempt to make immigration enforcement impossible. The Portland ICE headquarters was completely shut down during the occupation, and two years later, amid months of uninterrupted protests following the murder of George Floyd, protesters would attack the building once again, smashing windows and confronting federal agents. In Philadelphia, movements successfully leveraged protests to force the city to cancel its agreement with ICE for shared access to what is known as the Preliminary Arraignment Reporting System, or PARS, in August 2018.

Nationwide, calls to abolish ICE quickly went mainstream, with all of the opportunities and pitfalls this entailed. Polls showed nearly half of Americans, and nearly three-quarters of Democrats, favored dismantling the agency. At the height of the protests, Alexandria Ocasio-Cortez won an uphill New York congressional primary on a radical platform that included eliminating the agency, and within weeks, House Democrats introduced a bill to that effect. A full half of the candidates in the Democratic presidential primary would ultimately embrace the call. There were plenty of good reasons that ICE became a target of widespread indignation: mass workplace raids to intimidate workers, accusations of widespread physical and sexual assault, the apparent impunity of ICE's operations, and its management of massive detention centers, which have often been compared with concentration camps. At the same time, it was also a strange choice on some level.

In the first place, with some exceptions, it *wasn't* ICE that was separating families—it was Border Patrol. While both operate under the umbrella of Homeland Security, and CBP detainees are often transferred to ICE custody, lost amid calls to abolish ICE was CBP's long-standing role. This was no accident of course, especially for congressional Democrats to whom abolition meant breaking up ICE but keeping most of the pieces. The problem, as they saw it, was ICE's lack of transparency and Trump's abuse of the agency's functions. The draft legislation therefore proposed a committee empowered to determine which of ICE's functions were "essential" and didn't violate due process and human rights, placing these under new authority. This is a far cry from abolition or even significant reform, and has more in common with those city administrations like New York or Philadelphia that "defunded" the police by shuffling budget lines around.

When it comes to ICE, this has looked like attempting to distinguish enforcement and removal (ERO) from the agency's investigatory (HSI) and legal (OPLA) wings. Controversy over enforcement is nothing new within ICE; indeed, HSI had previously changed its name to remove affiliations with ICE, and more recently a group of investigators pressed for it to leave ICE entirely. This was not due to moral outrage at ICE's enforcement activities, of course, but a practical consideration—no one wants to collaborate with investigators tied to ICE. For Representative Mark Pocan, a self-styled "progressive" and co-sponsor of the Democratic bill to dismantle ICE, this comes down to a question of branding: "A part of your policy is the brand. If you can't get information by working with certain communities because they think you may be deporting them, you're not getting information that could help you go after someone who really is a threat to this country."[20]

HSI's stated goal of investigating weapons proliferation and drug and human trafficking, for example, furnishes an easy alibi for centrist Democrats who have no intention of actually abolishing ICE, while also revealing just how naturalized ICE's functions have become. Take for example the 2018 outrage over 1,475 children allegedly "lost" by the federal government. In reality, this meant that the Office of Refugee Resettlement was unable to locate the children. In their anti-Trump zeal, few well-meaning liberals bothered to ask *why* we would want those children under the watch of ORR, working hand in hand with ICE; most weren't lost at all, but were simply free of government oversight. Such exaggerated fears about child trafficking have been explicitly weaponized to justify and naturalize ICE's functions. Similarly, it's absurd to draw a line between OPLA and ERO, between the more than 1,100 lawyers overseeing mass deportation proceedings and the jackbooted thugs who carry out the orders.

As Pocan tacitly admits, Democratic proposals to abolish ICE, like proposals to reform the police, are more brand than substance. This isn't surprising: Hillary Clinton, who supported child deportation before it was cool, hasn't changed her tune all that much. Two decades after her husband blew wind into nativist sails, she went so far as to blame the victim, suggesting that "migration . . . is what lit the flame" of the racist right. Perhaps it was a gift, then, that within a few short months, and faced with midterm elections, the call to abolish ICE had all but disappeared from Democratic Party talking points. And just when it seemed that the use and abuse of abolition could not get any worse, Juliette Kayyem, a former Obama-era DHS official, reached new heights of absurdity by writing in *The Atlantic*, in July 2020, that rather than taking aim at ICE or DHS, "the only thing that needs to be abolished is the Trump administration."[21] With Biden in control of the deportation machine today, such partisan alibis lose their force.

There is no question that ICE *should* be abolished, immediately and unconditionally, but lost in the widespread outrage was the question of what abolition means. Abolition is about more than enforcement, and it is far broader than even ICE itself. Of course, it's a *good* thing that ICE is an easy target today—the strengths and weaknesses of calls to abolish ICE are one and the same. After all, as a relatively young institution—younger indeed than many of those reading this book—it's easy to imagine a world without ICE. It's much harder to imagine a world without border patrol, much less a world without a border to be patrolled. The task of abolition is to build bridges that connect the widespread outrage at exceptional evil to the banality of its everyday function. This means shifting the focus from those wrongly imprisoned to the entire system of mass incarceration. It means connecting individual instances of police murder to policing as a murderous system. It means leveraging the momentum of calls to abolish ICE toward the abolition of DHS as a whole; abolishing border patrol rather than renaming those overseeing it; and ultimately abolishing the border itself.

As with all abolition, moreover, this is about more than eliminating institutions—and certainly more than simply rebaptizing them with new names. For Uhlmann, "it is also about building

anew," about reimagining—and reorganizing—our understanding of the borderlands as a whole.[22]

—

Abolishing the police, ICE, Border Patrol, and the border—all
are part of a single struggle against a shared process of criminalization: an interlocking bipartisan effort to demonize
migrants, people of color, and the poor. This process has seen
millions deported or allowed to die in the desert while others
are earmarked from birth for mass incarceration, and in all cases
at the hands of police. But the similarities run deeper still.

The police were born when poor whites chose their race over
their class, and even today anyone that does so is the police. For
W.E.B. Du Bois, this betrayal rested on the myth that Black
slaves represented competition and that, if freed, they would
drive wages down to the detriment of white workers. "What
they failed to comprehend," Du Bois wrote with a palpable exas-
peration, "was that the black man enslaved was an even more
formidable and fatal competitor than the black man free."[23] In
other words, it was not slaves but their *condition* as slaves, as the
cheapest of cheap labor, that drove down wages across the board.
The point was so simple and so obvious, but capitalism loves
nothing more than a working class divided, and sowing this
confusion was enough to provoke bloody race riots across the
North.

Even Abraham Lincoln felt the need to respond to the "imaginary, if not sometimes malicious" argument that free slaves
"would injure and displace white labor more by being free than by
remaining slaves . . . Emancipation . . . would probably enhance
the wages of white labor and very surely would not reduce
them."[24] Despite this, the Great Emancipator himself favored
shipping slaves out of the country—a process often euphemis-
tically described as "colonization," but which here he at least
called by its true name: "deportation." As legal theorist K-Sue
Park has shown, today's self-deportation policies—which entail

making migrants' lives so intolerably harsh or dangerous that they will choose to leave and discourage others from coming—originated with similar strategies deployed historically against slaves, Indians, and Chinese people.[25]

By arguing that migrants threaten American workers by stealing jobs and driving down wages, anti-migrant rhetoric today traffics in precisely the same kind of myth. But just as it was not free slaves but the slave *system* that drove wages down, the same goes for migrants today. Study after study has shown that migration has little to no impact on wages, because it isn't migration, but border policing and enforcement, that weakens workers and drives wages down. What the border does is to *segment* the labor force, introducing an artificial divide among workers that the bosses can leverage to increase profits and exert control. By casting many migrants into a gray area—no labor protections, no minimum wage, no right to unionize—criminalization creates an ideal situation for capitalists, who can pay the bare minimum and hire and fire at will. A defenseless and deportable class is in no position to demand higher wages, and the bosses know it. Research bears this out, showing a clear correlation between immigration enforcement and wage stagnation among undocumented workers, but here's the kicker: by holding down the wages of undocumented workers, immigration enforcement suppresses wages across entire branches of industry, impacting both documented and undocumented workers.[26]

Criminalization is the *cause* of low wages, not the solution. The absurdity of a myth doesn't make it any less tenacious, however, especially when coupled with a desire to believe. The idea that migrants are to blame for low wages is at the very heart of Trump's faux populism, and remains prevalent among his more nativist supporters. His handlers, namely Steve Bannon and Stephen Miller, made this claim a central plank of their ostensibly colorblind "economic nationalism," which sought to scramble class solidarities and convert at least a sector of Black and Brown workers to the anti-immigrant cause. Migrants, they argued, compete with Black and established Latinx workers, driving their wages down. While both Bannon and Miller are undeniably white nationalists, they distanced themselves from ethno-nationalism—what Bannon called a "collection of clowns"—in favor of a broader electoral strategy. In Bannon's own words, "when we get to 25 and 30 percent of the black working class and the Hispanic working class voting for us, we will have a realignment like 1932," referring to Franklin Delano Roosevelt's landslide victory and the period of Democratic hegemony it inaugurated—"we'll govern for fifty years."[27]

This strategy, which Daniel HoSang and Joseph Lowndes call a "multicultural right-wing populism," even appeals to the history of anti-Black racism to divide communities of color along national lines. Black Americans are portrayed as "law-abiding citizens preyed upon by undocumented immigrants" even as they are described as victims of racial violence within American society.[28] At its worst, as with Black Trump mouthpieces like vloggers Diamond and Silk, this has taken the form of a resentful politics that, rather than recognizing a shared process of criminalization, instead asks: If *we* break the law *we* go to jail, so why don't they? More perversely still, this same logic can be found in the ostensibly radical American Descendants of Slavery (ADOS) movement, which shatters even Black internationalism by demanding reparations be reserved *only* for Black Americans. Appeals to Black nativism against migrant communities are nothing new, HoSang and Lowndes insist, and they "ultimately reward white supremacy," and—we could add—capitalism as well.[29] Luckily, these appeals don't seem to have much traction: Black support for Trump's border wall is only half that of even Latinx respondents, and the project of economic nationalism faltered at the ballot box in November 2020.

Occasionally, anti-migrant arguments infiltrate sectors of the self-described left as well. This is the case for Angela Nagle, who published a now-notorious article in the conservative *American Affairs* journal entitled "The Left Case against Open

Borders." The venue, once known as the *Journal of American Greatness*, was a strange choice, but the arguments are stranger still. The left, Nagle insists, has always been against open borders, because—in her view—migration weakens union bargaining power. It is the right, by contrast, that wants to abolish borders in favor of the free movement of capital. By neglecting the concrete demands of labor unions to restrict migration in favor of an abstract moral imperative to defend migrants at all costs, Nagle concludes, the left has become "useful idiots" for capitalism's own strategy of globalization.

On every point, Nagle is comically wrong. The left has a long history of internationalism, notably among radical unions like the Industrial Workers of the World (IWW), which explicitly rejected "race prejudice and imaginary boundary lines." Nagle's attempt to conscript an entire radical pantheon into her anti-immigrant crusade—from Marcus Garvey and Frederick Douglass to Karl Marx himself—falls flat, since none opposed *migration* per se, only capitalism's *use* of migrants as weapons.[30] Nagle is wrong that migrants drive wages down—they don't—although she doesn't hesitate to appeal to George Borjas, the same discredited economist cited by Trump advisor Stephen Miller. And she misses the mark wildly when she suggests that the right supports open borders. The bosses don't want open borders; they want NAFTA, and for the same reasons that the left abhors it: because while capital moves freely, the border remains—and is increasingly militarized—to provide leverage in the form of wage differentials. US companies would never set up shop in Mexican *maquilas* if it didn't mean crossing a border for lower-wage and less-protected workers. And they want their migrants undocumented by design.[31]

Speaking at the 1907 International Socialist Congress in Stuttgart, Germany, Karl Liebknecht recognized clearly what Nagle apparently cannot grasp more than a century later: that the "sword of deportation" hangs over the working class like that of Damocles, and that overcoming it was "the first condition for foreigners to stop being predestined to squeeze wages and break strikes." Workers will continue to migrate—the question is how to prevent them from becoming a weapon in the enemy's arsenal. Looking back on the Stuttgart resolution, Lenin himself later insisted that "one cannot be internationalist and be at the same time in favor of such restrictions" on migration, sparing no venom for the likes of Nagle: "Such Socialists are in reality jingoes."[32] Angela Nagle is Bannon-lite, a "useful idiot" of white nationalism whose arguments could be just as easily used to oppose the abolition of slavery, the Great Migration, and workplace desegregation.[33]

While Nagle was quickly ostracized by the left, however, similar arguments remain among those who downplay police racism, who discredit calls to defund and abolish the police, and who welcome police within labor unions—all in the name of a wooden class-first politics. Ironically, what all these approaches share is an impoverished view of the working class as mostly white members of conservative unions—a vision that stops at the border and excludes undocumented people within. They neglect the stratification by race and status and misunderstand how the police powers of the state uphold these divisions—which only hurt workers and the poor. And all paradoxically in the service of a watered-down social democratic politics, a glorified liberalism that sacrifices so much to demand so little. Such an amputated view of the working class of today occludes the radical potential of the working class of the future: a transnational, multiracial, and militant class that far exceeds whiteness, the police, and the border.

Also left out is the fact that this horizon is also a living, breathing reality, as became apparent on May Day 2006, when "Latinx workers initiated the largest general strike in the history of the Americas ... this mass action breathed new life into a labor movement that had been in disarray for decades."[34] Its closest, indeed its *only* rival to that claim, was the mass labor walkout of the Civil War, in which hundreds of thousands of slaves abandoned plantations for freedom, and which Du Bois insisted was also a "general strike." This image of a hemispheric, even global, working class shares nothing with the globalization from above of NAFTA or Fortress Europe, which masquerade as borderless while immiserating workers and throwing up ever more walls.

It is not migrants who drive wages down, but the criminalization of migration and the permanent, unprotected underclass it produces. By confronting, attacking, and abolishing those barriers dividing the global poor, the class as a whole grows stronger.

—

Why talk about the border in a book about the police? Because the police were born from the division of the working class, and because without police, the border is just a line on a map or in the sand, an unthreatening cable sagging loosely between two posts. Which is basically how the southern border functioned for a century. As scholar A. Naomi Paik notes: "For most of the United States' history, its borders have been as porous as they've been mobile. People crossed them without a marker, a checkpoint, or border patrol officer in sight; for much of the country's history, people may not have been aware that they were even crossing a border."[35]

This porosity served a function: as historian Greg Grandin shows in *The End of the Myth*, this was less a border than a frontier, an outward-oriented and expansive reflection of imperial white personhood. From Indian Removal and Manifest Destiny to the infiltration and seizure of Texas, the frontier underwrote a massive, colonial land grab—that is, until the land ran out, the myth of expansion came to an end, and colonial contradictions were internalized in the resentful nativism of today. Border policing was essentially nonexistent until the late nineteenth century, and even after the US Border Patrol was formally established in 1924, setting into motion the long process of criminalization that would reach its apex in 1996, it was less concerned with policing the border line than with policing the boundaries of whiteness and disciplining the racialized labor force of the borderlands. In other words, they did exactly what police do, and have always done, everywhere.

These new border police drew their recruits from the same wellspring of resentment as slave patrols in the South: poor white men. Kelly Lytle Hernández tells of young white boys who grew up fighting Mexicans on the playground before joining the ranks of the Border Patrol to do essentially the same.[36] The policing of slaves, moreover, was synonymous with the wages of whiteness, providing both a psychological sense of superiority and a material wage, and consolidating a cross-class alliance in which poor whites did the work of their class enemies. While the relationship between Border Patrol and agribusiness was certainly more complex—these were not the mercenaries of capital that the Texas Rangers had been—the function was the same: to discipline a racialized labor force while elevating themselves to middle-class status.[37] And in the end, to police the border was to police that division internal to the class that was the most powerful weapon in the arsenal of the bosses.

For Daniel Denvir, the deep resonances between the criminalization of poor people of color within the United States and the migrants crossing the border can be traced, in large part, to the question of migration more broadly. "The logic animating white resistance to the black Great Migration and freedom struggle," Denvir writes, "has been similar to that behind the anti-immigrant movement—and that the latter in many ways grew out of and alongside the former."[38] Black Americans, previously contained to plantations by the proto-police, moved north to segregated communities with equally policed boundaries. If those boundaries have been relaxed today, their armed custodians remain, and struggles over desegregation, busing, policing, and mass incarceration map onto broader nativist sentiments. "Segregation was and remains a system of domestic bordering,"

Denvir concludes, to which we can add that border enforcement was and remains a system for *policing* whiteness and labor.[39]

If US policing and US imperialism were born on the same day, border policing followed close behind, and if policing the population and policing the planet shared so much, policing the border lay squarely between the two. As historian Kathleen Belew demonstrates in *Bring the War Home*, the biggest predictor for the growth of the Ku Klux Klan and other racist paramilitaries was the aftermath of war, when the violence workers tasked with imposing global white power returned home to do the same. It was no coincidence that the first border fence would be built with materials recycled from the wartime internment camps built for Japanese Americans, or that Border Patrol commander John P. Longan, who helped spearhead the mass deportation campaign known as Operation Wetback in 1954, would deploy many of the same methods a decade later in a wave of counterinsurgent terror across Latin America.[40] Or that after Vietnam, the KKK formed a Klan Border Watch that harassed not only Latinx migrants but also Vietnamese refugees. And it's absolutely no surprise that today's ICE agents are "predominantly male and have often served in the military, with a police department or both."[41]

Like the police and the military, Border Patrol and ICE uphold racial divisions among the global poor, upholding the barriers of segregation dividing Du Bois's "dark proletariat." The Fraternal Order of Police and the "unions" representing ICE and Border Patrol enthusiastically embraced Trump's 2016 candidacy, but their enthusiasm didn't stop there. Some agents "thumped their chest as if they had just won the Super Bowl" after Trump emerged victorious, and former ICE director Thomas Homan praised Trump for "taking the handcuffs off" border agents.[42] In a joint statement, the CBP and ICE unions reported that "morale amongst our agents and officers has increased exponentially."[43] In other words, they didn't need to be asked to do their violent work—a fact that became viciously apparent in the peculiar temporality of the Muslim Ban, which CBP began to voluntarily enforce hours *before* it was required to do so (and continued to do so even in violation of several court orders). These were Trump's most willing executioners, a fact only underlined when the then-president deployed elite Border Patrol agents to the George Floyd protests in Portland, Oregon.

Abolishing the police *means* abolishing ICE and Border Patrol, and it starts the same way: by cracking the foundations of their power. Pressure should immediately be brought to bear within the labor movement to disaffiliate the so-called unions representing ICE and Border Patrol from the American Federation of Government Employees (AFGE) and its parent federation, the AFL-CIO. For journalist Kim Kelly,

> a genuinely radical labor movement should group police, prison guards, border patrol agents, and ICE agents in the same category . . . They are an occupying military force, sworn to serve only the interests of capital and the state to the detriment of humanity. They protect and serve property, not people, and the only solidarity they feel is with their own kind.[44]

Pressure to disaffiliate is already building, and as growing sectors of the labor movement, including the New York Teamsters, embrace sanctuary and refuse to enable ICE raids on their members, Kelly foresees a "divorce in the making."

Disaffiliating and abolishing the ICE and CBP unions is a first step toward targeting the institutions more directly. Building on calls from the grassroots, we must demand the immediate abolition of ICE—*not* the restructuring of its "essential" functions under a new name: we must abolish enforcement and removal, abolish investigations, and abolish the legal apparatus underpinning both. Abolition cannot be limited to ICE and CBP, either. We must also demand the immediate abolition of the overarching monstrosity that is DHS, which coincides with and has only further naturalized the idea that we should look upon borders primarily as a security threat to be closed off.[45] We must demand an immediate, total, and unconditional amnesty for *all* migrants as a step toward the full decriminalization of the border and those symbolically associated with it by race and language. Doing so would eliminate, in a stroke, the leverage the border provides to drive down the wages of all workers.

Demands are one thing, however; making it happen is another. If one thing is clear, it's that we can't expect solutions from policymakers. As the specter of Trump recedes, President Biden and the Democratic Party will offer little more than empty words at best, technologically rationalized border fascism at worst. While every minute of the twenty-four-hour news cycle is dedicated to the insistence that change comes only from above, from backroom deals, pragmatic negotiation, and congressional horse-trading, no amount of ruling-class propaganda can conceal the fact that we are *only* talking about ICE today because of the intransigent demands and direct action from the grassroots. The imperative for radical change can only come from below. Luckily, this strategy doesn't have to start from zero. Movements for and by migrants have a long history of direct struggle against the border and its police stretching back long before the #AbolishICE encampments.

Recent years have seen a variety of escalating campaigns to discredit, defund, and isolate ICE and border enforcement. Under legal and public pressure, city and county jails nationwide have ended ICE contracts; under pressure from residents, cities have declared noncooperation with ICE raids. Corporations like CoreCivic and GEO Group that have made billions from private migrant detention have come under increased scrutiny for neglect and widespread abuse, leading JPMorgan Chase to cut off financing streams to both in 2019.[46] Around the same time, workers at the furniture giant Wayfair opted to walk out rather than supply ICE detention centers. Movimiento Cosecha, which campaigns for permanent legal protections for undocumented migrants, has spearheaded a consumer boycott of ICE-related business, and universities have come under pressure for their collaboration with the deportation apparatus.

The machinery of border policing is particularly vulnerable when it comes to technology. DHS has the largest tech budget of any government agency, Amazon is notoriously friendly with ICE, and almost all major tech companies also have contracts with border enforcement agencies. But in 2018, Google employees pressed the company to break ties with the Defense Department; and the next year, alongside workers at Microsoft and Amazon, they began to target ICE cloud contracts as well. Amid the public scrutiny of recent years, defunding ICE itself is squarely on the table, and efforts to do so are being spearheaded under the banner of the Defund Hate Campaign. In 2018, the campaign mobilized sufficient grassroots energy to pressure Congress into blocking a special request for $1 billion by ICE, and it continues to push for defunding the agency.[47]

Our task today is to build on the spontaneous and organized efforts of communities nationwide while continuing to break down the boundaries dividing abolitionist movements. Here the ultimate horizon is the same as it is for police abolition: to make ICE and Border Patrol obsolete by building strong communities. For years, organizers across the Southwest and beyond have been deepening resistance networks in undocumented communities, beginning with an everyday culture of resistance and disobedience: neighbors warn neighbors when they see ICE in the neighborhood, some with papers refuse to show them, and it's not uncommon to see someone on the side of the road with an improvised sign warning of checkpoints ahead. Other, more organized efforts have seen the establishment of nascent rapid-response networks that have sought to directly prevent deportation raids from being carried out.

Even before Arizona leapt to national attention with the approval of the anti-migrant SB 1070 legislation in 2010, ICE was actively carrying out raids with the support of local law enforcement, and communities were organizing to resist them. One organization involved at the time is Arizona's Repeal Coalition, which came together in 2007 around the demand to repeal all anti-migrant legislation, coupled with the sweeping insistence that all communities be able to "live, love, and work wherever they please." Cecilia Sáenz Becerra, a member of Phoenix Repeal at the time, explained to me how Repeal's capacity to resist ICE didn't emerge overnight, but was built gradually over time through the slow work of relationship-building with undocumented women in a trailer park community: "by accompanying folks to get state benefits for their children, helping find loved ones in the deportation system, being there emotionally, playing with children, and sharing meals."

According to Repeal member Luis Fernández, those organizing further north in Flagstaff began with a door-knocking campaign in those communities most likely to be targeted by raids. "The night we held a community meeting with some eighty people, ICE raided the neighborhood that Repeal was working in. As an immediate response, young activists in town organized an ICE watch, driving around the neighborhoods and observing the movements of the ICE officers." Communicating by text message, organizers and community members formed a rapid-response network that alerted neighbors and sought to obstruct raids when they happened. According to a Freedom of Information Act (FOIA) request filed by the American Civil Liberties Union, ICE admitted that community resistance had dramatically limited the agency's ability to carry out raids. Building strong communities can make ICE's work impossible.

Further north in Canada, Vancouver's No One Is Illegal network was simultaneously engaged in an inspiring display of mass civil disobedience to prevent the deportation of a paralyzed refugee, Laibar Singh. Through a combination of street protest and direct action, organizers quickly mobilized 2,000 supporters to blockade Vancouver's international airport on December 10, 2007, forcing the government to back down by surrounding the vehicle in which Singh was traveling.[48] While Singh ultimately self-deported due to state harassment and racist demonization by Canadian society more broadly, the case was a flashpoint for struggles around Canadian immigration and deportation policy. In the words of Harsha Walia, a key organizer in the blockade to defend Singh: "Direct action is not only an effective form of resistance, but an inherent part of the broader process of nurturing our individual and collective revolutionary consciousnesses. In this sense, direct actions aren't simply about militancy but about building our collective power to feel emboldened rather than disempowered." Feeling emboldened means building a culture of resistance that only leads to more power in the long run. For Walia, the task is not simply to prevent deportations, but to abolish "border imperialism" as a whole.[49]

Direct action against deportation *works*—not only tactically, by hindering ICE's ability to function while concretely protecting some from the hell of deportation, but also politically, as a tool for mass mobilization and for provoking a broader national debate. Moving forward, organizations with deep roots in local communities will prove crucial relay points for a broader anti-deportation strategy, building the local infrastructure needed to shepherd volunteers into mobile flying squads capable of obstructing ICE's work by warning communities and physically preventing raids. Direct action means gradually weaving this dense fabric of community out of thousands of existing threads. It means transforming rescue and recovery missions like Águilas del Desierto into channels for safe passage across the desert, demanding more than the right to simply provide food and water, but to provide sanctuary as well. In the short term, it means redirecting 911 calls to grassroots organizations—today, 911 operators often route calls directly to Border Patrol without informing the caller. Just as we advocate rerouting 911 calls away from the police, border rescue needs to be taken out of the hands of the enforcers.

Direct action against the deportation machine is a dangerous undertaking, however. From the scorching sun beating down on those aiding and rescuing migrants to targeted repression by the state and murder by white vigilantes, the risks are many. In the early years of the sanctuary movement, activists were subjected to FBI harassment and federal prosecution. In the late 1980s, eight organizers were convicted for "running a modern-day underground railroad," but the prosecutions backfired, and the movement only grew further.[50] Today, organizers are being targeted similarly: in 2018, nine No More Deaths volunteers were charged with federal misdemeanors, including Scott Warren, who faced twenty years on felony charges before his acquittal in 2019.

After several weeks camped out at the #OccupyICE protests in San Antonio, a young activist known as Mapache was snatched off a nearby street the day after his DACA (Deferred Action for Childhood Arrivals) application was scheduled for renewal. His application had been denied, an agent told him, because he was a "bad person," and officers pressured Mapache to hand over information about other local organizers. At eighteen years old and barely speaking any Spanish, he eventually opted for deportation to Monterrey, Mexico.[51] Mapache's fate was not new: as Uhlmann writes, "ICE has a long-standing—and intensifying—practice of silencing activists."[52] In recent years, ICE has detained several organizers from the New Sanctuary Coalition in New York, and in 2020 Nancy Nguyen, executive director of Philadelphia-based VietLead, was arrested after protesting outside of the home of the acting ICE director, himself a Vietnamese refugee.

—

For A. Naomi Paik, the ultimate horizon for these struggles is what she calls "abolitionist sanctuary," which stitches together the history of sanctuary movements with the abolitionist tradition, past and present. The Trump years saw an explosion of sanctuary cities, counties, and even states, provoking unhinged Twitter attacks and threats to withhold federal funding from the president. By refusing to participate in the policing of migrants and even directly disrupting the operations of ICE, Paik argues, sanctuary spaces provide "a ground floor for survival and a strategy of resistance" while also "forging thicker connections" with movements to abolish policing and the prison-industrial complex.[53]

When cities refuse to participate in ICE enforcement, they are also withholding matching resources in a way that severely hinders ICE's ability to seize and deport, and local strategies like the decriminalization of street vendors and providing driver's licenses to migrants can have a major impact on keeping them out of the waiting hands of ICE. For instance, Chicago's sanctuary city status has meant that the number of people held in Cook County Jail who were handed over to ICE fell from 1,400 annually to zero almost overnight. However, ICE has developed a host of administrative workarounds, and sanctuary doesn't apply to those listed in the city's sprawling gang database, making sanctuary more image than reality.[54] A truly abolitionist vision of sanctuary, in contrast, points us toward a world in which *la migra*, and indeed *all* police, are obsolete. Drawing inspiration from first-wave abolitionism, abolitionist sanctuary looks to the safe passage provided by the Underground Railroad and local jurisdictions that blocked enforcement of the Fugitive Slave Act—not to mention those who freed slaves through direct action.

Abolitionist sanctuary means reinforcing the already-strong bridges that connect migrant struggles to struggles against anti-Black police violence; and it means understanding that Black–Brown solidarity is a two-way street. On the one hand, organizers from Mijente, the UndocuBlack Network, and other groups have increasingly come to recognize and center anti-Blackness within the migrant struggle and to insist that ICE cannot be abolished without abolishing policing as a whole. And on the other hand, the Movement for Black Lives platform demanded an "end to all deportations, immigrant detention, and ICE raids."[55] Abolitionist sanctuary means a proliferation of know-your-rights trainings, legal workshops, and support escorts for ICE appointments—all of which are also essential to the broader police abolition struggle. It means refusing the double bind of criminalization that seeks to divide so-called good migrants worthy of status from bad "criminal aliens" earmarked for removal. Abolitionist sanctuary, moreover, is explicitly anti-colonial and builds outward toward broader solidarities with Indigenous struggles, including resistance to the Dakota Access Pipeline and the global struggle against US imperial power.

Abolitionist sanctuary, in other words, is about far more than migration, seeking instead to actively tear down the walls that separate our struggles. And like all abolition, Paik reminds us, border abolition means

> striv[ing] not only to break down the forms of oppressive power we don't want, but also to build the world we want in its place— where bans, walls, and raids are no longer needed . . . The goal is to make the whole world a sanctuary for all, everywhere. It seeks to create a world where cages, removals, and policing— whether of immigrants, migrants crossing national borders, people of color, gender nonconforming people, or any person made into a criminal by the laws of the state—no longer exist.[56]

A world in which the border, and its police, are obsolete.

—

What will we do without the border? Who and what will protect us from the nightmarish realities that lay on the other side—the faceless demons of MS-13, the heartless traffickers of drugs and of people who, we are told, have made the borderlands a veritable hell for so many? As with the police, the answer is far simpler than it seems, because we are asking the wrong question.

Like the police, the border doesn't protect against violence—it *creates* violence. In the words of geographer Reece Jones:

The existence of the border itself produces the violence that surrounds it. The border creates the economic and jurisdictional discontinuities that have come to be seen as its hallmarks, providing an impetus for the movement of people, goods, drugs, weapons, and money across it. The hardening of the border through new security practices is the source of the violence, not a response to it.[57]

The border, moreover, drives up the prices of illegally smuggled drugs, and it is in the space of this profit that violence becomes profitable, too. As with the police, this is the violence of armed impunity, which leverages racial dehumanization to abuse the most vulnerable. So it comes as no surprise that the victims are the same: people of color, women, children, and queer and trans people, all of whom are subject to disproportionate physical and sexual abuse at the hands of border police. Abolition removes the entire incentive structure for border violence on the part of both state and extra-state forces. Abolition wipes away the leverage used by capitalists to drive wages down in maquilas on the Mexican side and for those left undocumented in the US. The partial legalization of marijuana, for example, has already led to a collapse in marijuana prices, undermining the profitability and role of cartels. Abolition would destroy this incentive and reduce border violence in the process.[58]

If police abolition means thinking harder about the causes of violence, it also means thinking harder about the causes of migration, and confronting the legacies of colonialism and US intervention that have impoverished communities, dislocated their inhabitants, and sown chaos across the hemisphere and the world. And just as policing and mass incarceration has created closed circuits from the ghetto to the prison and back, the same could be said of US imperialism and the deportation regime. Indeed, it was Bill Clinton's mass deportations that created MS-13—"bastard offspring" of the IIRIRA—while a decade later, Secretary of State Hillary Clinton oversaw a coup in Honduras.

As with the cycle of carceral violence, the impact of these twin interventions came full circle in the a mass exodus of Central Americans and widely publicized migrant caravans that have reverberated against the border in recent years.

The border doesn't solve any problems; it *is* the problem to be solved, and the solution is abolition. Once there was no border—and that day will come again.

Conclusion: Democracy or the Police?

Picture this: there's an armed gang roaming the streets, harassing the population, brutalizing the innocent, and taking more than a thousand lives each year—three Americans dead every day. No one would seriously propose reforming such a force. We wouldn't tolerate it—we would attack and dismantle it. This seems obvious enough, but we aren't talking about just any street gang, about the Bloods, Crips, or MS-13. We're talking about what Tupac Shakur once deemed "the biggest gang in America."

To call the police a gang is not hyperbole. As one recent headline put it, "Police killed more people in 2019 than Bloods, Crips combined."[1] It isn't just about the killing, either. When the police kill, maim, and brutalize, they refuse all accountability. We have seen how police and their not-so-benevolent associations organize, bargain, and lobby for absolute impunity and resist any attempts at civilian oversight. Where negotiation and lobbying aren't enough, they throw very public temper tantrums, taking to the literal bully pulpit of right-wing media or engaging in "blue flu" sick-out campaigns. And where all this fails or local elected officials are not sufficiently obedient, police and their unions don't hesitate to buck civilian authorities entirely, acting outside and against, rather than under the control of, democratic oversight.

Rather than deny the accusation that they are a gang, many officers embrace it. Former New York mayor Michael Bloomberg once even boasted, "I have my own army," and he wasn't lying. But this is an army that has never been faithful to the chain of command, and in recent years has gone fully rogue. Since literally turning their backs on Mayor Bill de Blasio during the attempted "blue coup" in 2014, the NYPD has continued to lash out at civilian oversight. In early 2020, Ed Mullins, head of the Sergeants Benevolent Association (SBA), tweeted that the NYPD was "declaring war" on the mayor. When the SBA doxed the mayor's daughter, Chiara, leaking records of her arrest during the George Floyd rebellions, this wasn't mere retribution: the SBA was demanding mounted horseback units to police protesters. The fact that the police don't work for the people but in their own interests, and that these interests involve repressing protest and resisting social change, is a frightening prospect in itself. Even more alarming, however, is that the bullying worked—they got their mounted units.[2]

As this case shows, police are more than willing to harass and even threaten elected leaders who cross them, a fact that the case of Vallejo, California, only drives home. As Shane Bauer recently documented for *The New Yorker*, Vallejo boasts one of the state's most violent police departments: so violent that officers bend the tips of their badges to keep track of fatal shootings; and so violent, in fact, that the insurance company covering settlements recently increased the city's deductible fivefold. For decades, the city council was effectively in the pocket of the Vallejo Police Officers' Association (VPOA)—as the former city manager Joe Tanner put it, "The cops owned the council." When former city council member Stephanie Gomes was running for office, the VPOA asked her, straight up: "If you win, will you stay bought?" As the city fell into a fiscal crisis and the budget was balanced on the backs of Vallejo's poorest, Gomes and Tanner struggled to rein in contractually protected police salaries—confronting this political power head-on in the process.

In response to their efforts, local police harassed both officials. Cops drove by Gomes's house repeatedly, casting intimidating glances inside while revving their engines. When her security alarm was tripped, police used this as a pretext to pry open a window and snoop around—anonymous posts later appeared online about personal items of hers found inside. And when Gomes proposed a civilian oversight board for police misconduct, police packed the chamber to heckle her. The threats against Tanner were more direct: as Bauer writes, "A Vallejo cop approached him in a restaurant in a nearby town and told him, 'You're gonna get yours.' An anonymous caller threatened to burn his house down. His Jeep was keyed several times and its tires were slashed." In order to circumvent the power of the VPOA, Vallejo had to file for bankruptcy and, eventually, declare a public safety emergency.[3] Cases like these are not the exception but the rule. Over at *The New Republic*, Sam Adler-Bell spoke to politicians nationwide who had confronted police power, noting that "their stories are remarkably similar. All expressed fear for their own safety and the safety of their families. They feel scrutinized by beat cops when they walk the streets and worry their movements are being surveilled."[4]

Where negotiating, lobbying, and bullying city officials fail, when it's not enough to have misconduct records scrubbed every few months, violent cops often resign and move rather than face discipline—passed around police departments like so many abusive Catholic priests. Timothy Loehmann, the Cleveland police officer who shot twelve-year-old Tamir Rice, had previously been forced out of another department, strategically resigning before he could be fired. After George Floyd was killed, nearly 200 officers resigned from the Minneapolis Police Department, fearing greater scrutiny. There is even an entire website—Law Enforcement Move—dedicated to the task of helping cops relocate to "police-friendly communities." The website's founder told Bauer that he had been contacted with more than a thousand requests in the course of a few short months.

———

Police are more than just a gang, however—policing is a racket. This is not merely a metaphor. The sociologist Charles Tilly famously argued that war making and state making can be viewed as protection rackets that meet all the criteria of organized crime. A racketeer offers protection from violence—which they themselves threaten to unleash if their victims don't pay up—and Tilly argues that governments do much the same:

> To the extent that the threats against which a given government protects its citizens are imaginary or are consequences of its own activities, the government has organized a protection racket. Since governments themselves commonly simulate, stimulate, or even fabricate threats of external war and since the repressive and extractive activities of governments often constitute the largest current threats to the livelihoods of their own citizens, many governments operate in essentially the same ways as racketeers.[5]

The only difference, Tilly concludes, is that governments do so under the cover of the law.

What about the police? After all, they do more than harass elected leaders—they also *extort* them, and the public purse at large. Police promise protection that they conspicuously fail to deliver, but even empty promises come with a hefty price tag in the form of endlessly expanding budgets, devouring funds that could otherwise be earmarked for essential social services or local infrastructure. Despite falling crime rates, police bankrolls have continued to grow—and spectacularly, increasing by nearly 50 percent per capita since the 1990s. Per capita spending on Chicago's notoriously violent police has *tripled* since the 1960s, and currently eats up 40 percent of the city's budget.[6] New York shells out nearly $6 billion annually, while spending in Los Angeles has doubled in just a few decades to $3 billion.

Not content to extort the public through the political system, many police departments steal in more direct ways, with entire departments nationwide funding their operations through the system of legalized theft known as civil asset forfeiture, in which police seize—and *keep*—assets that they claim to be involved in criminal activity, even where the owners are not convicted, or even arrested. As of 2014, civil asset forfeiture surpassed total losses from all burglaries nationwide—some $5 billion annually. So egregious is this practice that the Supreme Court stepped in with a unanimous 2019 ruling in the case of *Timbs v. Indiana*. Tyson Timbs had been convicted of a minor drug crime carrying a maximum fine of $10,000, but police had also seized his legally purchased Land Rover worth some $42,000. The court found that forfeiture can violate the Eighth Amendment prohibition on excessive fines.

Occasionally, such extortion happens through collaboration with the powers that be, a scenario that was most notoriously true in Ferguson. There, police worked directly with the courts and under pressure from city administrators to squeeze nearly a quarter of the city budget, like blood from a stone, out of an already-poor and majority-Black population. Through bogus fines and exorbitant court fees, Ferguson police oversaw the collection of what Robin D.G. Kelley has called "a kind of racial tax, an extraction of surplus directly by the state without producing anything besides discipline and terror and the reproduction of the state." Kelley, evoking Marx's classic description of the use of state violence in the service of wealth, describes this as "revenue by primitive accumulation."[7]

As a protection racket, however, policing is a dismal failure— all racket, no protection, beyond the wealthiest and whitest segments of society. Where threats of community violence are real and imminent, police offer notoriously little help. But where they can be leveraged into broader impunity and expanding budgets, police routinely exaggerate existing threats or fabricate entirely new ones. And, whether it's harassing and brutalizing people of color and the poor, or extorting resources that could otherwise be earmarked for early intervention, youth programs, drug treatment, social justice, or mental health care, the police produce the same violence they claim to prevent. The result, as we have seen, is a more dangerous world.

Police power is well-organized criminal blackmail, and police unions its ringleaders, taking to the media to stoke fear about imaginary threats or a "war on police"—and to communicate ransom demands.

—

This is all true even when the police aren't breaking the law—but they do so all the time. As we might expect in a job defined by access to both weapons and impunity, corruption is rife, and police have always been deeply embedded in organized crime as both "meat eaters" complicit in high-level crime and as small-scale bribe-takers, or "grass eaters." Police nationwide, past and present, have planted drugs and guns for false convictions—notoriously in Chicago, where more than a hundred felony drug convictions linked to a single disgraced sergeant, Ronald Watts, have recently been vacated. Policing is corrupt and corrupting; and lawbreaking by the cops isn't an exception—it's the rule.

But while many police break the law for their own benefit or simply because they *can*, police lawbreaking plays a deeper role in fabricating the world of police that we inhabit today. Walter Benjamin argued that the police not only uphold but also *remake* the law every day, because "the separation of lawmaking and law-preserving violence is suspended" by street-level police discretion and prerogative.[8] The past century has only confirmed this fact. Policing walks the line between the law and lawlessness, but also *shifts* that line, breaking and reshaping the law every day through a million discretionary acts. But while police lawbreaking is often rationalized, and indeed lionized, in popular culture and even academic studies as what is known as "Dirty Harry Syndrome"—heroic cops breaking the law in the unflinching pursuit of a higher justice—the reality is far different. Police don't break the law in the name of a more just world, but to transform the world in ever more authoritarian and anti-democratic directions. While crowing endlessly about law and order, they break the law in the name of the capitalist, white supremacist, and patriarchal orders governing our world. As the attack dogs of racial capitalism, police power tends naturally toward fascism: a permanent hierarchy of well-behaved white citizens.

The consistently reactionary orientation of police and their unions—their permanent hostility to labor movements and racial equality—is therefore no mistake. And it's no surprise that the Fraternal Order of Police (FOP), alongside the Border Patrol and Immigration and Customs Enforcement (ICE) unions, heartily endorsed a violent bully like Donald Trump, for whom law-and-order and lawbreaking were nearly synonymous. One of Trump's first acts in office, in fact, was to issue an executive order denouncing the "dangerous anti-police atmosphere in America," making perfectly clear that he would be the president of the police and not of the rioters and the looters—a thinly veiled threat directed at Black Lives Matter. While the lawlessness of the cops reached new heights under Trump, however, it's a mistake to believe—as many liberals do—that Trump himself was the cause. Policing didn't fundamentally change under Trump—he simply unleashed the police to do what police do best, and all indications suggest that Biden will do much the same.

Of course, the horizon of police fascism is far broader than policing. The FOP's wish list for Trump's first one hundred days in office was a truly intersectional pile of shit that extended well beyond police power. The FOP called for Trump to repeal the Deferred Action for Childhood Arrivals (DACA) program, tighten immigration restrictions, ease oversight of privately run migrant detention centers, attack sanctuary cities, strengthen sanctions on Cuba, expand the 287(g) program to deepen relations between local police and ICE, and reverse a Bush-era ban on racial profiling.[9] In short, they offered an overarching program for racial and class hierarchy in which the police are above the law, but the vast majority of us must obey or suffer the consequences. This thirst for obedience and social order, which combines racial resentment with a bootlicking fealty toward the rich, underlines the fascist tendency of policing in general, which manifests in the explicit sympathy many individual cops display toward openly racist and fascist organizations.

A recent report from the Brennan Center entitled *Hidden in Plain Sight* makes this astonishingly clear: "Since 2000, law enforcement officials with alleged connections to white supremacist groups or far-right militant activities have been exposed in Alabama, California, Connecticut, Florida, Illinois, Louisiana, Michigan, Nebraska, Oklahoma, Oregon, Texas, Virginia, Washington, West Virginia, and elsewhere."[10] These relationships are nothing new: police and far-right organizations have long been brothers-in-arms, intertwined branches of the same white supremacist tree. Police chiefs often led local Klan chapters, and as late as the 1980s Klan activity in police departments in Kentucky was found to be widespread. Police nationwide continue to work closely with far-right groups today, with new cases of ongoing police ties to the Klan and neo-Nazi organizations surfacing daily.

Los Angeles alone has seen a string of violent neo-Nazi gangs within its police forces, from the Lynwood Vikings to the Compton Executioners implicated in the 2020 killing of Andrés Guardado. After a 2016 clash between antifascists and white nationalists at the California state capitol that left several injured, court documents revealed how police later collaborated with and expressed sympathy for neo-Nazis while pursuing charges against the left.[11] In 2017, right-wing militias were spotted helping the Department of Homeland Security arrest counterprotesters in Portland, and in 2019 a Portland Police Bureau lieutenant was found to have collaborated with the far-right group Patriot Prayer, exchanging hundreds of friendly text messages and even filing charges against antifascists at the group's behest.[12]

If police in the past often looked on as Black people were publicly lynched, they do the same today as armed fascists attack Black Lives Matter and antifascists. The police know which side they are on, and sometimes they do more than just watch. Members of the Proud Boys, self-described "Western chauvinists," have been seen fist-bumping DC police and attending a FOP event in Philadelphia, and cops nationwide have been sacked for direct membership in the far-right organization. During the George Floyd protests, Minnesota state troopers and other police retaliated against protesters by slashing the tires of every car in a Kmart parking lot—in their words, they "strategically deflated tires to keep vehicles from being used in attacks."[13] According to one militia member patrolling the streets of Kenosha alongside Kyle Rittenhouse on the day he killed two demonstrators, police had announced their plans to push protesters toward the militias and then leave.[14] Indeed, such police collaboration with militias is widespread and well documented.

The so-called Patriot movement epitomizes this symbiotic relationship between police and the far right, and the lawless law-and-order vision they preach. The contradiction is right in the name: while professing loyalty to the US Constitution, many "patriots" are more than willing to take up arms against the government and others. This is even more explicit for groups like the Three Percenters and Oath Keepers, which recruit heavily from the ranks of current and former law enforcement while decrying the government as tyrannical. The United States is no stranger to self-proclaimed prophets, its hyper-individualism fertile soil for those claiming to be the sole interpreters of the word of God. For groups like the Oath Keepers, whose "oath" is to uphold the Constitution, every "sovereign citizen" is a constitutional scholar, empowered to interpret the scripture and strike down some laws in favor of others. This is the lawmaking prerogative of the police on steroids (often literally so).

Police routinely display far-right insignia—and notably the "III" logo of the Three Percenters—in tattoos and on uniforms, tactical gear, and bumper stickers. During the Ferguson rebellion, armed Oath Keepers were spotted on rooftops with semi-automatic rifles, and while the St. Louis County police chief ordered them to stand down, it turned out that he had Oath Keepers among his own ranks. One, Dan Page, was seen live on CNN shoving and threatening to arrest host Don Lemon and would later be fired after video of a violent racist tirade was leaked to the press. The contradictions of the Patriot movement were on full display when these avowed defenders of the Constitution stormed the US Capitol in early January 2021, in a quixotic attempt to overturn the results of the presidential election. Crowds of vehement Blue Lives Matter supporters fought uniformed police, killing one, and an Air Force veteran was shot and killed while invading the seat of government in whose name she had served four tours of duty in Iraq and Afghanistan.

What explains such close collaboration, even complicity, between law enforcement and the far right? The assumption is often that white supremacist have "infiltrated" police departments. While this is certainly true on some level, it neglects the historical function of policing and the ideology it produces. According to the Centre for the Analysis of the Radical Right, the presence of white supremacists in law enforcement has reached "epidemic" levels, but not due to infiltration from the outside. Instead, as we've seen, "links between the police and organized racism are as old as the institutions themselves," and police forces "have been breeding grounds for far-right ideology for decades."[15] We can't argue that the police have been taken over by white supremacists when their day-to-day function is to enforce racial domination, and it should come as no surprise that ideological adherents of white supremacy would be drawn to the job.

The police aren't being invaded by anti-democratic fascists; they *are* the fascists, and are busily training new recruits for the far right every day. If anything, the arrow of this violent symbiosis moves in the other direction. As Melissa Gira Grant has argued, "Far-right militias are learning impunity from the cops." While militias have been buoyed by support from Trump, who famously tweeted, "When the looting starts, the shooting starts," it is the history of policing and the systematic impunity police enjoy that matters most: "When these people kill, like police have, they can rest easy in the knowledge that it will take the same criminal legal system that supports them to convict them. They know that for everyone who condemns such a killing as murder, there will be some—maybe more—who welcome it as justice."[16] As I have shown, police impunity doesn't stop with the police, but spills over dangerously, extending to self-appointed deputies of whiteness and protectors of private property, to organized militias and lone wolf vigilantes.

On the global level, the circle widens further still as the imperialist policing of the planet proceeds without even the slightest pretense of democratic oversight. The presence of white supremacists in the military, not to mention the institutional cultivation of a martial culture of authoritarian violence in the armed forces, produces an inevitable anti-democratic creep across society. As Kathleen Belew shows, military intervention abroad is often the most powerful determinant of white nationalist violence at home. When Garrett Foster attended a BLM protest in Austin armed with an AK-47 to defend the crowd, he was shot dead by Daniel Perry, an active duty Army sergeant who had previously tweeted violent threats about protesters. And while global policing has always been a bipartisan affair, it reached aggressive new heights under Trump: in the midst of the George Floyd rebellions at home, Trump authorized sanctions on the International Criminal Court for having the temerity to investigate US troops for war crimes in Afghanistan and elsewhere. Moreover, one of his last acts in office was to pardon the Blackwater mercenaries implicated in the 2007 Nisour Square massacre that left seventeen Iraqi civilians dead.

The global police state operates with even more impunity than at home, and that's saying a whole hell of a lot.

—

At every level, policing conceals its fundamentally anti-democratic character under the veil of democratic legality, but that veil has never fit and today hangs in tatters. The police bristle at even minimal civilian oversight, and they misrepresent reality—stoking fear of a "war on police" or a "Ferguson effect"—to leverage special treatment under the law. A Georgia law signed in mid 2020, for example, criminalizes "bias-motivated intimi-dation" against police—provisions that state Republicans had earlier attempted to slide into broader hate crime legislation. Police power breaks down all limits and barriers and aspires to a world of total impunity, as the NYPD's war on de Blasio made perfectly clear. Even their extortion isn't purely financial: wages, overtime, and retirement benefits take a backseat to ensuring that cops are not accountable for their actions.

The implications are clear: the police are not answerable to the people and instead represent a permanent, rolling assault on the *demos* of democracy. Such aggressive impunity is not compatible with even the stunted farce of a democratic system that we enjoy in the United States, where political participa-tion is limited to an occasional choice between candidates preselected by wealth and power, much less a more radically democratic vision. It's high time to choose between democracy and the police. However, this doesn't mean fighting to defend a corrupt and exclusionary two-party system that masquerades as democratic while attempting to monopolize the name. If the cops were born from the wreckage of Reconstruction and the betrayed promise of abolition democracy, this tragedy was also a testament to far more ambitious horizons of democratic possibility.

Abolition democracy was the first real attempt to include *everyone* in the political community. But you can't simply make citizens of slaves—the "mudsill" or foundation of the entire system—without radically destabilizing the architectonics of white supremacy and transforming the very meaning of democracy in the process. At some point, quantity becomes quality. For Marx, workers constitute a universal class, since to fight for their own liberation is to fight for the liberation of all—the abolition of the world as it exists. Workers, he famously observed, have nothing to lose but their chains, and when it comes to the brutally literal chains of slavery, this is even more evidently true. This is why, for W.E.B. Du Bois, abolition democracy was democracy of a specifically expansive type, the kind of democracy that becomes possible only through abolition. And this is why, under Reconstruction governments, emancipation for the most oppressed meant expanded rights for *all*: poor people, white and Black alike, women, men, and children. And this is why the unmatched experiment of abolition democracy was eradicated by white terror—by the nascent cops and the Klan, hand in hand.

In other words, the police emerged historically not as a supplement to abolition democracy but a substitute for it; not to safeguard the demos but to patrol its divisions and exclusions, ensuring Black subjection and white rule, to the detriment of all poor and working people. We haven't seen democracy of this kind ever since. Instead, we have seen the police enforce Jim Crow in the South and patrol territorial segregation in the North—and do the same in the name of gentrification today. Police who once openly cowed Black voters away from the polls today oversee school resegregation and the boundaries of increasingly gerrymandered electoral districts. Not only is this policing and mass incarceration complex responsible for rolling back democratic participation through the systematic disenfranchisement of millions; but when people take to the streets to fight back, it is the cops that loudly criminalize and brutally repress those movements. Whether by their lobbying foundations and fraternal orders or with shields and batons, the police mark the boundary of who gets to participate in political life and whose voices matter most.

Today, abolition democracy isn't about the democracy we have, but the democracy we can *imagine*. It's about what new kinds of democratic participation become possible when we roll back police power, the stifling burden of whiteness, and capitalist exploitation. It means building an ambitious democratic vision that remains faithful to the legacy of past freedom struggles and those looming on the horizon. On the crushing of abolition democracy nearly a century and a half ago, Du Bois wrote that "democracy died save in the hearts of Black folks" and that "the plight of the white working class throughout the world" suffered immeasurably as a consequence. But today, this radically democratic contraband, hidden away at the heart of Black struggle and the "dark proletariat" across the globe, offers the key to a new democratic horizon that is synonymous with a world without police.[17]

As should be clear by now, a world without police is also a world without capitalism, and without that structure of unearned power and privilege we call "whiteness." We can't abolish one part of this deadly triad while leaving the others untouched: where economic and racial inequality exist, so too will there be those hired to police those boundaries, even if they go by another name. And where these are not understood in relation to patriarchal power, policing will draw ever more from the wellspring of masculine authority and incel resentment. This is why the idea of getting rid of the police can seem so impossibly utopian—for most people, it's just plain crazy talk. Policing is as American as apple pie, and it has wormed its way to the very core—*all* the apples are bad apples.

If we can't abolish the police without also abolishing capitalism, patriarchy, and whiteness, then ours is a daunting task indeed. But here's the trick: it is precisely *because* the police are so central for American capitalism that even apparently small changes can have far broader impacts. Indeed, the police are so overwhelmingly important for the American power structure that even the smallest cracks and fissures in their power can unleash dramatic repercussions and unforeseeable changes. While the power police wield can seem natural, overwhelming, and unassailable, we mustn't forget that the police guard their power so jealously because it is also incredibly fragile. Even minor oversight makes it more difficult for the police to use their everyday discretion to ensure obedience through fear and to uphold the color line, while giving communities expanding room to maneuver and struggle.

We find this confirmed in their panicked reaction to every wave of mass resistance against police murder, and to those movements today demanding defunding and abolition. We can read our own power in their desperate exhortations to "back the blue"; we can sense our own systolic rush in the blood that floods their pink faces as they squeal loudly on *Fox News*. But despite liberal handwringing that militant Black rebellion is counterproductive and produces only reactionary white back-lash, the balance sheet of US history arcs toward a frustratingly evasive, but real freedom. And as the past year has shown, when the police react ferociously to the most human of demands, they do our work for us, making the case for abolition all the more clear. If policing is the Achilles' heel of the US racial order, it sometimes seems more like plastic explosives pressed against the foundation.

As the old saying goes, policing is the third rail of American politics because that's where the power is.

—

A world without police is not a utopia. It is *real*, and in some sense, it already exists. It is all around us, from our families, blocks, and community organizations to broader experiments across the globe and the powerful wave of abolitionist struggle that surged forth to demand justice for George Floyd, Breonna Taylor, and so many others—a real, lasting justice in which *we keep us safe.* What seems utopian to us is the idea that these small glimpses might become something much bigger, that the amorphous world we share with those we trust could become *the* world. But this is because we are told every day that there is no alternative to the devastation of the present, no possible world without police.

When Octavia Butler set pen to paper to write *Parable of the Sower,* she detailed the wreckage of a future characterized by scarcity and insecurity—a description that rings all too true in the present. Even in her dystopian imagination, however, Butler couldn't even make the police sound any worse than they are today. She simply described them exactly as they exist and have always existed: as corrupt and self-interested, useless at best but devastatingly harmful at worst. The police, she wrote, placing the words carefully in the mouths of her protagonists, "may be able to avenge you, but they can't protect you . . . They never helped when people called for help. They came later, and more often than not, made a bad situation worse." *Parable of the Sower* is not pure dystopia, however, but attests to the fragments of community that persist, like so many seeds, just below the surface, waiting to sprout forth from the sheer impossibility of things continuing as they are. "We can't live this way," one character insists, before another offers the sharp counterpoint: "We *do* live this way."

Radical alternatives to the world of police today emerge not as a distant dream or impossibly detached horizon, but as the lived reality of moments of resistance—no matter how small—struggles unfolding in the streets and in communities. The police are a living nightmare, and the world they work to build every day, from street-level brutality to federal legislation, is a radically dystopian project that forecloses on human possibility in favor of institutionalized hierarchy and control. This project stalks dreams of human equality and freedom without ever fully defeating them, two possible futures pinballing off one another in the dialectics of our political imagination. And as we have seen, some of the most ambitious experiments in building communities without police have emerged not from a position of security and comfort, but out of the direst of circumstances. As the Minneapolis-based abolitionist organization MPD150 describes it: "Millions of us already live in a world where we don't even think about calling on the police for help; it isn't some kind of far-future fantasy."

Abolition is not a distant utopia, however. The reality is that nothing could be more utopian than believing that things could continue as they are. Abolition means reckoning with the wreckage of the present and assuming the ultimately unavoidable task of fashioning this wreckage into liberation. Rather than simply prefiguring a future world, abolition *is* that world, as an expansive, material force.

—

"What do you do with an institution whose core function is the control and elimination of black people specifically, and people of color and the poor more broadly?" This is the question posed by Mychal Denzel Smith, and his answer unhesitating: "You abolish it." You don't reform it, you don't negotiate with it, you don't split the difference. You don't fight inhumanity halfway. This was true of slavery in the past and remains true of the police today. More than fifty years ago, James Baldwin wrote that "the police treat the Negro like a dog" and little has changed. We need look no further than Mike Brown's lifeless body lying in the street for four hours to see how true Baldwin's words ring today—indeed, more than true: it is only in the most forgotten neighborhoods that even a dead animal would be treated so badly.

What would a world in which the police are obsolete look like? Smith admits that we don't have all the answers. "I only know there will be less dead black people," and that this would be a world marked by "full social, economic, and political equality." While the details remain hazy, he insists, "it's a world worth imagining."[18] The task before us is to bind this imagination to construction, to dare to dream and dare to build. A world without police would be a world without poverty and hunger, in which everyone would have enough, and no one would need to look over their shoulder. It would be a world without white supremacy, in which no one is viewed as dispensable or as deserving anything less than a fully human life. It would be a world without the violence of patriarchy, in which women, children, and those gendered otherwise are not seen as objects for possession—economic or sexual. Without capitalism, white supremacy, and patriarchy, why on earth would we need the police? And since the police exist to govern and reinforce barriers, boundaries, and borders, to fight the police is to fight those divisions racking our world as well.

Police abolition is a wager, but like any wager, it's a question of the odds. The police simply don't do what they claim to do, nor what many people believe they do. They don't protect and they don't serve; they *do* dehumanize and brutalize entire communities, and target the vulnerable for physical and sexual abuse with near-total impunity. The stakes and the odds both become sharper as a result: Are you going to bet on something that has failed systematically, or on the possibility that we might be able to build something different? The world without police might seem far away—but, as we have seen, it already exists, here and now. It might seem expensive, but we already throw billions of dollars down the insatiable black hole of policing while getting nothing but more violence in return.

What would happen if the billions of dollars spent on the police annually were instead dedicated to community safety in the short term and to building a community of equals in the future? And while full economic, racial, and gender equality may seem impossible, nothing is more far-fetched than the belief that we could go on like this forever. While radical change can sometimes seem impossible, we have already accomplished just that: we've changed so much so quickly, and more than anything else, we have changed minds, broken down barriers, and opened up new vistas of possibility where impossibility had previously reigned. We have pried open the door of the new with the leverage of mass struggle. And the tide is turning, as it did with prisons: in the United States and across the globe, people are sick of the cops, and abolition is on the table before us as never before.

As Ruth Wilson Gilmore tells us, "Abolition requires that we change one thing: everything."[19] Let's get to it.

Acknowledgments

This book is a product of the upsurge. Its pace was quickened by street rebellion, its temperature raised by the warmth of burning cop cars. It was written under quarantine lockdown but also under curfew and National Guard occupation. Its sentences are punctuated by rubber bullets, tear gas, and concussion grenades, but also by the sound of breaking windows and the ringing of a single hammer battering a statue of Frank Rizzo into a well-deserved historical oblivion. This is to say, it was written in Philadelphia, a city where the MOVE bombing still resounds like a subterranean thunderclap—a city of political resistance and of political prisoners, a city that has changed dramatically in the decade I have spent here.

This is a book, and here I should just be brutally honest, that is motived by an outrage bordering on hatred. My thanks to the police for every day proving their inhumanity and obsolescence. They have done far more than anyone else to show that the world of police is not a world worth inhabiting. It's not often that your enemies lay their necks so voluntarily on the chopping block.

It was as a member of Bring the Ruckus, and from the late Joel Olson, that I first learned how the police hold together the global capitalist monstrosity, and how this hatred of the police thus holds the key to revolutionary strategy. My deepest gratitude to the many comrades alongside whom I have struggled in the years since, as the long global upsurge has gained pace: Raider Nation Collective, Trayvon Martin Organizing Committee, Free the Streets, Action Against Black Genocide, and the Abolition Journal Collective.

This book draws inspiration from the many heirs of Tubman and Du Bois whose names seem almost redundant since their brilliance flows like an undercurrent throughout, but here are some: Ruth Wilson Gilmore, Mariame Kaba, Robin D.G. Kelley, and Angela Davis. This book draws insights, moreover, from an entire generation of comrade-scholars of policing: Kristian Williams, whose authoritative work I first read as a young organizer, and more recently Alex Vitale, Ben Brucato, David Correia, and Tyler Wall.

Concretely, this book would never have been written were it not for the patient efforts of both my agent Róisín Davis from Roam Agency and my editor Ben Mabie at Verso, who helped transform my involuntary exile from academia into the words you are reading here. Róisín has been a thoughtful, creative, and persistent sounding-board and advocate; Ben is a truly gifted and intuitive editor who grasped the essence of this project and has helped to shape it indelibly.

This book has benefited from a decade of conversations—some short, others endless—with countless comrades, especially Christina Heatherton, Jordan Camp, Sina Kramer, Joe Lowndes, Andrew Dilts, Charmaine Chua, and of course Viktoria Zerda. Thanks as well to those who provided useful commentary and insights: Ian Schiffer, Laleh Khalili, Ashley Bohrer, Marisol LeBrón, Kali Akuno, Zach Levenson, Richard Pithouse, Bret Grote, and Mae Boda. For leading by example and for her unflinching generosity and support, I owe an enormous debt to Keeanga-Yamahtta Taylor.

Thanks, finally and as always, to my parents who, by teaching me to love equality, also taught me to hate its opposite.

May we live life according to the late Fred Hampton's golden rule: "I am the people, I am not the pig."

Notes

Introduction

1. Joshua Clover, *Riot. Strike. Riot. A New Era of Uprisings* (London and New York: Verso, 2016), 180.
2. "'We're Not Abolishing Safety': Minneapolis Councillor Explains Plan to Dismantle Police," CBC, June 9, 2020, cbc.ca.
3. Julia Lurie, "They Built a Utopian Sanctuary in a Minneapolis Hotel. Then They Got Evicted," *Mother Jones*, June 12, 2020, motherjones. com. This has been a difficult experiment indeed. Security became a central challenge at the Sheraton, both internally and from cops and vigilantes threatening from the outside, and the same was true of the encampments that emerged at Powderhorn Park and elsewhere. One, in Brackett Park, sought to provide a safe haven for largely Indigenous women without involving the police—surveys of the encampments showed that nearly half of residents were Indigenous.
4. A Bloomberg investigation concluded that, despite embracing the language of defunding, most departments in fact *increased* police budgets. Sarah Holder, Fola Akinnibi, and Christoper Cannon, "'We Have Not Defunded Anything': Big Cities Boost Police Budgets," *Bloomberg CityLab*, September 22, 2020, bloomberg.com.
5. Miles Parks, "Confederate Statues Were Built to Further a 'White Supremacist Future,'" NPR, August 20, 2017, npr.org.
6. Angela Davis, *Are Prisons Obsolete?* (New York: Seven Stories Press, 2003).
7. Mariame Kaba, "Yes, We Mean Literally Abolish the Police," *New York Times*, June 12, 2020, nytimes.com.
8. W.E.B. Du Bois, *Black Reconstruction in America, 1860–1880* (New York: The Free Press, 1998), 346.
9. Du Bois, *Black Reconstruction*, 239.
10. Du Bois, *Black Reconstruction*, 30.

11. Angela Y. Davis, *Abolition Democracy: Beyond Empire, Prisons, and Torture* (New York: Seven Stories Press, 2005), 73–4.

12. See the late comrade Joel Olson, "The Freshness of Fanaticism: The Abolitionist Defense of Zealotry," *Perspectives on Politics* 5, n. 4 (December 2007).

13. A 2017 ACLU poll showed that 91 percent of Americans support criminal justice reform, while 71 percent support reducing the prison population.

14. "What Is the PIC? What Is Abolition?," Critical Resistance official website, criticalresistance.org.

15. As Robin D.G. Kelley reminds us, such calls go back at least as far as the 1968 vice presidential bid of Black socialist Paul Boutelle (later Kwame Somburu). "Insecure: Policing under Racial Capitalism," *Spectre* 1, n. 2 (Fall 2020), 16.

16. "The Strategy," A World without Police official website, aworldwithout-police.org.

17. Kaba, "Yes, We Mean Literally Abolish the Police."

1. The Pig Majority

1. Naomi Murakawa, *The First Civil Right: How Liberals Built Prison America* (Oxford: Oxford University Press, 2014), 68. As Ida B. Wells described it in 1893: "Over a thousand black men, women and children have been thus sacrificed the past ten years. Masks have long since been thrown aside and the lynchings of the present day take place in broad daylight. The sheriffs, police and state officials stand by and see the work well done." *The Light of Truth* (New York: Penguin, 2014). And as David Correia and Tyler Wall put it, "Lynching was lawmaking." *Police: A Field Guide* (London and New York: Verso, 2017), 53.

2. Simon Purdue, "The Other Epidemic: White Supremacists in Law Enforcement," *Open Democracy*, August 6, 2020, opendemocracy.net.

3. Haley Willis et al., "Tracking the Suspect in the Fatal Kenosha Shootings," *New York Times*, August 27, 2020, nytimes.com.

4. Ta-Nehisi Coates, *Between the World and Me* (New York: Spiegel & Grau, 2015), 79.

5. W.E.B. Du Bois, *Black Reconstruction in America, 1860–1880* (New York: The Free Press, 1998), 12.

6. W.E.B. Du Bois, *The Souls of Black Folk* (New York: Penguin, 1996), 145.

7. Du Bois, *Black Reconstruction*, 700, 12.
8. Du Bois, *The Souls of Black Folk*, 145; *Black Reconstruction*, 12. More than sixty years later, James Baldwin succinctly summarized the two functions of the police: "to keep the Negro in his place and to protect white business interests." "A Report from Occupied Territory," *The Nation*, July 11, 1966.
9. James Forman Jr., *Locking Up Our Own: Crime and Punishment in Black America* (New York: Farrar, Straus & Giroux, 2017), 9.
10. W.E.B. Du Bois, *The Philadelphia Negro: A Social Study* (Philadelphia: University of Pennsylvania Press, 1996), 132.
11. Well-known studies have shown how participants in video game simulations are more likely to shoot unarmed Black suspects and less likely to shoot armed white suspects, and that Black participants are as likely as white participants to exhibit these biases. Joshua Correll et al., "The Police Officer's Dilemma: Using Ethnicity to Disambiguate Potentially Threatening Individuals," *Journal of Personality and Social Psychology* 83, n. 6 (2002). One study even shows how Korean participants are more likely to shoot suspects if the police officer they are *playing* in a simulation is white instead of Black. S.H. Park and H.J. Kim, "Assumed Race Moderates Spontaneous Racial bias in a Computer-based Police Simulation, *Asian Journal of Social Psychology* 18, n. 3 (2005).
12. Terrence McCoy, "Ferguson Shows How a Police Force Can Turn Into a Plundering 'Collection Agency,'" *Washington Post*, March 5, 2015, washingtonpost.com.
13. Keeanga-Yamahtta Taylor, *From #BlackLivesMatter to Black Liberation* (Chicago: Haymarket, 2016), 76–9.
14. Brian Mann, "Charles Rangel: America's 'Front-Line General' in the Drug War," *North Country Public Radio*, August 19, 2013, northcountrypublicradio.org.
15. Taylor, *From #BlackLivesMatter to Black Liberation*, 100–1.
16. Taylor, *From #BlackLivesMatter to Black Liberation*, 78–9.
17. Forman, *Locking Up Our Own*, 11.
18. Alex S. Vitale, *The End of Policing* (London and New York: Verso, 2017), 2.
19. Forman, *Locking Up Our Own*, 157. Vesla Weaver paints an even more sympathetic picture of Black leadership, although one wonders on what level leaders should have known that their demands would be only selectively embraced. "The Untold Story of Mass Incarceration," *Boston Review*, October 24, 2017, bostonreview.net.

20. Elizabeth Hinton, "The Minneapolis Uprising in Context," *Boston Review*, May 29, 2020, bostonreview.net.
21. Between 1972 and 1991, Chicago Police Department officer Jon Burge, a Korea and Vietnam military police veteran, oversaw the torture and coerced confessions of dozens. See Kelly Hayes, "Chicago Police Torture: Explained," *The Appeal*, December 5, 2019, theappeal.org. Burge's methods were drawn from the arsenal of global counterinsurgency warfare, and like many Latin American countries that have experienced brutal dictatorships, Chicago too has an entire institution, the Chicago Torture Justice Center, dedicated to victims of police torture. Burge himself learned torture techniques at Fort Benning, Georgia, home to the infamous School of the Americas.
22. Alex Vitale makes this point eloquently in an interview with Madison Pauly, "What a World without Cops Would Look Like," *Mother Jones*, June 2, 2020, motherjones.com.
23. "Criminal Justice Expenditures: Police, Corrections, and Courts," Urban Institute, urban.org.
24. Carlos Ballesteros, "Chicago Has Nearly Tripled Per Capita Police Spending since 1964, data show," *Injustice Watch*, June 9, 2020, injusticewatch.org.
25. Brian Barrett, "The Pentagon's Hand-Me-Downs Helped Militarize Police. Here's How," *Wired*, June 2, 2020, wired.com. For the full article, see Casey Delehanty et al., "Militarization and Police Violence: The Case of the 1033 Program," *Research and Politics* 4, n. 2 (April 2017).
26. "Criminalizing Children at School," *New York Times*, April 18, 2013, nytimes.com.
27. Maya Lindberg, "False Sense of Security," *Teaching Tolerance* (Spring 2015), 24.
28. Melinda D. Anderson, "The Rise of Law Enforcement on College Campuses," *The Atlantic*, September 28, 2015, theatlantic.com. In Philadelphia, controversy erupted when it was revealed that local universities like the University of Pennsylvania had been involved in policing the George Floyd protests far off campus. As Anderson explains, the University of Chicago Police Department (UCPD), whose patrol areas are home to far more nonstudents than students, are notorious for off-campus enforcement. While local critics assert that UCPD "systematically racially profiles and harasses ... with complete impunity ... Under current Illinois law, as a private institution the university is not required to disclose arrest reports, traffic stop data, or information concerning its off-campus patrols."

29. Emma Reynolds, "Calls Are Growing to Defund Police in the US. Here Are Some Lessons from Overseas," CNN, June 24, 2020, cnn. com.

30. Mark Neocleous, *The Fabrication of Social Order: A Critical Theory of Police Power* (London: Pluto, 2000), xi.

31. Correia and Wall, *Police: A Field Guide.*

32. Peter Linebaugh, "Police and Plunder," *Counterpunch*, February 13, 2015, counterpunch.org.

33. Kelley, "Insecure," 19.

34. Beth E. Richie and Kayla M. Martensen, "Resisting Carcerality, Embracing Abolition: Implications for Feminist Social Work Practice," *Affilia: Journal of Women and Social Work* 35, n.1 (2020), 12, 14.

35. See especially Dorothy Roberts, *Shattered Bonds: The Color Of Child Welfare* (New York: Basic Civitas, 2002).

36. Vitale, *The End of Policing*, 42.

37. Roberto González, Hugh Gusterson, and David Price, "Introduction," in Network of Concerned Anthropologists, ed., *The Counter-Counterinsurgency Manual, or, Notes on Demilitarizing American Society* (Chicago: Prickly Paradigm, 2009), 13.

38. Alfredo Mirandé, *Gringo Justice* (Notre Dame, IN: University of Notre Dame Press, 1987), 67, 72.

39. Kelly Lytle Hernández, *Migra! A History of the U.S. Border Patrol* (Berkeley: University of California Press, 2010), 20.

40. Mirandé, *Gringo Justice*, 74.

41. Mirandé, *Gringo Justice*, 146.

42. Ryan Devereaux, "The Bloody History of Border Militias Runs Deep—and Law Enforcement Is Part of It," *The Intercept*, April 23, 2019, theintercept.com.

43. Michael Muskal and Lauren Raab, "Cleveland blames Tamir Rice, 12, for his own death, then apologizes," *Los Angeles Times*, March 2, 2015, latimes.com.

44. Du Bois, *Black Reconstruction*, 42, 631.

45. Stuart Schrader, *Badges without Borders: How Global Counter-insurgency Transformed American Policing* (Oakland: University of California Press, 2019), 13.

46. Jordan T. Camp and Christina Heatherton, *Policing the Planet: Why the Policing Crisis Led to Black Lives Matter* (London and New York: Verso, 2016).

47. Schrader, *Badges without Borders*, 25.

48. Sean McFate, "Mercenaries and War: Understanding Private Armies

Today," National Defense University Press, December 4, 2019, ndupress.ndu.edu.

49. Schrader, *Badges without Borders*, 24.
50. Du Bois, *Black Reconstruction*, 16.

2. Who Do You Serve? Who Do You Protect?

1. Thanks in large part to the efforts (or lack thereof) of the police themselves, there is no good overall data on killings by police, but a growing consensus places that number around twice previously existing official and self-reported data, somewhere around 1,000 deaths annually. See the methodological discussion in Franklin E. Zimring, *When Police Kill* (Cambridge, MA: Harvard University Press, 2017).
2. Ryan Gabrielson et al., "Deadly Force, in Black and White," *ProPublica*, October 10, 2014, propublica.org; Gabriel L. Schwartz and Jaquelyn L. Jahn, "Mapping Fatal Police Violence across U.S. Metropolitan Areas: Overall Rates and Racial/Ethnic Inequities, 2013–2017," *PLOS ONE*, June 24, 2020, journals.plos.org.
3. The relationship between many Asian American communities and the police is complex, as underlined recently by Tou Tho's complicity in George Floyd's death, and by NYPD officer Peter Liang's killing of Akai Gurley in East New York—not to mention the defense of Liang by many in the Chinese American community. Polling shows, however, that younger Asian Americans are more attuned to racial discrimination in policing: whereas 40 percent of elderly Asians believe the police treat different races equally, this number is as low as 15 percent for younger generations. Hansei Lo Wang, "On Police Treatment, Asian-Americans Show Ethnic, Generational Splits," NPR, April 18, 2017, npr.org.
4. Heather Mac Donald, "The Myth of Systemic Police Racism," *Wall Street Journal*, June 2, 2020, wsj.com.
5. See Andrew Gelman et al., "An Analysis of the New York City Police Department's 'Stop-and-Frisk' Policy in the Context of Claims of Racial Bias," *Journal of the American Statistical Association* 102, n. 479 (2007).
6. Dean Knox et al., "Administrative Records Mask Racially Biased Policing," *American Political Science Review* 114, n. 3 (August 2020).
7. This is what Aubrey Clayton calls "the statistical paradox of police killings," *Boston Globe*, June 11, 2020, bostonglobe.com.
8. Mapping Police Violence, "2020 Police Violence Report," policeviolencereport.org.

9. Rob Arthur, "New Data Shows Police Use More Force against Black Citizens Even Though Whites Resist More," *Slate*, May 30, 2019, slate.com.

10. Heather Mac Donald, "I Cited Their Study, So They Disavowed It," *Wall Street Journal*, July 8, 2020, wsj.com. One of the authors, Joseph Cesario, responded that "the reason for the retraction had nothing to do with the claims made by Heather Mac Donald," but instead that the authors had "overstepped with the inferences we made from our data." Cesario further revealed that he had informed Mac Donald of this decision, and the reasons for it, before her op-ed misrepresenting and denouncing the decision. "Why We Withdrew the Police Shooting Study," *Wall Street Journal*, July 14, 2020, wsj.com. The official *PNAS* retraction statement is available at psyarxiv.com/dj57k.

11. Chris Polansky, "TPD Major: Police Shoot Black Americans 'Less Than We Probably Ought To,'" Public Radio Tulsa, June 9, 2020, publicradiotulsa.org.

12. Adolph Reed Jr., "How Racial Disparity Does Not Help Make Sense of Patterns of Police Violence," *Nonsite*, September 16, 2016, nonsite.org.

13. New Mexico routinely boasts the highest rate of police killings in the country, with Albuquerque police killing at a rate eight times that of the NYPD—much of it directed against Latinx and Indigenous people. See Rachel Aviv, "Your Son is Deceased," *The New Yorker*, January 26, 2015, newyorker.com.

14. Schwartz and Jahn, "Mapping Fatal Police Violence."

15. German Lopez, "Why Police So Often See Unarmed Black Men as Threats," *Vox*, September 20, 2016, vox.com.

16. Jamelle Bouie, "Michael Brown Wasn't a Superhuman Demon," *Slate*, November 26, 2014, slate.com. Racism is nothing if not opportunistic. When LAPD chief Daryl Gates sought to excuse deaths caused by police chokeholds, he argued that "in some blacks when it is applied, the veins or arteries do not open up as fast as they do in normal people." "Coast Police Chief Accused of Racism," *New York Times*, May 13, 1982, nytimes.com.

17. "Black Boys Viewed as Older, Less Innocent Than Whites, Research Finds," *American Psychological Association* (March 2014), apa.org; Naa Oyo A. Kwate and Shatema Threadcraft, "Perceiving the Black female body: Race and Gender in Political Constructions of Body Weight," *Race and Social Problems* 7, n. 3 (July 2015); Tom Jacobs, "The Dangerous Delusion of the Big, Scary Black Man," *Pacific Standard*, June 14, 2017, psmag.com.

18. Taylor, *From #BlackLivesMatter to Black Liberation*, 211. Somewhat

embarrassingly, Reed appears to have criticized Taylor's book without having read it, or even perused the table of contents. He writes that her "point of departure requires harmonizing the interests of the black poor and working class with those of the black professional-managerial class," when much of the book—and the entirety of the third and fifth chapters—makes the opposite argument. "On the End(s) of Black Politics," *Nonsite*, September 16, 2016, nonsite.org.

19. Alex S. Vitale, *The End of Policing* (London and New York: Verso, 2017), 76.

20. Bill Hutchinson, "'They Didn't Give a Damn': Mother of Slain Walter Wallace Says Police Knew Her Son Was in a Mental Crisis," ABC, October 28, 2020, abcnews.go.com.

21. Doris A. Fuller et al., *Overlooked in the Undercounted: The Role of Mental Illness in Fatal Law Enforcement Encounters* (Treatment Advocacy Center, 2015), treatmentadvocacycenter.org. Some estimates, moreover, indicate that one-third of those killed by police—including Sandra Bland, Eric Garner, and Freddie Gray—suffered from a disability broadly understood, leading campaigners to draw attention to the connections between disability and police murder. Dominic Bradley and Sarah Katz, "Sandra Bland, Eric Garner, Freddie Gray: The Toll of Police Violence on Disabled Americans," *Guardian*, June 9, 2020, theguardian.com.

22. Jacob Bor et al., "Police Killings and Their Spillover Effects on the Mental Health of Black Americans: A Population-Based, Quasi-Experimental Study," *Lancet* 392, n. 10144.

23. Kristian Williams, *Our Enemies in Blue: Police and Power in America* (Cambridge: South End Press, 2007), 70–1; Mike Davis, *City of Quartz: Excavating the Future in Los Angeles* (London: Verso, 1990), 294.

24. See Victoria Law, "Against Carceral Feminism," *Jacobin*, October 17, 2014, jacobinmag.com.

25. I vividly remember the cynicism of Philadelphia Police during the Occupy movement, who shrugged off reports of sexual assault in the camp until Mayor Michael Nutter found it convenient to publicly denounce the occupation as unsafe and demand its eviction. An earlier report showed "that the Philadelphia police department harbored a culture where rape victims were routinely belittled and their cases ignored by patrol officers and detectives, while predators got away with sexual assault and, literally, murder." Joanna Walters, "Investigating Rape in Philadelphia," *Guardian*, July 2, 2013, theguardian.com.

26. Caroline Mimbs Nyce, "These Attacks Could've Been Prevented," *The*

Atlantic, July 15, 2019, theatlantic.com.

27. Jim Mustian and Michael R. Sisak, "'Clearance Rate' For Rape Cases Fell Last Year to Its Lowest Point since at Least the 1960s, according to FBI Data," *Chicago Tribune*, December 27, 2018, chicagotribune. com.

28. Exceptional clearance gives local police broad power to mark cases as cleared even when no arrest has been made, and this power is abused by some cities in particular. A data set compiled by *Newsy* and *ProPublica* showed wide discrepancies between official and real clearance rates: in Oakland, where the official clearance rate was 60 percent, some 47 percent were cleared exceptionally, meaning that only 13 percent of cases saw arrests. This abysmal clearance rate was similar to many other large cities: 14 percent in Los Angeles, an astonishing 8 percent in Seattle and Chicago, with Phoenix, Tucson, and other cities even lower. Many, New York included, refused to provide data. Lena V. Groeger et al., "Could Your Police Department Be Inflating Rape Clearance Rates," *ProPublica/Newsy*, November 15, 2018, propublica.org.

29. Andrew Van Dam, "Less than 1% of Rapes Lead to Felony Convictions. At Least 89% of Victims Face Emotional and Physical Consequences," *Washington Post*, October 6, 2018, washingtonpost. com. According to the Rape, Abuse and Incest National Network (RAINN), this number is even lower: of 1,000 assaults only 230 are reported, 46 lead to arrest, only 9 of these are referred to prosecutors, only 5 lead to felony conviction, and only 4.6 are incarcerated—less than one-half of one percent. See "The Criminal Justice System: Statistics," RAINN official website, rainn.org.

30. Norm Stamper, *Breaking Rank: A Top Cop's Exposé of the Dark Side of American Policing* (New York: Nation Books, 2006), 123.

31. Cato Institute, National Police Misconduct Reporting Project, *2010 Annual Report*; Correia and Wall, *Police: A Field Guide*, 47–9.

32. Zoë Carpenter, "The Police Violence We Aren't Talking About," *The Nation*, August 27, 2014, thenation.com. See also Philip M. Stinson et al., "Police Sexual Misconduct: A National Scale Study of Arrested Officers," *Criminal Justice Policy Review* 26, n. 7 (2014).

33. Correia and Wall, *Police: A Field Guide*, 49.

34. Matthew Spina, "When a Protector Becomes a Predator," *Buffalo News*, November 22, 2015.

35. Matt Sedensky, "AP: Hundreds of Officers Lose Licenses over Sex Misconduct," *AP News*, November 1, 2015, apnews.com. As a recent

ProPublica report has demonstrated, sexual assault by police is not solely targeted at women: Joaquin Sapien, Topher Sanders, and Nate Schweber, "Over a Dozen Black and Latino Men Accused a Cop of Humiliating, Invasive Strip Searches," September 10, 2020, propublica.org.

36. Isidoro Rodriguez, "Predators behind the Badge: Confronting Police Sexual Misconduct," *The Crime Report*, March 12, 2020, thecrimereport.org.

37. Natasha Lennard, "Police Reportedly Claim a Brooklyn Teen Consented to Sex in Custody. That's Impossible," *The Intercept*, October 20, 2017, theintercept.com.

38. Natasha Lennard, "In Secretive Court Hearing, NYPD Cops Who Raped Brooklyn Teen in Custody Get No Jail Time," *The Intercept*, August 30, 2019, theintercept.com.

39. L.B. Johnson, *On the Front Lines: Police Stress and Family Well-Being*, Hearing before the Select Committee on Children, Youth, and Families House of Representatives, 102nd Congress, First Session (Washington, DC: US Government Printing Office, 1991); P.H. Neidig et al., "Interspousal Aggression in Law Enforcement Families: A Preliminary Investigation," *Police Studies* 15, n.1 (1992).

40. National Center on Domestic and Sexual Violence, "When the Batterer Is a Cop," ncdsv.org. Philadelphia District Attorney Larry Krasner explained to the writer Eve Ewing how he himself had defended two women who, "after finding their police officer husbands cheating and trying to divorce them, had been arrested by those same husbands. One was arrested twice." "Blue Blood: America's Brotherhood of Police Officers," *Vanity Fair*, August 25, 2020, vanityfair.com.

41. See "Police Family Violence Fact Sheet," National Center for Women and Policing official website, womenandpolicing.com.

42. National Coalition against Domestic Violence, "Domestic Violence in the Military," ncdsv.org. A recent review of existing (similarly self-reported and recent) data shows "rates of past-year perpetration of IPV [Intimate Partner Violence] ranged from 13.3 percent to 47 percent among male active duty servicemembers and 13.5 percent to 42 percent among male Veterans." Jennifer M. Gierisch et al., "Intimate Partner Violence: Prevalence among U.S. Military Veterans and Active Duty Servicemembers and a Review of Intervention Approaches," Department of Veterans Affairs (August 2013).

43. Manny Fernandez, "'You Have to Pay with Your Body': The Hidden Nightmare of Sexual Violence on the Border," *New York Times*, March

3, 2019, nytimes.com. Lomo Kriel, "ICE Deported a Key Witness in Investigation of Sexual Assault and Harassment at El Paso Detention Center," *Texas Tribune*, September 15, 2020, texastribune.org.

44. National Center for Transgender Equality, *Blueprint for Equality* (October 2016), 28.

45. National Coalition of Anti-violence Programs, "Hate Violence against Transgender Communities" (April 2017), avp.org.

46. Melissa Gira Grant, *Playing the Whore: The Work of Sex Work* (London and New York: Verso, 2014), 4–6.

47. Nicole Reinert, "Why the 'Celeste Guap' Scandal Isn't Only about Her," KQED, September 29, 2016, kqed.org.

48. Correia and Wall, *Police: A Field Guide*, 255.

49. Isabel Cristo, "Policing Doesn't Protect Women," *The New Republic*, July 6, 2020, newrepublic.com.

50. Davis, *City of Quartz*, 126, 271.

51. David Bayley, *Police for the Future* (New York: Oxford University Press, 1994), 3.

52. Christopher M. Sullivan and Zachary P. O'Keeffe, "Evidence That Curtailing Proactive Policing Can Reduce Major Crime," *Nature Human Behavior* 1 (2017). The parallels to an earlier NYPD "blue flu" in 1971 are eerie: emerging similarly in the wake of struggles for civil rights and Black power, 25,000 NYPD officers called in sick for five days. But as an article at the time put it, "it didn't seem to make much difference ... There was no crime wave, no massive traffic jams, no rioting ... the experience inspired a wry joke in the form of a question: Do we really need police?" Ricard Reeves, "Maybe They Should Be Doing Something Different," *New York Times*, January 24, 1971.

53. Shima Baradaran Baughman, "How Effective Are Police? The Problem of Clearance Rates and Criminal Accountability," *Alabama Law Review* 72, n. 1 (2020).

54. Michelle Alexander, *The New Jim Crow: Mass Incarceration in the Age of Colorblindness* (New York: New Press, 2010), 236–7.

55. Lisa J. Huriash, "Cops and Schools Had No Duty to Shield Students in Parkland Shooting, Says Judge Who Tossed Lawsuit," *South Florida Sun Sentinel*, December 17, 2018, sun-sentinel.com. This contradicted a simultaneous ruling by a county court on another case brought against Peterson for negligence, which was later upheld by an appeals court on the grounds that qualified immunity has an exception if someone "acted in bad faith or with malicious purpose or in a manner

exhibiting wanton and willful disregard of human rights, safety, or property." The court ruled that it's plausible that Peterson did. Peterson was later criminally charged with neglect under a caregiver statute. Sheriff's deputy Brian Miller, who was fired for sitting in his car and slowly putting on his bulletproof vest rather than intervening, was reinstated through union arbitration with back pay.

56. Seth W. Stoughton, "How Police Training Contributes to Avoidable Deaths," *The Atlantic*, December 12, 2014, theatlantic.com.

57. Vaidya Gullapalli, "Spending Billions on Policing, Then Millions on Police Misconduct," *The Appeal*, August 9, 2020, theappeal.org.

58. Stuart Schrader, "To Protect and Serve Themselves," *Public Culture* 31, n. 3 (September 2019).

3. The Mirage of Reform

1. Boots Riley, Facebook post, April 8, 2015, facebook.com/TheCoup/posts /939269816107473.

2. Christina Elmore and David MacDougall, "N. Charleston Officer Fatally Shoots Man," *Post and Courier*, April 3, 2015, postand courier.com.

3. Jon Swaine, "Walter Scott Shooting: Officer Laughs about Adrenaline Rush in Recording," *Guardian*, April 13, 2015, theguardian.com.

4. Chloé Cooper Jones, "Fearing For His Life," *The Verge*, March 13, 2019, theverge.com.

5. Parts of the preceding paragraphs appeared previously in George Ciccariello-Maher, "We Must Disband The Police," *Salon*, April 24, 2015, salon.com.

6. Michel Foucault once said much the same of prisons, noting how: "Prison 'reform' is virtually contemporary with the prison itself: it constitutes, as it were, its programme ... mechanisms, whose purpose was apparently to correct it, but which seem to form part of its very functioning, so closely have they been bound up with its existence throughout its long history." *Discipline and Punish: The Birth of the Prison* (New York: Vintage, 1995), 234.

7. Rachel Herzing, "The Magical Life of Broken Windows," in Jordan T. Camp and Christina Heatherton, *Policing the Planet: Why the Policing Crisis Led to Black Lives Matter* (London and New York: Verso, 2016).

8. Kristian Williams, *Our Enemies in Blue: Police and Power in America* (Cambridge: South End Press, 2007), 32.

9. Williams, *Our Enemies in Blue*, 51.
10. Stuart Schrader, "To Protect and Serve Themselves," *Public Culture* 31, n. 3 (September 2019), 67, 217.
11. Robert M. Fogelson, *Big-City Police* (Cambridge: Harvard University Press, 1977), 16.
12. Alene Tchekmedyian, "LASD Deputy Gang at Compton Station Lied about Guns and Hosted Inking Parties, Deputy Says," *Los Angeles Times*, August 21, 2020, latimes.com. Few have connected the dots between this killing, the later killing of Dijon Kizzee, and an ambush targeting two Compton Sheriff's deputies.
13. United States Department of Justice, Civil Rights Division, *The Ferguson Report* (New York: New Press, 2015), 141.
14. Stuart Schrader, "The Liberal Solution to Police Violence: Restoring Trust Will Ensure More Obedience," *Indypendent*, June 30, 2015, indypendent.org.
15. Tracey L. Meares, "Policing: A Public Good Gone Bad," *Boston Review*, August 1, 2017, bostonreview.net.
16. Taylor, *From #BlackLivesMatter to Black Liberation*, 129.
17. Barak Ariel, William A. Farrar, and Alex Sutherland, "The Effect of Police Body-Worn Cameras on Use of Force and Citizens' Complaints against the Police: A Randomized Controlled Trial," *Journal of Quantitative Criminology* 31 (2015).
18. Ben Brucato, "Policing Made Visible: Mobile Technologies and the Importance of Point of View," *Surveillance and Society* 13, n. 3/4 (2015). Not only was there clear bias in the authorship, but the "experiment" took place amid a total overhaul stemming from prior sexual misconduct, in which officers' jobs were threatened if they didn't change their behavior, leading predictably to reductions in use of force unrelated to the cameras.
19. Patricia J. Williams, "The Rules of the Game," in R. Gooding-Williams, ed., *Reading Rodney King / Reading Urban Uprising* (London: Routledge, 1993), 51–2.
20. Min-Seok Pang and Paul A. Pavlou, "Armed with Technology: The Effects on Fatal Shootings of Civilians by the Police," Bureau of Justice Assistance, bja.ojp.gov. Another macro-analysis of 70 recent studies showed that cameras had no effect on use of force whatsoever. Lindsey Van Ness, "Body Cameras May Not Be the Easy Answer Everyone Was Looking For," *Pew Stateline*, January 14, 2020, pewtrusts.org.
21. Brucato, "Policing Made Visible," 467.

22. Jamelle Bouie, "The Militarization of the Police," *Slate*, August 13, 2014, slate.com.

23. Rania Khalek, "Israel-Trained Police 'occupy' Missouri after Killing of Black Youth," *Electronic Intifada*, August 15, 2014, electronicintifada.net.

24. Brendan McQuade, "The Demilitarization Ruse," *Jacobin*, May 24, 2015, jacobinmag.com.

25. Alex S. Vitale, *The End of Policing* (London and New York: Verso, 2017), 12.

26. Jamelle Bouie, "Why More Diverse Police Departments Won't Put an End to Police Misconduct," *Slate*, October 13, 2014, slate.com. See also Brad W. Smith, "The Impact of Police Officer Diversity on Police-Caused Homicides," *Policy Studies Journal* 31, n. 2 (2003).

27. *The Ferguson Report*, 151.

28. Simone Weichselbaum, "One Roadblock to Police Reform: Veteran Officers Who Train Recruits," *The Marshall Project*, July 22, 2020, themarshallproject.org.

29. Emily Green, "Another Case Involving Ex-Atlanta Officer Garrett Rolfe Is Scrutinized," NPR, July 7, 2020, npr.org.

30. For one meta-analysis of 492 scientific studies, see Patrick S. Forscher et al., "A Meta-Analysis of Procedures to Change Implicit Measures," *Journal of Personality and Social Psychology*, 117 (2019).

31. Rhea Mahbubani, "Officers Already Get Training to Deal With Biases They May Not Know They Have, but There's No Evidence It Actually Works," *Insider*, June 16, 2020, insider.com.

32. Emily R. Siegel et al., "Minneapolis Police Rendered 44 People Unconscious with Neck Restraints in Five Years," *NBC News*, June 1, 2020, nbcnews.com.

33. David Correia and Tyler Wall, *Police: A Field Guide* (London and New York: Verso, 2017), 64.

34. Vitale, *The End of Policing*, 16–17.

35. Justin Hansford, "Community Policing Reconsidered: From Ferguson to Baltimore," in Camp and Heatherton, eds., *Policing the Planet*, 218–19.

36. Mariame Kaba, "Yes, We Mean Literally Abolish the Police," *New York Times*, June 12, 2020, nytimes.com.

37. Correia and Wall, *Police: A Field Guide*, 2–3, 5.

38. Correia and Wall, *Police: A Field Guide*, 166, 171.

39. Andy Mannix, "Killing of George Floyd Shows That Years of Police Reform Fall Far Short," *Star Tribune*, June 20, 2020, startribune.com.

40. Pilar Melendez, "Minneapolis Man: Cop Who Kneeled on George Floyd 'Tried to Kill Me' in 2008," *The Daily Beast*, May 29, 2020, thedailybeast.com.

41. Mark Joseph Stern, "Democrats' Police Reform Bill Lets Federal Agents Off the Hook," *Slate*, June 8, 2020, slate.com.

42. Derecka Purnell, "The George Floyd Act Wouldn't Have Saved George Floyd's Life. That Says It All," *Guardian*, March 4, 2021, theguardian.com.

43. Ruth Wilson Gilmore and Craig Gilmore, "Restating the Obvious," in Michael Sorkin, ed. *Indefensible Spaces* (New York: Routledge, 2007), 145.

44. Mariame Kaba, "Police 'Reforms' You Should Always Oppose," *Prison Culture*, December 1, 2014, usprisonculture.com.

45. Critical Resistance, "Reformist Reforms vs. Abolitionist Steps in Policing," criticalresistance.org.

46. For an overview, see Sarah Holder et al., "'We Have Not Defunded Anything': Big Cities Boost Police Budgets," *Bloomberg*, September 22, 2020, bloomberg.com.

4. Breaking Police Power

1. Between 2011 and 2019, the Philadelphia FOP "successfully fought to have police discipline overturned or reduced about 70% of the time, even in some instances where Internal Affairs investigators determined that officers had committed crimes," and when Ramsey himself had pledged to "melt their badges." David Gambacorta, "Philly's Police Union Spent Decades Amassing Power. Reforms Could Cut Its Clout," *Philadelphia Inquirer*, June 19, 2020, inquirer.com.

2. James Surowiecki, "Why Are Police Unions Blocking Reform?" *The New Yorker*, September 12, 2016, newyorker.com.

3. Jim Dalrymple II, "Here's What Police Actually Planned To Say If Darren Wilson Was Indicted," *Buzzfeed*, December 10, 2014, buzzfeed-news.com.

4. K. Rambo, "Portland Police Union Chief Introduces 2022 Ballot Initiative to Limit Right to Assemble," *Oregonian*, September 29, 2020, oregonlive.com.

5. Alex S. Vitale, *The End of Policing* (London and New York: Verso, 2017), 40–1.

6. Kristian Williams, *Our Enemies in Blue: Police and Power in America*

(Cambridge: South End Press, 2007), 110, 92.

7. Williams, *Our Enemies in Blue*, 121–2.

8. Williams, *Our Enemies in Blue*, 135.

9. Williams, *Our Enemies in Blue*, 124–5.

10. Williams, *Our Enemies in Blue*, 134.

11. Williams, *Our Enemies in Blue*, 136.

12. Williams, *Our Enemies in Blue*, 141.

13. "A Tale of Two St. Louis Police Unions," *St. Louis American*, January 23, 2020, stlamerican.com; Eli Hager and Weihua Li, "White US Police Union Bosses Protect Officers Accused of Racism," *Guardian*, June 10, 2020, theguardian.com.

14. See Ezra Marcus, "The War on Frats," *New York Times*, August 1, 2020, nytimes.com.

15. Surowiecki, "Why Are Police Unions Blocking Reform?"

16. David Correia and Tyler Wall, *Police: A Field Guide* (London and New York: Verso, 2017), 164.

17. Stephen Rushin, "Police Arbitration," *Vanderbilt Law Review* (forthcoming), available at papers.ssrn.com/sol3/papers.cfm?abstract_id=3654483.

18. Reade Levinson, "Across the U.S., Police Contracts Shield Officers from Scrutiny and Discipline," *Reuters*, January 13, 2017, reuters.com.

19. Eli Hager, "Blue Shield," *The Marshall Project*, April 27, 2015, themarshallproject.org.

20. Hager, "Blue Shield."

21. Hager, "Blue Shield."

22. Hager, "Blue Shield."

23. Surowiecki, "Why Are Police Unions Blocking Reform?"

24. Surowiecki, "Why Are Police Unions Blocking Reform?"

25. J. Justin Wilson, "Institute for Justice Asks U.S. Supreme Court to Hold Government Officials Accountable For Destroying Idaho Home with Grenades," Institute for Justice, January 16, 2020, ij.org.

26. International Union of Police Associations, "The International Union of Police Unions Association Formally Endorses the Campaign for the Re-election of Donald Trump" (press release), iupa.org.

27. Sam Adler-Bell, "How Police Unions Bully Politicians," *The New Republic*, October 20, 2020, newrepublic.com.

28. Kim Kelly, "No More Cop Unions," *The New Republic*, May 29, 2020, newrepublic.com.

29. Dhammika Dharmapala et al., "Collective Bargaining Rights and Police Misconduct: Evidence from Florida," *Journal of Law, Economics,*

and Organization (forthcoming). The study uses already unionized police departments as a control group, thereby allowing researchers to isolate the impact of a 2003 Florida Supreme Court decision allowing sheriff's deputies to unionize on violent misconduct.

30. Williams, *Our Enemies in Blue*, 139.
31. "Black Lives Matter," Association of Flight Attendants official website, June 5, 2020, afacwa.org.
32. Hamilton Nolan, "Workers United Branch Calls on AFL-CIO to Expel Police Unions," *In These Times*, June 17, 2020, inthesetimes.com.
33. "AFSCME Members Call on Union Leadership to Support the Movement for Black Lives and Demand a Cop-Free AFSCME," *Left Voice*, September 1, 2020, leftvoice.org. While AFSCME approved progressive statements on police reform at its 2020 convention, just six years earlier it had approved a resolution calling for increased efforts to organize among law enforcement.
34. Felix Thompson et al., "Why and How SEIU Members Are Calling on Our Union to Expel Cops," *Labor Notes*, July 10, 2020, labornotes.org.
35. "Out of more than a dozen surveyed, just one Philadelphia local said it had supported calls to defund the police and to expel police unions from the labor movement: AFT Local 2026, representing 1,300 faculty and staff at the Community College of Philadelphia." Juliana Feliciano Reyes, "Philadelphia's Labor Movement Faces a Reckoning over the City's Powerful Police Union," *Philadelphia Inquirer*, July 17, 2020, inquirer.com.
36. Matthew Cunningham-Cook, "The AFL-CIO's Police Union Problem Is Bigger Than You Think," *The Intercept*, June 18, 2020, theintercept.com.
37. Benjamin Levin, "What's Wrong with Police Unions?" *Columbia Law Review* 120, n. 5 (2020), 1398.
38. Ilya Somin, "How to Curb Police Abuses—And How Not To," *Reason*, May 31, 2020, reason.com.
39. Bill Fletcher Jr., "The Central Issue Is Police Repression, Not Police Unions," *In These Times*, June 12, 2020, inthesetimes.com.
40. Cunningham-Cook, "The AFL-CIO's police union problem."
41. Cedric Johnson, "Ending the Violence," *Jacobin*, July 20, 2016, jacobinmag.com.
42. Shawn Gude, "Why We Can't Support Police Unions," *Jacobin*, July 31, 2015, jacobinmag.com.
43. Williams, *Our Enemies in Blue*, 141.
44. Kim Kelly, "The AFL-CIO's Untenable Stance on Cops," *The New*

Republic, August 5, 2020, newrepublic.com.

45. Cunningham-Cook, "The AFL-CIO's police union problem."
46. Adeshina Emmanuel, "Why Black Lives Matter Is Taking On Police Unions," *In These Times*, July 22, 2016, inthesetimes.com.
47. Alex Press, "Why the Left Opposes Police Unions," August 8, 2017, *Alex Press* (blog), saxlepres.wordpress.com.
48. Cunningham-Cook, "The AFL-CIO's police union problem."
49. Williams, *Our Enemies in Blue*, 136–7.
50. Robin D.G. Kelley, "Insecure: Policing under Racial Capitalism," *Spectre* 1, n. 2 (Fall 2020), 16, 34.
51. Eve Ewing, "Blue Bloods: America's Brotherhood of Police Officers," *Vanity Fair*, August 25, 2020, vanityfair.com.
52. Surowiecki, "Why Are Police Unions Blocking Reform?"
53. "To Hold Police Accountable, Ax the Arbitrators," *New York Times*, October 3, 2020, nytimes.com.
54. For Stuart Schrader, this also means greater scrutiny toward the International Association of Chiefs of Police (IACP), which has played a key role in global, US-led counterinsurgency. "Police Reform Won't Fix a System That Was Built to Abuse Power," *The Nation*, June 12, 2020, thenation.com.
55. See Josmar Trujillo "Do Cops Serve the Rich? Meet the NYPD's Private Piggy Bank," *Gothamist*, October 24, 2019, gothamist.com.
56. Kelley, "Insecure," 26.
57. Adler-Bell, "How Police Unions Bully Politicians."
58. Andrew Grim, "What Is The 'Blue Flu' and How Has It Increased Police Power?" *Washington Post*, July 1, 2020, washingtonpost.com.
59. Adler-Bell, "How Police Unions Bully Politicians."
60. Gambacorta, "Philly's Police Union Spent Decades Amassing Power."

5. Building Communities without Police

1. John Steinbeck, *The Grapes of Wrath* (New York: Penguin, 1992), 419.
2. Salar Mohandesi, "Party as Articulator," *Viewpoint Magazine*, September 4, 2020, viewpointmag.com.
3. Benjamin Wallace-Wells, "Can Minneapolis Dismantle Its Police Department?" *The New Yorker*, August 8, 2020, newyorker.com.
4. Wallace-Wells, "Can Minneapolis Dismantle Its Police Department?"
5. Steve Fletcher, "I'm a Minneapolis City Council Member. We Must Disband the Police—Here's What Could Come Next," *Time*, June 5,

2020, time.com.

6. Wallace-Wells, "Can Minneapolis Dismantle Its Police Department?"

7. Haven Orecchio-Egresitz, "Vote to Disband Minneapolis Police Lets City Council Members 'Pose as Great Reformers While Doing Absolutely Nothing,' Police Brutality Research Group Says," *Insider*, June 11, 2020, insider.com.

8. Tiffany Bui, "What to Do about the MPD? How Three Activist Groups Are Rethinking Public Safety," *MinnPost*, July 1, 2020, minnpost.com.

9. Alleen Brown, "We Don't Have Time to Wait," *The Intercept*, June 5, 2020, theintercept.com.

10. Gili Ostfield, "We Can Solve Our Own Problems," *The New Yorker*, August 31, 2020, newyorker.com.

11. Eddie Chuculate, "In Minneapolis It's AIM That Serves and Protects," *Indian Country Today*, May 30, 2020, indiancountry today.com.

12. Justin Glawe and Kate Briquelet, "Minneapolis Neighborhood Patrols Fear White Supremacists Are Infiltrating to Derail Protests," *The Daily Beast*, June 6, 2020, thedailybeast.com.

13. MPD150, "What Are We Talking about When We Talk about 'a Police-Free Future?,'" mpd150.com.

14. MPD150, "10 Action Ideas for Building a Police-Free Future," mpd150.com.

15. MPD150, "What Are We Talking about When We Talk about 'a Police-Free Future?'"

16. Garrett Felber, "The Struggle to Abolish the Police is Not New," *Boston Review*, June 9, 2020, bostonreview.net.

17. Kristian Williams, *Our Enemies in Blue: Police and Power in America* (Cambridge: South End Press, 2007), 227.

18. Robin D.G. Kelley, *Hammer and Hoe: Alabama Communists During the Great Depression* (Chapel Hill: University of North Carolina Press, 1990).

19. Robert F. Williams, *Negroes with Guns* (New York: Marzani & Munsell, 1962).

20. See Lance Hill, *The Deacons for Defense* (Chapel Hill: University of North Carolina Press, 2004), and Charles E. Cobb, *This Nonviolent Stuff'll Get You Killed* (New York: Basic Books, 2014).

21. Cle Sloan, *Bastards of the Party* (documentary film, 2005).

22. The full plan is available at gangresearch.net/GangResearch/Policy/cripsbloodsplan.html.

23. Rose City Copwatch, *Alternatives to Policing* (2008), 12.

Notes for Pages 142 to 147

24. See MASK official website, ontheblock.org.
25. Nissa Rhee, "Despite Spike in Shootings, a Chicago Community Gets a Handle on Violence," *Christian Science Monitor*, August 8, 2018, csmonitor.com.
26. Manny Ramos and Sam Kelly, "Disheartening Week—and Year—for Mothers Against Senseless Killings, but Their Work Continues," *Chicago Sun Times*, July 26, 2020, chicago.suntimes.com.
27. Ramos and Kelly, "Disheartening Week."
28. "What Is Cahoots?," White Bird Clinic official website, whitebirdclinic.org.
29. "MH First Oakland," Anti Police-Terror Project, antipoliceterrorproject.org. In 2020 alone, cities like Portland, Oregon, established a similar grassroots People's Crisis Line, Denver created a similar program called STAR which reduced arrests for mental health emergencies to zero, and democratic socialist Chicago alderman Rossana Rodríguez spearheaded a pilot program to divert emergency calls away from the police.
30. Rose City Copwatch, *Alternatives to Policing*, 7–8.
31. See, for instance, the Portland Bad Date Line, facebook.com/PDXbaddateline.
32. Alisa Bierria, "Pursuing a Radical Anti-Violence Agenda inside/outside a Non-Profit Structure," in INCITE!, ed., *The Revolution Will Not Be Funded: Beyond the Non-Profit Industrial Complex* (Durham: Duke University Press, 2017).
33. CARA, "Taking Risks," *The Revolution Starts at Home: Confronting Intimate Violence Within Activist Communities* (Oakland: AK Press, 2016).
34. Restorative Response Baltimore official website, restorativeresponse.org.
35. Cass Balzer, "Rethinking Police Presence: Libraries Consider Divesting from Law Enforcement," *American Libraries*, July 8, 2020, americanlibrariesmagazine.org.
36. Andrew Dilts, "Death Penalty 'Abolition' in Neoliberal Times: The SAFE California Act and the Nexus of Savings and Security," in Geoffrey Adelsberg, Lisa Guenther, and Scott Zeman, eds., *Death and Other Penalties: Philosophy in a Time of Mass Incarceration* (New York: Fordham University Press, 2015), 128.
37. "Critical Resistance–INCITE! Statement on Gender Violence and the Prison Industrial Complex," (2001), available at incite-national.org.
38. Dorothy Roberts, "Abolishing Policing Also Means Abolishing Family

Regulation," *The Imprint*, June 16, 2020, imprintnews.org. See also Mimi E. Kim, "Challenging the Pursuit of Criminalisation in an Era of Mass Incarceration: The Limitations of Social Work Responses to Domestic Violence in the USA," *British Journal of Social Work* 43, n. 7 (October 2013).

39. Shellsea Lomeli "We Are Deputies of the Police," *Davis Vanguard*, July 10, 2020, davisvanguard.org.
40. Brendan McQuade, "The Camden Police Department Is Not a Model for Policing in the Post-George Floyd Era," *The Appeal*, June 12, 2020, theappeal.org.
41. Nancy Solomon, "The Real Bosses of New Jersey," *ProPublica*, May 1, 2019, propublica.org.
42. Brendan McQuade, "The 'Camden Model' Is Not a Model. It's an Obstacle to Real Change," *Jacobin*, July 4, 2020, jacobinmag.com.
43. McQuade, "Obstacle to Real Change."
44. McQuade, "Obstacle to Real Change."
45. One overlooked consequence of the George Floyd rebellions has been the immediate appearance of large-scale cluster hires in anti-racism and new tenure-track positions in Black studies where university administrators had previously insisted no new hiring was possible. Magic!
46. Keeanga-Yamahtta Taylor, "Five Years Later, Do Black Lives Matter?" *Jacobin*, September 30, 2019, jacobinmag.com.
47. While 92 percent of white officers believe that the United States has already achieved equal rights, only 29 percent of Black officers do, numbers which are almost exactly reversed when it comes to the legitimacy of movements for police accountability. Rich Morin et al., "Behind the Badge," *Pew Research Center*, January 11, 2017, pewsocialtrends.org.
48. Robin D.G. Kelley argues that while Black police protective leagues were not strictly abolitionist, they often understood themselves as protecting "Black communities rather than their own jobs." Some, like the Afro-American Patrolmen's League (AAPL), even developed structural critiques of policing—and were punished unsparingly as a result. Robin D.G. Kelley, "Insecure: Policing under Racial Capitalism," *Spectre* 1, n. 2 (Fall 2020), 32.
49. Raider Nation Collective, *Raider Nation, Volume 1: From The January Rebellions to Lovelle Mixon and Beyond* (2010), available at georgecic-cariello.files.wordpress.com/2012/06/rnc04_13 edit.pdf.

6. Self-Defense and Abolition

1. Alejandro Velasco, *Barrio Rising: Urban Popular Politics and the Making of Modern Venezuela* (Berkeley: University of California Press, 2015).
2. Jacquelyn Dowd Hall, "The Long Civil Rights Movement and the Political Uses of the Past," *Journal of American History* 91, n. 4 (2005).
3. Frantz Fanon, *The Wretched of the Earth* (New York: Grove, 2004), 4.
4. Tamara K. Nopper, "Abolition Is Not a Suburb," *The New Inquiry*, July 16, 2020, thenewinquiry.com.
5. Phil A. Neel has charted this history and its tactical implications in "New Ghettos Burning," *Ultra*, August 17, 2014, ultra-com.org.
6. Ed Moloney, "Kneecapping, Yes, but a Victim's Wellbeing Wasn't an IRA Priority," *Irish Times*, October 25, 2014, irishtimes.com.
7. Kristian Williams, *Our Enemies in Blue: Police and Power in America* (Cambridge: South End Press, 2007), 232.
8. Michael Neocosmos, "From the Archive, Part 1," *New Frame*, newframe.com.
9. Colin Knox and Rachel Monaghan, *Informal Justice in Divided Societies: Northern Ireland and South Africa* (London: Palgrave MacMillan, 2002), 29.
10. Michael Neocosmos, "From the Archive, Part 2," *New Frame*, newframe.com.
11. Hawzhin Azeez, "Police Abolition and Other Revolutionary Lessons from Rojava," *ROAR Magazine*, June 6, 2020, roarmag.org.
12. Laleh Khalili and Jillian Schwedler, *Policing and Prisons in the Middle East: Formations of Coercion* (New York: Columbia University Press, 2010), 15.
13. Anya Briy, "Zapatistas: Lessons in Community Self-organisation in Mexico," *Open Democracy*, June 25, 2020, opendemocracy.net.
14. César Enrique Pineda, "Acapatzingo: Construyendo comunidad urbana," *Contrapunto* 3 (November 2013), 49, 55.
15. Pineda, "Acapatzingo," 49.
16. Pineda, "Acapatzingo," 56–8.
17. Gerardo Rénique and Deborah Poole, "The Oaxaca Commune: Struggling for Autonomy and Dignity," *NACLA Report on the Americas*, May 1, 2008, nacla.org.
18. Barucha Peller, "Self-Reproduction and the Oaxaca Commune," *ROAR Magazine* 1 (Spring 2016), roarmag.org.
19. See Dawn Paley, *Drug War Capitalism* (Oakland: AK Press, 2014).
20. María Teresa Sierra, "Indigenous Justice Faces the State: The Community

Police Force in Guerrero, Mexico," *NACLA Report on the Americas*, September 2, 2010, nacla.org.

21. Gilberto López y Rivas, "Cherán: Cinco años de autonomía y dignidad," *La Jornada*, April 15, 2016, jornada.com.mx.

22. Linda Pressly, "Cheran: The Town That Threw Out Police, Politicians and Gangsters," BBC, October 12, 2016, bbc.com.

23. Raúl Zibechi, *Dispersing Power: Social Movements as Anti-state Forces* (Oakland: AK Press, 2010), 92.

24. Marisol LeBrón, *Policing Life and Death: Race, Violence, and Resistance in Puerto Rico* (Berkeley: University of California Press, 2019), 4.

25. LeBrón, *Policing Life and Death*, 202, 204.

26. LeBrón, *Policing Life and Death*, 228.

27. See Scott Crow, ed., *Setting Sights: Histories and Reflections on Community Armed Self-Defense* (Oakland: PM Press, 2018).

28. LeBrón, *Policing Life and Death*, 238.

29. Naomi Klein, *The Shock Doctrine: The Rise of Disaster Capitalism* (New York: Picador, 2008).

30. Gerald Horne, *The Apocalypse of Settler Colonialism* (New York: Monthly Review Press, 2018).

31. James Baldwin, "A Report from Occupied Territory," *The Nation*, July 11, 1966.

32. Kali Akuno, "Casting Shadows," *Jackson Rising: The Struggle for Economic Democracy and Black Self-Determination in Jackson, Mississippi* (Cantley, QC: Daraja Press, 2017). After the passing of Chokwe Lumumba and the election of his son Chokwe Antar Lumumba, relations with police warmed and a more traditional policy was pursued.

7. Abolish ICE, Abolish the Border

1. Puck Lo, "For Migrants in Arizona Who Call 911, It's Border Patrol on the Line," *Al-Jazeera America*, March 25, 2015, america.aljazeera.com.

2. Puck Lo, *After/Life* (documentary film, 2018), available at pucklo.com/afterlife/.

3. "Military Cover-Up? 100s of Migrants Feared Dead in Mass Grave at AZ's Barry Goldwater Bombing Range," *Democracy Now*, August 15, 2018, democracynow.org.

4. Jean Guerrero, "Death at the Border: A Brother's Fatal Journey Inspires Altruism," KPBS, December 14, 2016, kpbs.org.

5. Óscar Martínez, *The Beast: Riding the Rails and Dodging Narcos on the*

Migrant Trail (London and New York: Verso, 2013), 169.

6. Guerrero, "Death at the Border."

7. No More Deaths, *The Disappeared*, 6, thedisappearedreport.org.

8. Testimony from INS commissioner Doris Meissner, calling for stronger enforcement in the short and medium term, confirms this. Joseph Nevins, *Operation Gatekeeper* (London: Routledge, 2002), 115.

9. Nevins, *Operation Gatekeeper*, 10, 148.

10. Daniel Denvir, *All-American Nativism: How the Bipartisan War on Immigrants Explains Politics as We Know It* (London and New York: Verso, 2020), 50–7.

11. Kari Hong, "The Absurdity of Crime-Based Deportation," *UC Davis Law Review* 50 (2017), 2145.

12. Michelle Alexander, *The New Jim Crow: Mass Incarceration in the Age of Colorblindness* (New York: New Press, 2010), 199.

13. Bianca Bruno, "Human Cost of Border-Protection Policies High, Immigrant Advocates Reveal," *Courthouse News*, October 1, 2019, courthousenews.com.

14. Kelly Lytle Hernández, *Migra! A History of the U.S. Border Patrol* (Berkeley: University of California Press, 2010), 44–5.

15. Chris Cillizza, "The Remarkable History of the Family Separation Crisis," CNN, June 18, 2018, cnn.com.

16. Denvir, *All-American Nativism*, 70.

17. Natascha Elena Uhlmann, *Abolish ICE* (New York: OR Books, 2019), 30.

18. Uhlmann, *Abolish ICE*, 49.

19. Maria Sacchetti, "Deportations from the Interior of the United States Are Rising under Trump," *Washington Post*, October 7, 2017, washingtonpost.com.

20. Benjy Sarlin, "This Democrat Is Writing a Bill to 'Abolish ICE.' Here's How It Would Work," NBC, June 30, 2018, nbcnews.com.

21. Juliette Kayyem, "Trump Is the Problem," *The Atlantic*, July 23, 2020, theatlantic.com.

22. Uhlmann, *Abolish ICE*, 8.

23. Du Bois, *Black Reconstruction*, 20.

24. Du Bois, *Black Reconstruction*, 148.

25. K-Sue Park, "Self-Deportation Nation," *Harvard Law Review* 132, n. 7 (May 2019).

26. See Douglas S. Massey and Julia Gelatt, "What Happened to the Wages of Mexican Immigrants? Trends and Interpretations," *Latino Studies* 8, n. 3 (Autumn 2010).

27. Daniel Martinez HoSang and Joseph E. Lowndes, *Producers, Parasites, Patriots: Race and the New Right-Wing Politics of Precarity* (Minneapolis: University of Minnesota Press, 2019), 105–7.
28. HoSang and Lowndes, *Producers, Parasites, Patriots*, 111.
29. HoSang and Lowndes, *Producers, Parasites, Patriots*, 114.
30. Garvey was himself a Jamaican-born migrant, and Douglass advocated what Juliet Hooker has recently characterized as a "universal right to migration." Juliet Hooker, *Theorizing Race in the Americas: Douglass, Sarmiento, Du Bois, and Vasconcelos* (New York: Oxford University Press, 2019), 51.
31. Nagle's fixation on Cesar Chavez is revealing. While Chavez's prime concern was the way that so-called "wetback" labor was being weaponized by the bosses to break strikes, he stood out nevertheless for his stubborn opposition to newer waves of migrant labor. What Nagle fails to mention is that Chavez's anti-migrant politics were part of cozying up to the Democratic Party and proved increasingly unpopular among the grass roots. As Justin Akers Chacón has shown, "most farmworkers had familial and other social ties to undocumented populations and resented collaboration with *la migra*," and the broader movement opted to build expansive transnational solidarities rather than embracing the divisions imposed by the bosses. Ultimately, the case of Chavez proves exactly the opposite of what Nagle seems to think: that capitalists can leverage so-called "illegals" against documented workers not despite the border, but because of it.
32. V.I. Lenin, "Letter to the Secretary of the Socialist Propaganda League" (1915), available at marxists.org.
33. Brianna Rennix and Nathan J. Robinson, "Responding to 'The Left Case Against Open Borders,'" *Current Affairs*, November 29, 2018, currentaffairs.org.
34. Paul Ortiz, *An African American and Latinx History of the United States* (Boston: Beacon, 2018), 163.
35. A. Naomi Paik, *Bans, Walls, Raids, Sanctuary: Understanding US Immigration for the Twenty-First Century* (Berkeley: University of California Press, 2020), 50.
36. Lytle Hernández, *Migra!*, 45.
37. Lytle Hernández, *Migra!*, 41.
38. Denvir, *All-American Nativism*, 11.
39. Denvir, *All-American Nativism*, 28.
40. Greg Grandin, "The Border Patrol Has Been a Cult of Brutality Since 1924," *The Intercept*, January 12, 2019, theintercept.com.

41. Nicholas Kulish et al., "Immigration Agents Discover New Freedom to Deport Under Trump," *New York Times*, February 25, 2017, nytimes.com.

42. Franklin Foer, "How Trump Radicalized ICE," *The Atlantic*, September 2018, theatlantic.com. Travis Linneman describes a monthly podcast put out by the National Border Patrol Council called *The Green Line*, an explicit analogy to the "blue line" of policing. The podcast, however, opens with audio from the Night's Watch from HBO's *Game of Thrones*—guardians of a massive wall that separates humanity from a world of monsters and zombies. *The Horror of Police* (Minneapolis: University of Minnesota Press, forthcoming).

43. "Joint Press Release Between Border Patrol and ICE Councils," iceunion.org.

44. Kim Kelly, "Abolish ICE's Union," *The New Republic*, September 2, 2019, newrepublic.com.

45. Matt Ford, "Dismantle the Department of Homeland Security," *The New Republic*, February 21, 2018, newrepublic.com.

46. Emily S. Rueb, "JPMorgan Chase Stops Funding Private Prison Companies, and Immigration Activists Applaud," *New York Times*, March 6, 2019, nytimes.com.

47. Uhlmann, *Abolish ICE*, 130.

48. "Laibar Sing Airport Action Dec 10," YouTube, uploaded December 9, 2010, youtube.com/watch?v=ywWVquJeUGw.

49. Harsha Walia, *Undoing Border Imperialism* (Oakland: AK Press, 2013).

50. Paik, *Bans, Walls, Raids, Sanctuary*, 107.

51. P.E. Moskowitz, *The Case against Free Speech* (New York: Bold Type, 2019), 181–3.

52. Uhlmann, *Abolish ICE*, 100.

53. Paik, *Bans, Walls, Raids, Sanctuary*, 103.

54. Paik, *Bans, Walls, Raids, Sanctuary*, 109–10.

55. Paik, *Bans, Walls, Raids, Sanctuary*, 124.

56. Paik, *Bans, Walls, Raids, Sanctuary*, 104, 128.

57. Reece Jones, *Violent Borders: Refugees and the Right to Move* (London and New York: Verso, 2016), 5.

58. Keith Humphreys, "How Legalization Caused the Price of Marijuana to Collapse," *Washington Post*, September 5, 2017, washingtonpost.com.

Conclusion: Democracy or the Police?

1. Michael Coard, "Police Killed More People in 2019 Than Bloods, Crips Combined," *Philadelphia Tribune*, October 21, 2019, phillytrib .com.

2. Sam Adler-Bell, "How Police Unions Bully Politicians," *The New Republic*, October 20, 2020, newrepublic.com.

3. Shane Bauer, "How a Deadly Police Force Ruled a City," *The New Yorker*, November 16, 2020, newyorker.com.

4. Adler-Bell, "How Police Unions Bully Politicians."

5. Charles Tilly, "War Making and State Making as Organized Crime," in *Bringing the State Back In*, Peter B. Evans, Dietrich Rueschemeyer, and Theda Skocpol, eds. (Cambridge, UK: Cambridge University Press, 1985), 171.

6. "Criminal Justice Expenditures: Police, Corrections, and Courts," Urban Institute, urban.org; Carlos Ballesteros, "Chicago Has Nearly Tripled Per Capita Police Spending since 1964, data show," *Injustice Watch*, June 9, 2020, injusticewatch.org.

7. Robin D.G. Kelley, "Insecure: Policing under Racial Capitalism," *Spectre* 1, n. 2 (Fall 2020), 25.

8. Walter Benjamin, "Critique of Violence," in *Reflections* (New York: Schocken, 1986), 286.

9. "The Trump Administration: The First 100 Days," Fraternal Order of Police, fop.net.

10. Michael German, "Hidden in Plain Sight: Racism, White Supremacy, and Far-Right Militancy in Law Enforcement," *Brennan Center for Justice*, August 27, 2020, brennancenter.org.

11. Sam Levin, "California Police Worked with Neo-Nazis to Pursue 'Anti-Racist' Activists, Documents Show," *Guardian*, February 9, 2018, theguardian.com.

12. Alex Zielinski, "Texts Show Protective Relationship between Portland Cops and Patriot Prayer," *Portland Mercury*, February 14, 2019, port-landmercury.com.

13. Bill Chappell, "Police Officers Slashed Car Tires During Minneapolis Protests, Police Agencies Say," NPR, June 9, 2020, npr.org.

14. Dee J. Hall, "Militia Member Says Kenosha Police Sought to Push Protesters toward Them on Night of Deadly Shootings," *Wisconsin Watch*, September 5, 2020, wisconsinwatch.org.

15. Simon Purdue, "The Other Epidemic: White Supremacists in Law Enforcement," *Open Democracy*, August 6, 2020, opendemocracy.net.

16. Melissa Gira Grant, "Far-Right Militias Are Learning Impunity from the Cops," *The New Republic*, August 31, 2020, newrepublic.com.

17. W.E.B. Du Bois, *Black Reconstruction in America, 1860–1880* (New York: The Free Press, 1998), 30, 16.

18. Mychal Denzel Smith, "Abolish the Police. Instead, Let's Have Full Social, Economic, and Political Equality," *The Nation*, April 9, 2015, thenation.com.

19. Ruth Wilson Gilmore, *Change Everything: Racial Capitalism and the Case for Abolition* (Chicago: Haymarket, 2021).

Index

Index

Index

mass deportations, 192, 201, 210
self-deportation, 194–5, 206
statistics on, 190
sword of as hanging over working
class, 197
universities' collaboration with, 204
Desert Eagles (Águilas del Desierto),
184–5, 188
Detroit Police Officers Association, 103
Diamond and Silk (vloggers), 196
Dilts, Andrew, 146
Dinkins, David, 104
"Dirty Harry Syndrome," 218
disciplining, of police, 110
Discord (app), 134
Disu, Jessica, 16
diversification, as topic of police reform,
84
Dodd, Jed, 121
domestic violence, by officers on partners
or children, 58–9
Douglass, Frederick, 14, 197
Du Bois, W.E.B., 12, 13, 14, 23–5, 26, 27,
28, 39, 41–2, 45, 100, 194, 199, 225,
226
due process, for police, 109, 122
Duke, David, 188
Dunn, Michael, 21

e-carceration, 150
#8toAbolition, 92
Eighth Amendment (US Constitution),
217
Ellison, Jeremiah, 2
The End of the Myth (Grandin), 199
enforcement and removal (ERO), 191
Engels, Friedrich, 128
Esquivias, Ricardo, 184–5
Estrada, Hector, 148
Ewing, Eve, 121

Fagan, Jeffrey, 110–11
Fanon, Frantz, 5, 160
Farrar, William ("Tony"), 81
FBI's Uniform Crime Reporting
database, 32
Felber, Garrett, 138
Ferguson, Missouri
bogus fines and exorbitant court

fees collected by police in, 217
extortion by police in, 217
military force as used against
protesters in, 42, 83, 177, 178
police killing of Mike Brown in, 4,
15, 21, 28, 50, 78, 84, 98, 118,
229
police of as trained in Israel, 83
poor as pushed from city to
impoverished suburban areas of,
161
protests/rebellions in, 28, 42, 78, 81,
87, 222
Ferguson Commission, 78
"Ferguson effect," 224
Ferguson Report, 78, 84
Fernández, Luis, 205
Fetonte, Danny, 115
Fifteenth Amendment (US Constitution),
12
Fifth Amendment (US Constitution),
102, 109
Fletcher, Bill, Jr., 114, 120
Fletcher, Steve, 130, 131
Florida
killing of Trayvon Martin in
Sanford, 4, 20–1, 87
mass school shooting in Parkland,
66
Pulse nightclub massacre in
Orlando, 67
vigilante killing of Jordan Davis in
Jacksonville, 21
Floyd, George
police department reaction to
killing of, 8–9, 215
police killing of in Minneapolis,
1–2, 4, 5, 6, 50, 74, 85, 90, 112,
125, 130
protests/rebellions following death
of, 1–2, 3, 6–7, 20, 63, 84, 93, 99,
112, 129, 130, 134, 147, 151, 178,
180–1, 190, 202, 214, 221, 223,
227
Forman, James, Jr., 27, 30
Foster, Garrett, 8, 223
Foucault, Michel, 35, 37
Fourteenth Amendment (US Constitution), 12

Index

Index

Index

qualified immunity as topic of, 91
as requiring reckoning with police
    unions, 122
task of, 73
training as topic of, 84–5
police scientists/science, 35, 38
police strikes, 64, 101, 102, 120, 138
police unions
    according to Adler-Bell, 111–12
    actions of regarding Jonathan Josey
        case, 97–8
    agenda of, 104
    as albatross, 120
    on Black Lives Matter (BLM), 99
    as born full-grown as "labor"
        aristocracy, 119
    calls for expelling and abolishing of,
        115, 120
    calls for labor movement to disaffili-
        ate them, 122–3
    as central pillar of police power, 125
    confronting and destroying of, 100
    as on the defensive, 123
    growing strength of, 106
    as harassing and threatening elected
        officials who cross them, 99
    history of, 120–1
    as mediators, 104
    as not really unions, 106
    police power as expressed largely
        through, 36
policing. *See also* police
    as about controlling "dangerous"
        people, 25
    as about disciplining workforce,
        25–6
    as Achilles' heel of US racial order,
        227
    alternatives to. *See* alternatives, to
        policing
    American policing going global, 42
    Black leadership as supporting
        unchecked policing, 29
    border policing. *See* border policing
    broken windows policing. *See*
        broken windows policing
    as cancer/virus, 37–8
    colonialism as form of, 166
    community as antidote of, 155

community policing. *See* commu-
    nity policing
as dismal failure, 217
emergence of professional policing,
    25
as functioning as linchpin of US
    capitalism, 44
imperial policing, 38
as inseparable from whiteness
    (white power), 23–4
militarization of, 31, 32–3, 34
proactive policing, 42, 65, 74
as racist, 27–8
racist policing, 26, 51, 62
as racket, 215–16
regional policing strategies, 166–7
sanitized language of, 36
society as built around, 10
as third rail of American politics,
    227
tragic origin story of, 103
in US as vaster than any other in
    the world, 31
US budget for, 34
politics
    law-and-order politics, 22, 31, 43,
        51, 54, 102, 111, 183, 219, 221
    police as becoming local kingmak-
        ers, 104
    policing as third rail of American
        politics, 227
poor communities of color
    as bearing twin brunts of social
        abandonment and police
        violence, 34
    Black police commissioners in
        Philadelphia as heaping
        disproportionate brutality on, 27
    capitalism as abandoning of to
        radical vulnerability and early
        death, 162
    causes of violence within, 30
    criminalization of, 200
    disciplinary function of schools in,
        148
    dismantling of access to care and
        treatment for, 52
    police as exacerbating social
        inequalities in, 88

Index

Rangel, Charles, 29
rape, by cop, 56–8
rape crisis centers, 143–4
rape kits, 55, 130
rapid-response networks, 138
Rawlings-Blake, Stephanie, 108–9
Reagan, Ronald, 29
Real ID Act (2005), 189
Reclaim the Block, 130, 132
Reconstruction
    cops as born from wreckage of, 224
    as dyad with abolition, 12
    failure of, 13, 14, 24, 42
Red Guards, 139
Reed, Adolph, 49–50, 52
Regional Coordinator of Community
    Authorities (CRAC), 171, 172
Reinoehl, Michael Forest, 9
Repeal Coalition (Arizona), 205
restorative justice, 134, 136, 143, 163, 175
Restorative Response Baltimore, 144–5
Rice, Tamir, 21, 41, 177, 215
Richie, Beth, 36
Riley, Boots, 71
Ritchie, Andrea, 57–8
Rittenhouse, Kyle, 9, 20, 221
Rivera Cusicanqui, Silvia, 173
Rizzo, Frank, 6, 104, 141
Roberts, Dorothy, 147
Rolfe, Garrett, 84, 113
Roosevelt, Franklin Delano, 196
Royal Irish Constabulary, 166

Safe Neighborhood Campaign, 144
Safe OUTside the System (SOS)
    Collective, 144
salaries and wages, of police, 68, 101,
    103, 106, 107, 116, 117, 166, 214, 224
San Antonio, Texas, #OccupyICE
    protests in, 207
San Antonio Police Department, Jackie
    Neal case, 108
San Antonio Police Officers Association,
    108
San Cristóbal de las Casas (Chiapas), as
    self-governed territory, 168
sanctuary movement, 5, 202, 206, 207–8,
    209, 219
San Francisco Police Officers Associa-

tion, 98
Santana, Feidin, 72, 81
Saunders, Lee, 114
school police. See school resource officers
    (SRO)
school resource officers (SRO)
    history of, 33, 37
    and mass shootings, 66–7
    votes to eliminate contracts for, 5,
        145
school-to-prison pipeline, 37, 148
Schrader, Stuart, 42, 45, 79, 124
Scott, Walter, 37, 71, 72, 81
Scott-Heron, Gil, 93
Sculley, Sheryl, 108
Seattle Rape Relief, 143
security patrols
    in Seattle, 138
    by Zapatistas, 168
self-defense
    abolition as not possible without,
        180
    claims of, 9, 22, 39–40, 82, 86
self-defense networks/movements,
    138–40, 158, 159, 161, 167–8, 173, 175,
    179, 181
self-deportation, 194–5, 206
self-managed security collectives, 3, 134
self-organized experiments, in Latin
    America, 167–8, 169
Sergeants Benevolent Association (SBA),
    99, 214
Serpico, Frank, 76–7
sexual assault
    by on-duty officers, 56–8
    police as not preventing or often
        investigating, 55–6
sexual minorities, and police protection,
    59–60, 146
sex workers
    complex realities of, 146–7
    and police protection, 60, 143
Shakur, Tupac, 213
Sharecroppers' Union, 139
Sharpton, Al, 72
The Shock Doctrine (Klein), 175–6
sick-outs, 103, 213
Silvercorp, 44
Singh, Laibar, 205–6

Index

Index